UNDERSTANDING
by DESIGN

GRANT WIGGINS AND JAY MCTIGHE

Association for Supervision and Curriculum Development
Alexandria, Virginia USA

Association for Supervision and Curriculum Development
1703 N. Beauregard St. • Alexandria, VA 22311-1714 USA
Telephone: 1-800-933-2723 or 703-578-9600 • Fax: 703-575-5400
Web site: http://www.ascd.org • E-mail: member@ascd.org

Gene R. Carter, *Executive Director*
Michelle Terry, *Associate Executive Director, Program Development*
Nancy Modrak, *Director, Publishing*
John O'Neil, *Director of Acquisitions*
Julie Houtz, *Managing Editor of Books*
Margaret A. Oosterman, *Associate Editor*
Katherine George, *Copy Editor*
Charles D. Halverson, *Project Assistant*
Robert Land, *Proofreader*
Gary Bloom, *Director, Design and Production Services*
Karen Monaco, *Senior Designer*
Tracey A. Smith, *Production Manager*
Dina Murray, *Production Coordinator*
John Franklin, *Production Coordinator*
Eva Barsin, Judi Connelly, *Desktop Publishers*

ASCD publications present a variety of viewpoints. The views expressed or implied in this book should not be interpreted as official positions of the Association.

Printed in the United States of America.

September 1998 member book (pcr). ASCD Premium, Comprehensive, and Regular members periodically receive ASCD books as part of their membership benefits. No. FY99-1.

ASCD Stock No. 198199   ASCD member price: $16.95   nonmember price: $20.95

Library of Congress Cataloging-in-Publication Data
Wiggins, Grant P., 1950-
   Understanding by design / Grant Wiggins and Jay McTighe.
   p. cm.
  Includes bibliographical references

  ISBN 0-87120-313-8 (pbk.)
  1. Curriculum planning—United States. 2. Curriculum-based assessment—United States. 3. Learning. 4. Comprehension. I. McTighe, Jay. II. Title.
  LB2806.15 .W54 1998
  374'.001—ddc21   98-25513
                                              CIP

03 02 01 00 99 98   10 9 8 7 6 5 4 3 2 1

U N D E R S T A N D I N G
by D E S I G N

List of Figures

FOREWORD

TROUBLED BY THE INADEQUACY OF MULTIPLE-CHOICE tests, educators began in the 1980s to look for better ways to assess student learning. Now, after a decade of thoughtful experimentation with tasks, rubrics, exhibitions, and portfolios, our profession has reached a milestone. In numerous districts and schools, educators now feel comfortable developing, administering, and scoring performance tasks. And—because there is no point teaching to an ambitious standard if your assessment misses the mark—today's emphasis on standards is moving performance assessment from a trendy innovation to an accepted element of good teaching and learning.

Grant Wiggins and Jay McTighe have played starring roles in the growth and maturation of per-

formance assessment. As a respected speaker and consultant, Grant Wiggins has brought vision, conviction, and intellectual rigor to communities struggling with the effort to make schooling more authentic. Jay McTighe, who has also consulted with educators throughout North America, is especially known for his enterprising leadership of the Maryland Assessment Consortium, a statewide collaboration that began in 1991 to support educators working on standards-based education. Separately and together, Wiggins and McTighe refined processes for designing and scoring tasks, insisting on quality work not only from students and teachers but from themselves as well. And, though they focused on assessment, they were always concerned with the full range of teaching and learning. Educators who looked to them for guidance often began by asking about assessment but were soon deeply engaged with curriculum and instruction.

Which brings us to this book, and the milestone it represents. Beginning with a quest for alternatives to prevailing modes of assessment, the performance movement has put performance itself at stage center. It no longer makes sense, if it ever did, to call test scores "performance." Performance is doing something that is valued in the world outside schools. In a way, then, for our evaluations to be valid, we must assess performance. So what is new here? What kinds of performance have we been assessing all along, and what have we been trying to assess with conventional tests?

The milestone I am talking about is the simple but compelling insight that is the foundation for this book: Performance assessment is especially useful for assessing two types of learnings. One is very familiar. If you want to know whether students can give a persuasive speech, shoot a free throw, sing a tune, solve a quadratic equation, or perform a laboratory procedure, ask them to do it. If the performance is valued for its own sake and the curriculum is intended to help students learn it, assess the performance as directly as possible. That is one kind of performance assessment, and teachers have been using it for generations.

This book, though, focuses on a different use for performance assessment, which is less obvious but very powerful. From years of experience developing, testing, and critiquing assessment tasks, the authors have concluded that performance is the key to assessing understanding. This kind of performance is tricky, though. Yes, we certainly want students to understand, but exactly what is understanding? And how can we be sure that a particular performance reveals it?

Wiggins and McTighe offer us a framework for teacher planning quite different from the one we know all too well. Designing lessons for understanding begins with what we want students to be able to do and proceeds to the evidence we will accept that they have learned it. Only then does it turn to how they will learn it. Along the way we must be clear about what we want students to understand, and what we mean by understanding.

These are matters at the heart of our profession, but they are very demanding, so much so that we would rather avoid them. Luckily, Wiggins and McTighe not only raise tough issues—they help us think them through. They offer filters for each stage of the design process and criteria for essential questions. They propose six facets of understanding and show what each facet suggests about assessment. Finally, they consider the implications for organization of the curriculum and for instruction. Strong, solid stuff.

A milestone does not necessarily mark the end of the journey. Education has a long way to go before the ideas explained here become standard practice. But with this book, we are on our way, and an exhilarating journey it promises to be.

—Ron Brandt

ACKNOWLEDGMENTS

THANKS TO THE MANY INDIVIDUALS, PAST AND present, whose work has stimulated our thinking and deepened our understanding: Jerome Bruner, Arthur Costa, John Dewey, Howard Gardner, Madeline Hunter, Frank Lyman, Sandra Kaplan, Plato, David Perkins, Jean Piaget, Socrates, William Spady, Ted Sizer, and Ralph Tyler. Grant is particularly grateful for Howard Gardner's invitation a few years back to visit with the Harvard Teaching for Understanding group to provide feedback on their then-emerging work. That rich conversation was a seminal moment in the development of this book.

Thanks, too, to the members of the *Understanding by Design* cadre—John Brown, Hilarie Davis, David Grant, Bill O'Rourke, Fran Prolman, Eleanor Renee Rodrigues, and Elliot Seif—for their thoughtful feedback and guidance during the theoretical and practical evolution of the book and companion training program. Rich Strong and Everett Kline gave valuable feedback and encouragement early on and throughout the writing.

The Geraldine R. Dodge Foundation and the Pew Charitable Trusts provided direct and indirect support of the project; we are grateful to both. The Dodge Curriculum Design Awards led us to many outstanding teacher designers, some of whose work is presented in this book.

This book would never have come about had it not been for the enthusiastic promotion and support of this work by ASCD staff—Mikki Terry,

Agnes Crawford, and especially Sally Chapman. We thank them for the faith, good counsel, and cheerleading they have provided. Thanks, too, to Ron Brandt for his support along the way in past years and for his Foreword.

A special thanks to the ASCD editorial staff, especially John O'Neil. They have shown great patience and helpfulness throughout the long process leading to the final manuscript. Thanks, also, to editors Katherine George and Margaret Oosterman and to the ASCD design and production staff for their efforts on our behalf. And a tip of the hat to the Center on Learning, Assessment, and School Structure (CLASS) staff for their usual cheerful assistance in preparing the manuscript.

Finally, we thank our wives and children for their support. Many, many hours of late-night, early-morning, and weekend work went into the development of the ideas and the book—hours that should have been spent playing catch, timing laps, and cleaning closets. We trust that they . . . understand.

INTRODUCTION

CONSIDER THE FOLLOWING FOUR VIGNETTES AND WHAT they suggest about understanding and the design of curriculum and assessments. Two are true. Two are fictionalized accounts of familiar practice.

Vignette 1

As part of a workshop on "understanding," a veteran high school English teacher entered the following reflection in a learning log about her own experience as a high school student:

> I felt then that my brain was a way station for material going in one ear and (after the test) out the other. I could memorize very easily and so became valedictorian, but I was embarrassed even then that I understood much less than some other students who cared less about grades.

Vignette 2

For two weeks every fall, all the 3rd grade classes participate in a unit on apples. The students engage in a variety of activities related to the topic. In language arts, they read *Johnny Appleseed* and view an illustrated filmstrip of the story. They each write a creative story involving an apple and then illustrate their stories using tempera paints. In art, students collect leaves from nearby crab apple trees

and make a giant leaf print collage on the hallway bulletin board adjacent to the 3rd grade classrooms. The music teacher teaches the children songs about apples. In science, they use their senses to carefully observe and describe the characteristics of different types of apples. During mathematics, the teacher demonstrates how to "scale up" an applesauce recipe to make a quantity sufficient for all the 3rd graders.

A highlight of the unit is the field trip to a local apple orchard, where students watch cider being made and go on a hayride. The culminating unit activity is the 3rd grade apple fest, a celebration for which parent volunteers dress as apples and the children rotate through various activities at stations—making applesauce, competing in an apple "word search" contest, bobbing for apples, completing a math skill sheet containing word problems involving apples, and so on. The fest concludes with selected students reading their apple stories while the entire group enjoys candy apples prepared by the cafeteria staff.

Vignette 3

A test item on a national mathematics assessment presented the following question to 8th grade students:

"How many buses does the army need to transport 1,128 soldiers if each bus holds 36 soldiers?"

Almost one-third of the 8th graders answered the question, "31 remainder 12" (Schoenfeld, 1988, p. 84).

Vignette 4

It is late April and the panic is beginning to set in. A quick calculation reveals to the world history teacher that he will not finish the textbook unless he covers an average of 40 pages per day until the end of school. He decides, with some regret, to eliminate a mini-unit on the Caribbean and several time-consuming activities, such as a mock United Nations debate and vote, and discussions of current international events in relation to the world history topics students have studied. To prepare his students for the departmental final exam, the teacher will need to switch into a fast-forward lecture mode.

* * *

Each of these vignettes reveals some aspect of understanding and design. (By the way, the odd-numbered vignettes are true; the others may as well be, given common practice.)

A Familiar Truth

The reflection of the high school English teacher reveals a familiar truth—even good students don't always display a deep understanding of what's been taught even though conventional measures (e.g., course grades and cumulative GPA) certify success. In her case, testing focused predominantly on the recall of information from textbooks and class presentations. She reported that she rarely was given assessments that called for her to demonstrate deeper understanding.

The fictionalized apples unit presents a familiar scene—an activity-oriented curriculum—in which students participate in a variety of hands-on activities. Such units are often engaging for students. The units may be organized, as in this vignette, around a theme and provide interdisciplinary connections. But questions remain. To which ends is the teaching directed? What are the big ideas and important skills to be developed during the unit? Do the students understand what the learning targets are? How often does the *evidence* of learning from the unit (e.g., the leaf print collage, creative writing stories, and completed word searches) reflect worthwhile content standards? What understandings will emerge from all these activities and will endure?

The mathematics test item reveals another aspect of understanding, or lack of it. While the students computed accurately, they had not grasped the meaning of the question or had apparently not understood how to use what they knew to reach an answer of 32 buses. Could it be that these students had mastered the decontextualized drill problems in the math book and on worksheets but had little opportunity to apply mathematics in real-world applications? Should we conclude that the students who answered, "remainder 12," *really* understand division and its use?

Nearly every teacher can empathize with the world history teacher's struggle, given the pressures to cover textbook material. The challenge is exacerbated by the natural increase of knowledge in fields such as science and history, not to mention additions to the curriculum in recent years (e.g., computer studies and drug education). At its worst, a coverage orientation—marching through the chronology of a textbook irrespective of desired results, student needs and interests, or apt assessment evidence— may defeat its own aims. For what do students remember, much less understand, when surface coverage is valued over uncovering? Such an approach could be labeled "teach, test, and hope for the best."

What the Book Is About

This book is about understanding and its various facets. We think that understanding is not a single concept but a family of interrelated abilities—six different facets—and an education for understanding develops them all. This book is also about design—the design of curriculums to engage students in exploring and deepening their understanding of important ideas *and* the design of assessments to reveal the extent of their understandings. In this book, we explore a number of related ideas:

■ Explore common curriculum, assessment, and instruction practices that may interfere with the cultivation of student understanding.

■ Examine a *backward design* process and consider its value in helping to avoid common inadequacies in curriculum and assessment planning.

■ Present a theory of the six facets of understanding and explore its theoretical *and* practical implications for curriculum, assessment, and teaching.

■ Propose an approach to curriculum and instruction designed to engage students in inquiry, promote "uncoverage," and make the understanding of big ideas more likely.

■ Examine a continuum of methods for appropriately assessing the degree of student understanding.

■ Consider the role that predictable student misunderstandings should play in the design of curriculums, assessment, and instruction.

■ Offer a template to assist in designing curriculums and assessments that focus on student understanding.

■ Propose a set of design standards for achieving quality control in curriculum and assessment designs.

This book is intended for educators interested in enhancing student understanding and in designing more effective curriculums and assessments to promote understanding. The audience includes teachers at all levels (elementary through university), subject-matter and assessment specialists, curriculum directors, pre- and in-service trainers, and school-based and central office administrators and supervisors.

Terminology

A few words about terminology are in order. Educators involved in reform work know that the words *curriculum* and *assessment* have almost as many meanings as there are people using the terms. In this book, *curriculum* refers to a specific blueprint for learning that is derived from content and performance standards. Curriculum takes content and shapes it into a plan for effective teaching and learning. Thus, curriculum is more than a general framework, contrary to many state and district documents on curriculum; it is a specific plan with identified lessons in an appropriate form and sequence for directing teaching.

The etymology of the word *curriculum* suggests this meaning: A curriculum is a particular "course to be run," given a desired endpoint. A curriculum is more than a syllabus, therefore: Beyond mapping

out the topics and materials, it specifies the activities, assignments, and assessments to be used in achieving its goals. The best curriculums, in other words, are written from the learner's point of view and the desired achievements. They specify what the learner will do, not just what the teacher will do.

By *assessment* we mean the act of determining the extent to which the curricular goals are being and have been achieved. Assessment is an umbrella term we use to mean the deliberate use of many methods to gather evidence to indicate that students are meeting standards. When we speak of evidence of understanding, we are referring to information gathered through a variety of formal and informal assessments during a unit of study or a course. We are not alluding only to end-of-teaching tests or culminating performance tasks. Rather, the collected evidence we seek may well include observations and dialogues, traditional quizzes and tests, and performance tasks and projects, as well as students' self-assessments gathered over time. In fact, a central premise of our argument is that understanding can be developed and evoked only through multiple methods of assessment.[1]

By *achievement target* we mean what has often been termed "intended outcomes" or "performance standards." All three terms refer to the desired impact of teaching and learning—what a student should be able to do and what standard should be used to signify understanding. Achievement target properly suggests that we keep aiming for a result using curriculum and instruction. Note that content standards are different from performance standards. Content standards specify the inputs—What is the content that should be covered? Performance standards specify the desired output—What must the student do, and how well, to be deemed successful?

Many district and state documents unhelpfully blur this distinction.

The word *understanding* naturally deserves clarification and elaboration, but that work is the challenge for the rest of the book. Understanding turns out to be a complex and confusing target even though we aim for it all the time. In this book, we use "understand" to mean that a student has something more than just textbook knowledge and skill—that a student really "gets it." Understanding, then, involves sophisticated insights and abilities, reflected in varied performances and contexts. We also suggest that different kinds of understandings exist, that knowledge and skill do not automatically lead to understanding, that misunderstanding is a bigger problem than we realize, and that assessment of understanding therefore requires evidence that cannot be gained from traditional testing alone.

What the Book Is Not About

Understanding by Design is not a prescriptive program. Rather than offering a step-by-step guide, the book provides a conceptual framework, design process and template, and an accompanying set of design standards. We offer no specific curriculum but rather a way to design or redesign any curriculum to make student understanding more likely.

Understanding by Design, therefore, should not be seen as competing with other programs or approaches. In fact, its theory of understanding and the backward design process are compatible with several prominent educational initiatives, including problem-based learning (Stepien & Gallagher, 1997), Socratic seminar, 4-MAT (McCarthy, 1981),

Dimensions of Learning (Marzano & Pickering, 1997), *The Skillful Teacher* (Saphier & Gower, 1997), and the recently published book (Wiske, 1997) and workbook (Blythe & Associates, 1998) from the Project Zero team at the Harvard Graduate School of Education on teaching for understanding.

We are restricting our inquiry into understanding in an important way. While teaching for in-depth understanding is a vital aim of schooling, it is only one of many. We are thus not suggesting here that all teaching be geared at all times toward deep and sophisticated understanding. Clearly, there are circumstances when this depth is neither feasible nor desirable. For example, learning the alphabet, acquiring certain technical skills such as keyboarding, and developing the basics in foreign language do not call for in-depth understanding. In some cases, the developmental level of students will determine how much abstract conceptualization is appropriate. Sometimes familiarity as a goal, rather than depth, is quite sufficient for certain topics.

This book is thus built upon a conditional: *If educators wish to develop greater in-depth understanding in their students, then* how should they go about it?

One warning, though. All teachers talk about wanting to get beyond coverage to ensure that students really understand what they learn. Although we talk this way, readers may find that what they thought was effective teaching for understanding really wasn't. In fact, we predict that readers will be somewhat disturbed by how hard it is to specify what understanding looks like and how easily educators can lose sight of understanding even as they try to teach for it.

One further point about our approach. Throughout the book, we offer what we call

"misconception alerts" in which we try to anticipate reader misconceptions about the lines of argument and ideas being proposed. This format has a message: Teaching for understanding must successfully predict such misunderstandings if it is to be effective. Indeed, central to the design approach is the need to design lessons and assessments that anticipate, evoke, and overcome the most likely student misconceptions. We put the alerts in boxes for quick accessibility, and the first one is on this page.

Reader, brace thyself! We are asking you to think differently about time-honored habits and points of view about curriculum, assessment, and instruction. As you will see, teaching for understanding requires rethinking what we thought we knew—whether the "we" involves students or educators. But we believe that you will find much food for thought here as well as many practical tips on how to achieve student understanding by design.

Endnote

1. A more comprehensive discussion of assessment can be found in Wiggins (1998).

■ MISCONCEPTION ALERT

Only alternative methods of teaching and assessing can yield understanding. Nothing could be further from the truth. The challenge is to *expand* a teaching repertoire to make sure that a greater diversity of appropriate methods of instruction are used than are found in most classrooms. (See Chapters 6, 7, and 10.)

Our approach is against traditional testing. Not so. Here, too, we seek to expand the normal repertoire to make sure that more appropriate diversity is found in classroom assessment. The challenge is to know which method to use when, and why. (See Chapters 1 and 5.)

Our approach is against letter grades. Also not true. By and large, letter grades are here to stay, and nothing in this book is incompatible with grades, transcripts, and college admission requirements. The book should help teachers, especially those at the secondary level, better justify their grading system and provide students with improved feedback about what grades stand for.

WHAT IS BACKWARD DESIGN?

*To begin with the end in mind
means to start with a clear understanding of
your destination. It means to know where you're going so
that you better understand where you are now so that the steps
you take are always in the right direction.*
—STEPHEN R. COVEY
THE SEVEN HABITS OF HIGHLY EFFECTIVE PEOPLE

Design—(vb) To have purposes and intentions; to plan and execute
—*OXFORD ENGLISH DICTIONARY*

TEACHERS ARE DESIGNERS. AN ESSENTIAL ACT OF OUR profession is the design of curriculum and learning experiences to meet specified purposes. We are also designers of assessments to diagnose student needs to guide our teaching and to enable us, our students, and others (parents and administrators) to determine whether our goals have been achieved; that is, did the students learn *and* understand the desired knowledge?

Like other design professions, such as architecture, engineering, or graphic arts, designers in education must be mindful of their audiences. Professionals in these fields are strongly client centered. The effectiveness of their designs corresponds to whether they have accomplished their goals for the end users. Clearly, students are our primary clients, given that the effectiveness of curriculum, assessment, and instructional designs is ultimately determined by their achievement of desired learnings.

As with other design professions, standards inform and shape our work. The architect, for example, is guided by building codes, customer budget, and aesthetics. The teacher as designer is similarly constrained. We are not free to teach any topic we choose. Rather, we are guided by national, state, district, or institutional standards that specify what students should know and be able to do. These standards provide a framework to help us identify teaching and learning priorities and guide our

design of curriculum and assessments. In addition to external standards, we also consider the needs of our students when designing learning experiences. For example, student interests, developmental levels, and previous achievements influence our designs.

Are the Best Curricular Designs "Backward"?

How, then, do these design considerations apply to curriculum planning? We use curriculum as a means to an end. We focus on a particular topic (e.g., racial prejudice), use a particular resource (e.g., *To Kill a Mockingbird*), and choose specific instructional methods (e.g., Socratic seminar to discuss the book and cooperative groups to analyze stereotypical images in films and on television) to cause learning to meet a given standard (e.g., the student will understand the nature of prejudice, and the difference between generalizations and stereotypes).

Why do we describe the most effective curricular designs as "backward"? We do so because many teachers *begin* with textbooks, favored lessons, and time-honored activities rather than deriving those tools from targeted goals or standards. We are advocating the reverse: One starts with the end—the desired results (goals or standards)—and then derives the curriculum from the evidence of learning (performances) called for by the standard and the teaching needed to equip students to perform. This view is hardly radical. Ralph Tyler (1949) described the logic of backward design clearly and succinctly about 50 years ago:

Educational objectives become the criteria by which materials are selected, content is outlined, instructional procedures are developed, and tests and examinations are prepared. . . . The purpose of a statement of objectives is to indicate the kinds of changes in the student to be brought about so that instructional activities can be planned and developed in a way likely to attain these objectives (pp. 1, 45).

Backward design may be thought of as purposeful task analysis: Given a task to be accomplished, how do we get there? Or one might call it planned coaching: What kinds of lessons and practices are needed to master key performances? The approach to curricular design we are advocating is logically forward and commonsensical but backward in terms of conventional habits, whereby teachers typically think in terms of a series of activities (as in the apples unit presented in the Introduction) or how best to cover a topic (as in the world history vignette).

This backward approach to curricular design also departs from another common practice: thinking about assessment as something we do at the end, once teaching is completed. Rather than creating assessments near the conclusion of a unit of study (or relying on the tests provided by textbook publishers, which may not completely or appropriately assess *our* standards), backward design calls for us to operationalize our goals or standards in terms of assessment evidence as we *begin* to plan a unit or course. It reminds us to begin with the question, What would we accept as evidence that students have attained the desired understandings and proficiencies—*before* proceeding to plan teaching and learning experiences? Many teachers who have adopted this design approach report that the process of "thinking like an assessor" about evidence of learning not only helps them to clarify their goals but also results in a more sharply defined teaching and learning target, so that students perform better knowing their goal. Greater coherence among desired results, key performances, and teaching and learning experiences leads to better student performance—the purpose of design.

The Backward Design Process

The logic of backward design suggests a planning sequence for curriculum. This sequence has three stages, shown in Figure 1.1. In this section, we examine these stages and illustrate their application with an example of a design for a 5th grade unit on nutrition.

FIGURE 1.1 **STAGES IN THE BACKWARD DESIGN PROCESS**

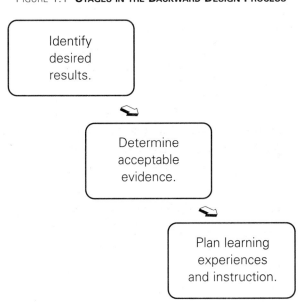

Stage 1. Identify Desired Results

What should students know, understand, and be able to do? What is worthy of understanding? What enduring understandings are desired?

In this first stage, we consider our goals, examine established content standards (national, state, and district), and review curriculum expectations. Given that there typically is more content than can reasonably be addressed, we are obliged to make choices. A useful framework for establishing curricular priorities may be depicted using the three nested rings shown in Figure 1.2 (see p. 10).

The empty background within the middle ring represents the field of possible content (topics, skills, and resources) that might be examined during the unit or course. Clearly, we cannot address all areas; thus, the largest ring identifies knowledge that students should find *worth being familiar with*. During the unit or course, what do we want students to hear, read, view, research, or otherwise encounter? For example, in an introductory course on classroom assessment, it makes sense for adult students to be conversant with the history of standardized testing in the United States and in other nations. Broad-brush knowledge, assessed through traditional quiz or test questions, would be sufficient, given the purpose of the course.

In the middle ring, we sharpen our choices by specifying *important knowledge* (facts, concepts, and principles) and *skills* (processes, strategies, and methods). We would say that student learning is incomplete if the unit or course concluded without mastery of these essentials. For instance, the characteristics of, and distinctions between, norm- and criterion-referenced assessments would be considered essential knowledge in the assessment course, and some use of that knowledge would properly be

FIGURE 1.2 **ESTABLISHING CURRICULAR PRIORITIES**

Worth being
familiar with

Important to
know and do

"Enduring"
understanding

expected. Here is another way to think about the middle ring: It specifies the prerequisite knowledge and skills needed by students for them to success-fully accomplish key performances.

The smallest ring represents finer-grain choic-es—selecting the "enduring" understandings that will anchor the unit or course. The term *enduring* refers to the big ideas, the important understand-ings, that we want students to "get inside of" and retain after they've forgotten many of the details. For the assessment course, students probably should be immersed in the principles of validity and reliabili-ty through extensive investigation, design work, and critique of sample tests, if they are to understand valid and reliable assessments.

How does one go about determining what is worth understanding amid a range of content stan-dards and topics? We offer four criteria, or filters, to use in selecting ideas and processes to teach for understanding.

Filter 1. To what extent does the idea, topic, or process represent a "big idea" having endur-ing value beyond the classroom? Enduring under-standings go beyond discrete facts or skills to focus on larger concepts, principles, or processes. As such, they are applicable to new situations within or beyond the subject. For example, we study the enactment of the Magna Carta as a specific histori-cal event *because* of its significance to a larger idea. That idea is the rule of law, whereby written laws specify the limits of a government's power and the rights of individuals—concepts such as due process. This big idea transcends its roots in 13th century England to become a cornerstone of modern democratic societies.

A big idea also can be described as a *linchpin* idea. The linchpin is the pin that keeps the wheel in place on an axle. Thus, a linchpin idea is one that is essential for understanding. For instance, without grasping the distinction between the letter and the spirit of the law, a student cannot understand the U.S. constitutional and legal system even if that student is highly knowledgeable and articulate about the facts of our history. Without a focus on linchpin ideas that have lasting value, students may be left with easily forgotten fragments of knowledge.

In sum, as Jerome Bruner (1960) put it bluntly in *The Process of Education*, "For any subject taught in primary school, we might ask [is it] worth an adult's knowing, and whether having known it as a child makes a person a better adult" (p. 52). A negative or ambiguous answer means the "material is cluttering up the curriculum."

Filter 2. To what extent does the idea, topic, or process reside at the heart of the discipline? By involving students in "doing" the subject, we provide them with insights into how knowledge is generated, tested, and used. Consider the ways professionals work within their chosen disciplines—conducting investigations in science, writing for different purposes (to inform, persuade, or entertain) to real audiences, interpreting events and primary source documents in history, applying mathematics to solve real-world problems, researching, critiquing books and movies, and debating issues of social and economic policy. Authentic learning experiences shift a student from the role of a passive knowledge receiver into a more active role as a constructor of meaning.[1]

Filter 3. To what extent does the idea, topic, or process require uncoverage? Think about the abstract ideas in the unit or course, those concepts and principles that are not obvious and may be counterintuitive. For example, in physics, students frequently struggle with ideas concerning gravity, force, and motion. When asked to predict which object—a marble or a bowling ball—will strike the ground first when dropped simultaneously, many students reveal a common misconception by incorrectly selecting the bowling ball.

What important concepts or processes do students often have difficulty grasping? What do they typically struggle with? About which big ideas are they likely to harbor a misconception? These are fruitful topics to select and uncover—by teaching for understanding.

Filter 4. To what extent does the idea, topic, or process offer potential for engaging students? Certain ideas are inherently interesting to students of various ages. And textbook knowledge that initially seems dry or inert can be brought to life by inquiries, simulations, debates, or other kinds of inherently engaging experiences. By having students encounter big ideas in ways that provoke and connect to students' interests (as questions, issues, or problems), we increase the likelihood of student engagement and sustained inquiry. For example, the question, What does it mean to be independent? not only serves as an essential question for the exploration of topics in social studies (Revolutionary War, slavery, and economics) but relates to a fundamental quest of adolescence. Ideas such as these are doorways to other big ideas, such as, What are the responsibilities and constraints that accompany increased freedoms?

None of these ideas for setting priorities and designing for better understanding is radical or new. Indeed, Bruner, in *The Process of Education* (1960), made an elegant case nearly 40 years ago for greater curricular focus on what matters most—powerful ideas with transfer:

> The curriculum of a subject should be determined by the most fundamental understanding that can be achieved of the underlying principles that give structure to a subject. . . . Teaching specific topics or skills without making clear their context in the broader fundamental structure of a field of knowledge is uneconomical. . . . An understanding of fundamental principles and ideas appears to be the main road to adequate transfer of training. To understand something as a specific instance of a more general case—which is what understanding a more fundamental structure means—is to have learned not only a specific thing but also a model for understanding other things like it that one may encounter (pp. 6, 25, and 31).

What is perhaps new is what we offer: a process and set of tools (templates and filters) to make the selection of curriculum priorities more likely to happen by design than by good fortune.

Stage 2. Determine Acceptable Evidence

How will we know if students have achieved the desired results and met the standards? What will we accept as evidence of student understanding and proficiency? The backward design approach encourages us to think about a unit or course in terms of the collected assessment evidence needed to document and validate that the desired learning has been achieved, so that the course is not just content to be covered or a series of learning activities.

This backward approach encourages teachers and curriculum planners to first think like an assessor before designing specific units and lessons, and thus to consider up front how they will determine whether students have attained the desired understandings. When planning to collect evidence of understanding, teachers should consider a range of assessment methods, depicted in Figure 1.3.

This continuum of assessment methods includes checks of understanding (such as oral questions, observations, and informal dialogues); traditional quizzes, tests, and open-ended prompts; and performance tasks and projects. They vary in scope (from simple to complex), time frame (from

FIGURE 1.3 **CONTINUUM OF ASSESSMENT METHODS**

Informal checks for understanding • Observation/Dialogue • Quiz/Test • Academic prompt • Performance task/project short-term to long-term), setting (from decontextu-alized to authentic contexts), and structure (from highly to nonstructured). Because understanding develops as a result of ongoing inquiry and rethink-ing, the assessment of understanding should be thought of in terms of a collection of evidence over time instead of an event—a single moment-in-time test at the end of instruction—as so often happens in current practice.

■ MISCONCEPTION ALERT

When we speak of evidence of understanding, we are referring to evidence gathered through a variety of formal and informal assessments during a unit of study or a course. We are not alluding only to end-of-teaching tests or culminating performance tasks. Rather, the collected evidence we seek may well include observations and dialogues, traditional quizzes and tests, performance tasks and projects, as well as students' self assessments gathered over time.

Given its focus on understanding, our unit or course will be anchored by performance tasks or pro-jects—these provide evidence that students are able to use their knowledge in context, a more appropri-ate means of evoking and assessing enduring under-standing. More traditional assessments (such as quizzes, tests, and prompts) are used to round out the picture by assessing essential knowledge and skills that contribute to the culminating perfor-mances. Figure 1.4 (see p. 14) shows the balanced use of different types of assessments. We can relate these various assessment types to the nested rings to show the relationship of curriculum priorities and assessments, as Figure 1.5 (see p. 15) illustrates.

Stage 3. Plan Learning Experiences and Instruction

With clearly identified results (enduring under-standings) and appropriate evidence of understand-ing in mind, educators can now plan instructional activities. Several key questions must be considered at this stage of backward design:

■ What enabling knowledge (facts, concepts, and principles) and skills (procedures) will students need to perform effectively and achieve desired results?

■ What activities will equip students with the needed knowledge and skills?

■ What will need to be taught and coached, and how should it best be taught, in light of perfor-mance goals?

■ What materials and resources are best suited to accomplish these goals?

■ Is the overall design coherent and effective?

Note that the teacher will address the specifics of instructional planning—choices about teaching methods, sequence of lessons, and resource materi-als—*after* identifying the desired results and assess-ments. Teaching is a means to an end. Having a clear goal helps us as educators to focus our planning and guide purposeful action toward the intended results.

Application of Backward Design

Setting: We are inside the head of a 5th grade teacher, Bob James, as he designs a three-week unit on nutrition.

Stage 1. Identify Desired Results

In reviewing our state standards in health, I found three content standards on nutrition that are benchmarked to this age level:

■ *Students will understand essential concepts about nutrition.*

■ *Students will understand elements of a balanced diet.*

■ *Students will understand their own eating patterns and ways in which these patterns may be improved.*

Figure 1.4 **TYPES OF ASSESSMENT**

Quiz and Test Items

These are simple, content-focused questions. They

- Assess for factual information, concepts, and discrete skill.
- Use selected-response or short-answer formats.
- Are convergent—typically they have a single, best answer.
- May be easily scored using an answer key (or machine scoring).
- Are typically secure (not known in advance).

Academic Prompts

These are open-ended questions or problems that require the student to think critically, not just recall knowledge, and then to prepare a response, product, or performance. They

- Require constructed responses under school or exam conditions.
- Are open. There is not a single, best answer or a best strategy for answering or solving them.
- Often are ill-structured, requiring the development of a strategy.
- Involve analysis, synthesis, or evaluation.
- Typically require an explanation or defense of the answer given or methods used.
- Require judgment-based scoring based on criteria and performance standards.
- May or may not be secure.

Performance Tasks and Projects

As complex challenges that mirror the issues and problems faced by adults, they are authentic. Ranging in length from short-term tasks to long-term, multistaged projects, they require a production or performance. They differ from prompts because they

- Feature a setting that is real or simulated: one that involves the kind of constraints, background noise, incentives, and opportunities an adult would find in a similar situation.
- Typically require the student to address an identified audience.
- Are based on a specific purpose that relates to the audience.
- Allow the student greater opportunity to personalize the task.
- Are not secure. Task, criteria, and standards are known in advance and guide the student's work.

Using these standards as the starting point, I need to decide what enduring understanding I want my students to take away from the unit. Although I've never deliberately thought about enduring knowledge, per se, I like the concept and think that it will help me focus my teaching and limited class time on the truly important aspects of this unit. As I think about the three content standards and the four filters for understanding, I think that what I'm really after is

Students will use an understanding of the elements of good nutrition to plan a balanced diet for themselves and others.

This understanding is clearly enduring, because planning nutritious menus is an authentic, lifelong

need and way to apply this knowledge. I'm still a little unclear about what "use an understanding" means, though. I'll need to reflect further on how an understanding goes beyond the use of specific knowledge. The basic concepts of nutrition are fairly straightforward, after all, as are the skills of menu planning. Does anything in the unit require, then, any in-depth and deliberate uncoverage? Are there typical misunderstandings, for example, that I ought to more deliberately focus on?

Well, as I think about it, I *have* found that many students harbor the misconception that if food is good for you, it must taste bad. One of my goals in this unit is to dispel this myth so that they won't have an automatic aversion to healthy food. In terms of the potential for engagement, no problem

---

Figure 1.5 **CURRICULAR PRIORITIES AND ASSESSMENTS**

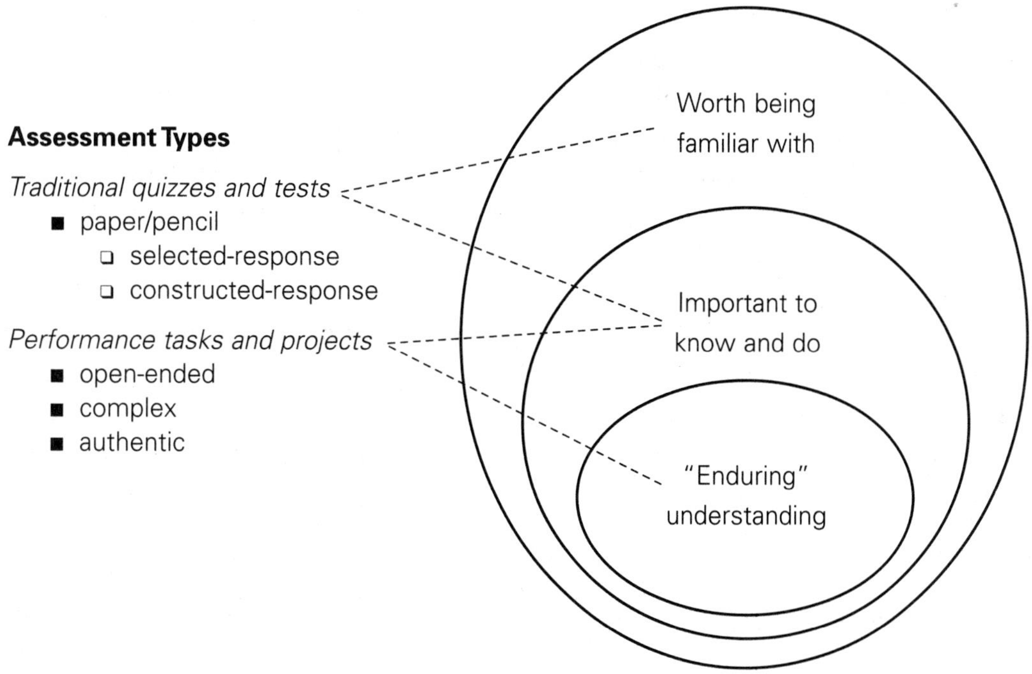

Assessment Types

Traditional quizzes and tests
- paper/pencil
  - selected-response
  - constructed-response

Performance tasks and projects
- open-ended
- complex
- authentic

Worth being familiar with

Important to know and do

"Enduring" understanding

there. Anything having to do with food is a winner with 10- and 11-year-olds. And there are some points to menu planning (such as balancing cost, variety, taste, and dietary needs) that are not at all obvious. This way of putting my goal will enable me to better focus on these points.

Stage 2. Determine Acceptable Evidence

This will be a bit of a stretch for me. Typically in a three- or four-week unit like this one, I give one or two quizzes; have a project, which I grade; and conclude with a unit test (generally multiple choice or matching). Even though this approach to assessment makes grading and justifying the grades fairly easy, I have come to realize that these assessments don't always reflect the most important understandings of the unit. I think I tend to test what is easy to test instead of assessing what is most important, namely the understandings and attitudes students should take away, above and beyond nutritional facts. In fact, one thing that has always disturbed me is that the kids tend to focus on their grades rather than on their learning. Perhaps the way I've used assessments—more for grading purposes than to document learning—has contributed somewhat to their attitude.

Now I need to think about what would serve as evidence of the enduring understanding I'm after. After reviewing some examples of performance assessments and discussing ideas with my colleagues, I have decided on the following performance task:

Because we have been learning about nutrition, the camp director at the outdoor education center has asked us to propose a nutritionally balanced menu for our three-day trip to the center later this year. Using the food pyramid guidelines and the nutrition facts on food labels, design a plan for three days, including the three meals and three snacks (a.m., p.m., and campfire). Your goal: a tasty and nutritionally balanced menu.

I'm excited about this task because it asks students to demonstrate what I really want them to take away from the unit. This task also links well with one of our unit projects: to analyze a hypothetical family's diet for a week and propose ways to improve their nutrition. With this task and project in mind, I can now use quizzes to check their prerequisite knowledge of the food groups and food pyramid recommendations, and a test for their understanding of how a nutritionally deficient diet contributes to health problems. This is the most complete assessment package I've ever designed for a unit, and I think that the task will motivate students as well as provide evidence of their understanding.

Stage 3. Plan Learning Experiences and Instruction

This is my favorite part of planning—deciding what activities the students will do during the unit and what resources and materials we'll need for those activities. But according to what I'm learning about backward design, I'll need to think first about what essential knowledge and skills my students will need to demonstrate the important understandings I'm after. Well, they'll need to know about the different food groups and the types of foods found in each group so that they will understand the USDA food pyramid recommendations. They will also need to know about human nutritional needs for carbohydrates, protein, sugar, fat, salt, vitamins, and minerals, and about the various foods that provide them. They'll have to learn about the minimum daily requirements for these nutritional elements and about various health problems that arise from poor nutrition. In terms of skills, they will have to learn how to read and interpret the nutrition fact labels on foods and how to scale a recipe up or down since these skills are necessary for their culminating project—planning healthy menus for camp.

Now for the learning experiences. I'll use resources that I've collected during the past several years—a pamphlet from the USDA on the food groups and the food pyramid recommendations; a wonderful video, "Nutrition for You"; and, of course, our health textbook (which I now plan to use selectively). As I have for the past three years, I will invite the nutritionist from the local hospital to talk about diet, health, and how to plan healthy menus. I've noticed that the kids really pay attention to a real-life user of information they're learning.

My teaching methods will follow my basic pattern—a blend of direct instruction, inductive (constructivist) methods, cooperative learning group work, and individual activities.

Planning backward has been helpful. I now can more clearly specify what knowledge and skills are really essential, given my goals for the unit. I'll be able to concentrate on the most important topics (and relieve some guilt that I am not covering everything). It is also interesting to realize that even though some sections of the textbook chapters on nutrition will be especially useful (for instance, the descriptions of health problems arising from poor nutrition), other sections are not as informative as other resources I'll now use (the brochure and video). In terms of assessment, I now know more clearly what I need to assess using traditional quizzes and tests, and why the performance task and project are needed—to have students demonstrate their understanding. I'm getting the feel for backward design.

Notice that the approach to design described in the nutrition unit has four essential features:

1. The assessments—the performance tasks and related sources of evidence—are designed *prior* to the lessons. These assessments serve as teaching targets for sharpening the focus of instruction, because we know in specific terms what we want students to understand and be able to do. These assessments also guide our decision making about what content needs to be emphasized versus content that is not essential.

2. Most likely, the familiar and favorite activities and projects will have to be modified in light of the evidence needed for assessing targeted standards. For instance, if the apple unit described in the Introduction were planned using this backward design process, we would expect some of the activities to be revised, to better support the desired enduring understandings.

3. The teaching methods and resource materials are chosen last, mindful of the work that students must produce to meet the standards. For example, rather than focusing on cooperative learning because it's the "in" teaching strategy, the question from a backward design perspective becomes, What instructional strategies will be most effective at helping us reach our targets? Cooperative learning may or may not be the best approach for a group of students and these particular standards.

4. The role of the textbook may shift from the primary resource to a supporting one. Indeed, in the

nutrition unit illustration, the 5th grade teacher realized the strengths and limitations of the text. Given other valuable resources (the nutritionist, the brochure, and the video), he didn't feel compelled to cover the book word for word.

We have presented a preliminary sketch of the big-picture design approach. Figure 1.6 shows how the three stages of design might look in practice.

Begin with a key design question; ponder how to narrow down the possibilities by setting intelligent priorities ("Design Considerations"); self-assess; self-adjust; and finally critique each element of design against appropriate criteria ("Filters"); and end up with a product that meets appropriate design standards in light of the achievement target ("What the Final Design Accomplishes").

Figure 1.6 **THE BIG PICTURE OF A DESIGN APPROACH**

Key Design Question	Design Considerations	Filters (Design Criteria)	What the Final Design Accomplishes
Stage 1. What is worthy and requiring of understanding?	National standards. State standards. District standards. Regional topic opportunities. Teacher expertise and interest.	Enduring ideas. Opportunities for authentic, discipline-based work. Uncoverage. Engaging.	Unit framed around enduring understandings and essential questions.
Stage 2. What is evidence of understanding?	Six facets of under-standing. Continuum of assessment types.	Valid. Reliable. Sufficient. Authentic work. Feasible. Student friendly.	Unit anchored in credible and educa-tionally vital evidence of the desired understandings.
Stage 3. What learning experiences and teaching promote understanding, interest, and excellence?	Research-based repertoire of learning and teaching strategies. Essential and enabling knowl-edge and skill.	WHERE Where is it going? Hook the students. Explore and equip. Rethink and revise. Exhibit and evaluate.	Coherent learning experiences and teaching that will evoke and develop the desired under-standings, promote interest, and make excellent perfor-mance more likely.

Take Stage 1, which concerns the targeted understanding. The designer must first clarify what is most worthy of understanding—in need of uncovering within a unit. Considering appropriate local, state, and national standards documents helps frame the target and prioritize instruction. The designer continues to refer to the design criteria to narrow and sharpen the focus of the unit, using the filters. The final product is a unit framed in terms of essential questions, which points clearly and explicitly toward a big idea. Refer to teacher Bob James's thinking about his nutrition unit in Stage 1 to see a hypothetical example.

In future chapters, we uncover this design process, examining its implications for the development and use of assessments, the planning and organization of curriculum, and the selection of powerful methods of teaching. In the closing chapters, we present a complete design template corre-sponding to each of the cells of Figure 1.6, a tool for designers that incorporates the elements of backward design. Finally, we visit the issue of quality control and offer a set of design standards by which assessments, curriculums, and teaching for understanding may be gauged—and improved.

Our first task, though, as the first cell in the figure suggests, is to better understand what content is worthy and needful of understanding. (Recall that teacher Bob James questioned how knowledge and skill differ from understanding.) Our first task for the next three chapters, then, is to better understand *understanding*.

Endnote

1. For greater insight into authenticity in learning and achievement, see Newmann & Associates (1997) and Wiggins (1998).

2

WHAT IS A MATTER OF UNDERSTANDING?

THIS CHAPTER FOCUSES ON THE FIRST PHASE OF curricular design: identifying our goals and determining what is worthy of understanding. Any complex unit of study will involve many targets simultaneously: knowledge, skills, attitudes, habits of mind, and understanding. We clarify how the goal of understanding differs from other achievement targets, when teaching for understanding is needed, and how to select the important understandings to focus upon. We also examine the power of essential questions for framing the curriculum and focusing instruction on matters of understanding.

What Should Be Uncovered?

Consider simple examples of our need to understand: We may read a text where we know all the words but cannot derive a meaning. We are puzzled by an unexpected comment from a friend. We have data that we cannot explain. We need to reach a decision regarding a perplexing issue. We must solve a problem with no pat solution.

The need to understand is heightened when an idea, fact, argument, or experience goes against our expectations or is counterintuitive. For instance, 12th grade students learn that a body's acceleration can decrease but its speed can still be increasing.

How can *that* be? Sixth graders multiply fractions using an algorithm. Although they have the formula, they have no clear idea why two numbers, when multiplied, yield a smaller result.

A curriculum designed to develop understanding would uncover complex, abstract, and counterintuitive ideas by involving students in active questioning, practice trying out ideas, and rethinking what they thought they knew. "Uncoverage" describes the design philosophy of guided inquiry into abstract ideas, to make those ideas more accessible, connected, meaningful, and useful. Uncoverage, then, must be done by design.

The Expert-Novice Gap

But our work as designers is complicated by the gap between expert and novice. What we as adults understand and appreciate seems of self-evident value and interest. But to the student the same idea can seem opaque, abstract—without meaning or value. A challenge we face as designers is to know the design *users* well enough—the students—to know what will need uncoverage from *their* point of view, not ours. In textbook writing, for example, important ideas are often reduced to summary sentences.

Thus, in addition to knowing our end users well, as educators, we must also know the subject well enough to get beyond inert textbook and curriculum framework language—to bring to life the important issues and people. Our designs must help the student see what is worth understanding, what needs further exploration and understanding from the activities and readings.

To begin our inquiry, let's uncover the weaknesses in these conventional curriculum designs by revisiting two vignettes from the Introduction. In the second vignette, the apples unit seems to focus in depth on a particular theme (harvest time), through a specific and familiar object (apples). But as the depiction reveals, there is no real depth because there is no enduring learning for the students to derive. The work is hands on without being "minds on," because students do not need to extract sophisticated ideas. They don't have to work at understanding; they need only experience.

Moreover, there are no clear priorities—the activities appear to be of equal value. The students' role is merely to participate in mostly enjoyable activities, without having to demonstrate that they understand any big ideas at the core of the subject (excuse the pun). All *activity-based*—as opposed to standards-based—teaching shares the weakness of the apples unit: Little in the design asks students to derive intellectual fruit from the unit. One might view this activity-oriented approach as "faith in learning by osmosis."

In the fourth vignette, the world history teacher covers vast amounts of content during the last quarter of the year. However, in his harried march to get through a textbook, the teacher apparently does not consider what the students will understand and apply from the material. Even if the course has some clear goals, how will students determine what is most important—by the number of paragraphs the textbook devotes to a topic? What kind of intellectual scaffolding is provided to guide students through the important ideas? In coverage-oriented instruction, the teacher, in effect, merely checks off topics that were covered and moves on, whether or not students understand or are confused. This approach might be termed "teaching by mentioning it."

Similar Results

Although the errors in design differ, in both units, the result is the same—student understanding of important ideas is not likely. Both the teacher of the apples unit and the history teacher would claim, if asked, that they want students to understand. "I want them to understand the importance of farming, harvesting, the role of the seasons," says the elementary school teacher. "I want students to understand the causes and effects of the two World Wars," says the high school history teacher. Yet, their curricular plans would show that understandings are more likely to occur through chance student interest and reflection than through the design of inquiry and performance. In neither case are all students guided to analyze their experience to derive understandings that the teachers claim the units are about.

Looking beyond these particular examples, let us summarize four common design flaws that work against understanding:

■ The design does not prioritize important ideas worthy of understanding. To the students, various activities and textbook topics appear of equal importance.

■ The design does not foster students' understanding because it does not encourage them to explore essential questions, link key ideas, or rethink their initial ideas or theories.

■ Students have no clear performance targets. They do not know the purpose of activities and lessons or the expected performance requirements, other than to participate in the activities and pay attention during lectures.

■ The necessary evidence that understanding has occurred has not been established. Without explicit performance goals or culminating assessments of understanding, teachers do not know which students understand what, and to what level of sophistication.

How, then, do we ensure that understanding is the true goal? We do so by knowing when to focus on understanding and when not to, and by knowing what subject matter needs uncoverage to be understood and learned.

Focusing on Priorities

Not everything we ask students to learn must be thoroughly understood. The purpose of a course or unit of study, the age of the learners, and the time available all determine how much or how little teachers can expect students to understand. But if we as educators seek greater depth and breadth, how do we set priorities amid so many content standards and despite little time? When is it worth the trouble to get students to understand? When is it sufficient for students to have only familiarity? Or acquaintance? In terms of curriculum design, how does understanding, as a target, differ from knowledge and skill?

If readers find the above questions difficult to answer, it might be because of three other complex questions:

■ What knowledge is *worth* understanding— worth spending time to uncover?

■ What kind of achievement target is understanding, and how does it differ from other targets or standards?

■ What are matters of understanding in *any*

achievement target? How does an educator identify or select the understanding element embedded or contained in *any* complex achievement target, such as state or district content standards?

Let us probe each of these questions.

What Knowledge Is *Worth* Understanding?

When should teachers require students to have an in-depth and broad understanding of something, and when should they be satisfied if students have only a superficial familiarity with it? How deep an understanding should teachers strive for in the available time? In other words, how can teachers identify the knowledge worth uncovering? Only by clarifying their priorities can teachers construct the most effective and efficient curriculum.

Earlier in this book, we stated four criteria for determining when material is worthy not just of covering but of understanding. The material should be

- Enduring.
- At the heart of the discipline.
- Needing uncovercoverage.
- Potentially engaging.

By coupling these criteria with the rings graphic introduced in Chapter 1 (Figure 1.2), we now offer a process for clarifying priorities and focusing on enduring understanding. While there are many fruitful topics worthy of understanding, the reality of teaching is that we cannot go into depth on everything. Figure 2.1 shows filters for arriving at enduring understanding. We need to make wise choices and stick with our priorities, based on the

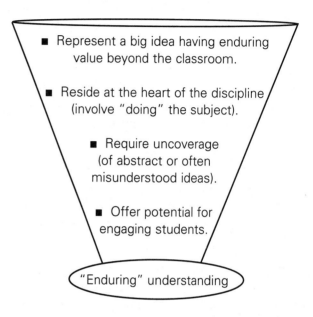

Figure 2.1 **FILTERS FOR SELECTING UNDERSTANDINGS**

- Represent a big idea having enduring value beyond the classroom.
- Reside at the heart of the discipline (involve "doing" the subject).
- Require uncoverage (of abstract or often misunderstood ideas).
- Offer potential for engaging students.

"Enduring" understanding

time available and any established curricular framework of content standards.

From a practical design point of view, a major challenge facing any designer is the inadequacy of most district, state, and national standards in helping clarify which are the big ideas and how best to uncover them. Many such statements are either too vague—"The student will be proficient in all genres of writing"—or they unhelpfully suggest that didactic teaching and rote learning will be sufficient for learning—"The student will know that there are three branches of government and why." Even when the standards identify a desired understanding, there is often too little guidance on what kinds of evidence are valid or adequate—"The student will understand that acceleration is a change in motion due to one or more forces acting on the body."

To more effectively craft and edit unit designs, we find that distinguishing three degrees of specificity and clarity in such standards is helpful. *Topical statements* are the least specific. They merely define the subject-area topic to be addressed without specifying what is to be understood and how—"Students will understand the Civil War." *General understandings* are a bit more specific. They identify what needs to be understood in an overall sense, but provide little help into the specific insights to be gained or the methods and assessments best used to gain and display such understanding—"Students will understand the causes and effects of the Civil War." *Specific understandings* not only summarize the particular understandings sought, they also suggest the kinds of work needed to achieve and show such an understanding— "Students will demonstrate through historical and social analysis and role-plays their understanding of the Civil War as a struggle of state versus federal power over economic and cultural affairs that continues to the present day."[1] Teacher-designers will likely need to amplify or sharpen the framing of the content standards into useful matters of understanding if they work in states or districts that provide less specific guidance.

Another way to frame a design issue at stake is to refer to our prioritization/assessment graphic (see Figure 1.5). Teacher-designers need to ask themselves the extent to which the standard merely requires students to be "familiar with" the textbook explanation of the Civil War—in which case a quiz on the textbook account will be sufficient—or the extent to which the standard requires the student to achieve a more complex and "enduring understanding" through analysis, synthesis, and evaluation of given accounts culminating in their own performance.

What Kind of Achievement Target Is Understanding, and How Does It Differ from Other Targets or Standards?

To understand a topic or subject is to use knowledge and skill in sophisticated, flexible ways. Knowledge and skill, then, are necessary elements of understanding, but they are not synonymous with understanding. Matters of understanding require more: Students need to make conscious sense and apt use of the knowledge they are learning and the principles underlying it.

By contrast, when we say we want students to know the key events of medieval history, to be effective touch typists, or to be competent speakers of French, the focus is on a set of facts, skills, and procedures that need only be internalized, as opposed to pondered and understood in terms of underlying principles or philosophy.

Understanding involves the abstract and conceptual, not merely the concrete and discrete: concepts, generalizations, theories, and mental links between facts. And understanding also involves the ability to use knowledge and skill in context, as opposed to doing something routine and on cue in out-of-context assignments or assessment items. So when we say we want students to understand the knowledge and skill they have learned, we are not being redundant. We want them to be able to use that knowledge in authentic situations as well as to understand the background of that knowledge. That background involves the theory or principles that give it importance, along with the reasons that justify our calling it knowledge as opposed to authoritative belief.

Because such matters of understanding are abstract and subtle, they are prone to student misunderstanding. In other words, students may know without understanding. For example, almost all students know how to multiply large numbers, but few know why the procedure works. All students know that the earth revolves around the sun, but few understand the evidence that was decisive in proving such a counterintuitive fact. Thus, a matter of understanding involves inquiring both into what makes knowledge knowledge and how to turn discrete skills into a purposeful repertoire.

What Are Matters of Understanding in *Any* Achievement Target?

Even fact-based objectives and straightforward skill development may contain latent matters of understanding. What conceptual or theoretical elements might lie within *any* objective? How can teachers identify those elements that require a more reflective understanding?

Consider, for example, persuasive writing as a desired achievement. At first blush, it would appear that we are dealing exclusively with a set of straightforward skills to be mastered. But on further reflection, we note a conceptual element here, something to intellectually uncover and better understand apart from the writing skill: The student must come to an understanding of *persuasion* and how it works if her writing is to be persuasive. The student must come to understand which techniques of persuasion work and why, and also must learn the subtleties in the role that audience, topic, and medium play in effective persuasion. In short, to learn to write persuasively, the student has to understand the *purpose* of the genre and the criteria by which we judge effectiveness of persuasion.

Also, understanding may well be developed by means other than writing. For example, to better understand persuasion, one might be asked to read famous speeches, critique TV commercials, and read and discuss such literature as Orwell's essay on language and politics. Thus, the skill goal of persuasive writing contains within it a conceptual matter of understanding.

Similarly, when working with factual knowledge or textbook summaries of big ideas, it often appears (especially to students) that there is nothing complicated about dates in history, vocabulary in language arts, or axioms in geometry. Here, too, it seems as if the only understanding that is required is attention, the need to grasp the meaning of the words in English and commit the facts to memory.

But underneath many straightforward facts is often a complicated and arguable matter of understanding, with a history worth knowing: What part of the fact might be embedded theory? For example, the "facts" of evolution are intertwined with a complex and arguable theory. Or, in vocabulary: Who determines legitimate and illegitimate meanings of words, and why do word meanings change, sometimes dramatically? For example, *objective* and *subjective* have reversed meaning from prior centuries. Or, in terms of axioms: What justifies an axiom? Why do we have the ones we have, and what makes them neither arbitrary nor true but important (e.g., the parallel postulate and its complex history)?

Problems for Understanding

In all three examples (facts, definitions, and axioms), problems for understanding lurk beneath *seemingly* unproblematic knowledge. In a curriculum for understanding, rethinking the apparently simple but actually complex is central to the nature of understanding and to a necessarily iterative approach to curricular design. Students continually must be led to recognize the *need* for uncoverage of

knowledge and skill they learn—the need for rethinking. For their part, teachers must be wary of the students' tendency to think of their own role as apprehension of textbook content as opposed to active inquiry into its justification, meaning, and value.

To put this in fancy philosophical language, the student brings a naive epistemology to the work, namely, that there is neat and clean knowledge out there and it is my job to learn (i.e., memorize) and use it as directed. A key challenge in teaching for understanding is to make the student's view of knowledge and coming-to-know more sophisticated by revealing the problems, controversies, and assumptions that lie behind much given and seemingly unproblematic knowledge. The work that teachers design should demonstrate to students that there is always a need to make sense of content knowledge through inquiries and applications—to get beyond dutiful assimilation to active reflection, testing, and meaning making.

To review, four criteria serve as filters to select ideas to teach for understanding. The idea, topic, or process

■ Represents a big idea with enduring value beyond the classroom.

■ Resides at the heart of the discipline, the "doing" of the subject in context.

■ Requires uncoverage.

■ Offers potential for engaging students.:

What specific curricular elements might meet these criteria? Here are some examples:

■ *Principles, laws, theories, or concepts* that are likely to have meaning for students if they appear to be sensible and plausible (not out of the blue or arbitrary pronouncements). In some sense, the student can verify, induce, or justify these ideas through inquiry and construction.

■ *Counterintuitive, nuanced, subtle, or otherwise easily misunderstood ideas,* such as gravity, evolution, imaginary numbers, irony, texts, formulas, theories, and concepts.

■ *The conceptual or strategic element of any skill* (e.g., persuasion in writing or "creating space" in soccer): the clarification of means and ends, and insight into strategy, leading to greater purposefulness and less mindless use of techniques. Such mindfulness can only come about by active reflection upon and analysis of performance (i.e., what works, what doesn't, and why).

Questions: Doorways to Understanding

Let me suggest one answer [to the problem of going into depth and avoiding excessive coverage] that grew from what we have done. It is the use of the organizing conjecture. They serve two functions, one of them obvious: putting perspective back into the particulars. The second is less obvious and more surprising. The questions often seemed to serve as criteria for determining where [students] were getting and how well they were understanding.

—BRUNER, 1973a, PP. 449–450

After we have identified an objective as requiring uncoverage, how do we more deliberately and practically design units and courses to develop student understanding? How might we take a mass of content knowledge and shape it to engage and focus student inquiry? One key design strategy is to build curriculum around the questions that gave rise to the content knowledge in the first place, rather than simply teaching students the "expert" answers found in textbooks.

Let's revisit the apples vignette (see Introduction) and consider possible key questions to use in framing the unit:

■ How have planting, growing, and harvest seasons affected life in the United States over the years? How have children's roles at harvest time changed? Do we still need to close schools for nearly three months in the summer?

■ How do geography and climate affect the growth of crops? Why is apple growing well suited to our region? What other regions support apple growing?

■ Who was the real Johnny Appleseed, and were there others? Will an "apple a day keep the doctor away"? Compared to other foods, how good for you are apples? Can today's apple farmers survive economically?

Notice how organizing the unit around questions such as these would provide teacher and students with a sharper focus and better direction for inquiry. The questions implicitly demand more than just a smorgasbord of activities found in the original unit. They call for students to make meaning of more carefully selected activities, and they call for teachers to devise assessment tasks related to answering them.

Regardless of which questions the teacher or class chooses, such questions render the unit design more coherent and make the student's role more appropriately intellectual. Without asking and pursuing such overarching questions, the student is confronted with a set of disconnected activities, resulting in minimal understanding of important

ideas. Without such questions to focus instruction, teaching easily falls into superficial and purposeless coverage. The world history unit in the opening vignettes (see Introduction) could be similarly improved by key questions that prioritize the textbook content for teachers and students.

At the heart of all uncoverage, then, is the deliberate interrogation of the content to be learned, as opposed to just the teaching and learning of the material. While this focus may sound odd, it points to an important truth about coming to understand: Knowledge must be more than mentioned or referred to in indiscriminate ways. Important ideas must be questioned and verified if they are to be understood. One might say that content that hasn't been questioned is like courtroom claims that are never examined, leading to a hodgepodge of opinions and beliefs instead of to knowledge.

Practically speaking, we must turn content standards and outcome statements into question form, and then design assignments and assessments that evoke possible answers. In contrast, most current curricular frameworks and standards documents make the mistake of framing core content as fact-like sentences rather than revealing them to be *culminating* summary insights, derived from questions and inquiries.[2] We should not be surprised, then, if we continue to see apple and world history units of the kind described in the Introduction. Only by framing our teaching around valued questions and worthy performances can we overcome activity-based and coverage-oriented instruction, and the resulting rote learning that produces formulaic answers and surface-level knowledge.

As Bruner's opening quote suggests, the best curriculum-guiding questions have another virtue— they serve as criteria against which to judge progress

in learning. For example, from the work to date, are we getting clearer about the apple's influence on our region's economy and culture? Do we yet have sufficient insight into the economics of farming? Student responses enable us to test our activity and assignment designs to ensure that learning is more than only engaging activity or indiscriminate coverage. Are we making headway in answering the questions? If not, students *and* teacher need to adjust.

Essential and Unit Questions

What types of questions might guide our teaching and engage students in uncovering the important ideas at the heart of each subject? We might begin to identify such questions by using the format found in the quiz show *Jeopardy*. Given the content found in a textbook—the answers to be learned—what is an important question for which the textbook provides an answer? For instance, if "balance of powers" (a core idea) is the answer, then what are some questions that give rise to it? Were there *other* answers that once seemed plausible but turned out to be less useful or correct? For the balance of power example, such a question might be: What structure of government best suits the fact that "all men are not angels" (to quote the *Federalist Papers*)?

Not just any question will do. Consider the following questions and notice how they differ from those typically posed during daily lessons and in textbooks:

■ Is there enough to go around (e.g., food, clothes, water?

■ Is history a history of progress?

■ Does art reflect culture or shape it?

■ Are mathematical ideas inventions or discoveries?

■ Must a story have a beginning, middle, and end?

■ When is a law unjust?

■ Is gravity a fact or a theory?

■ What do we fear?

■ Who owns what and why?

■ Is biology destiny?

These types of questions cannot be answered satisfactorily in a sentence—and that's the point. To get at matters of deep and enduring understanding, we need to use provocative and multilayered questions that reveal the richness and complexities of a subject. We refer to such questions as "essential" because they point to the key inquiries and the core ideas of a discipline. Figure 2.2 offers some tips for using essential questions.

Bruner (1996) suggests that questions of this type "are ones that pose dilemmas, subvert obvious or canonical 'truths' or force incongruities upon our attention" (p. 127). He provides an apt example of an essential question in biology, a recurring question that can be used to organize a unit, course, or entire program:

> One of the principal organizing concepts in biology is the question, "What function does this thing serve?"—a question premised on the assumption that everything one finds in an organism serves some function or it probably would not have survived. Other general ideas are related to this question. The student who makes progress in biology learns to ask the question more and more subtly, to relate more and more things to it (Bruner, 1960, p. 28).

Essential questions can and should be asked over and over. Practically speaking, they can recur across the curriculum (horizontally) and over the years (vertically). Central Park East Secondary School in New York, the school

Figure 2.2 **TIPS FOR USING ESSENTIAL QUESTIONS**

■ Organize programs, courses, units of study, and lessons around the questions. Make the *content* the answers to the questions.

■ Select or design assessment tasks, up front, that are explicitly linked to the questions. The tasks and performance standards should clarify what acceptable pursuit of, and answers to, the questions actually look like.

■ Use a reasonable number of questions per unit (between two and five). Make less be more. Prioritize content for students to make the work clearly focus on a *few* key questions.

■ Edit the questions to make them as engaging and provocative as possible for the particular age group. Frame the questions in "kid language" as appropriate.

■ Through a survey or informal check, ensure that every child understands the questions and sees their value.

■ Derive and design specific concrete exploratory activities and inquiries for each question.

■ Sequence the questions so they lead naturally from one to another.

■ Post the overarching questions in the classroom, and encourage students to organize notebooks around them to emphasize their importance for study and note taking.

■ Help students personalize the questions. Encourage them to share examples, personal stories, and hunches, and to bring clippings and artifacts to class to help the questions come alive.

■ Allot sufficient time for "unpacking" the questions—examining subquestions and probing implications. Be mindful of student age, experience, and other instructional obligations. Use question-concept maps to show relatedness of questions.

■ Share your questions with other faculty to make planning and teaching for cross-subject matter coherence far more likely. To promote essential questions schoolwide, ask teachers to post their essential questions in the faculty room or in department meeting and planning areas. Circulate questions in the faculty bulletin and present and discuss them at faculty meetings.

---

founded by Deborah Meier, builds its entire curriculum around a set of such essential questions linked to key "habits of mind":

> In every class and every subject, students will learn to ask and to answer these questions:
> a. From whose viewpoint are we seeing or reading or hearing? From what angle or perspective?
> b. How do we know when we know? What's the evidence, and how reliable is it?
> c. How are things, events, or people connected to each other? What is the cause and what is the effect? How do they fit together?
> d. What's new and what's old? Have we run across this idea before?

> e. So what? Why does it matter? What does it all mean? (Courtesy of Central Park East Secondary School.)

Essential questions may be characterized by what they do:

■ *Go to the heart of a discipline.* Essential questions can be found in the most historically important and controversial problems and topics in various fields of study: Is a "good read" a great book? Was arithmetic an invention or a discovery? Is history always biased? Do men naturally differ from women?

■ *Recur naturally throughout one's learning and in the history of a field.* The same important questions are asked and re-asked as an outgrowth of the work. Our answers may become increasingly sophisticated, and our framing of the question may reflect a new nuance, but we return again and again to such questions.

■ *Raise other important questions.* They invariably open up a subject, its complexities, and its puzzles; they suggest fruitful research rather than lead to premature closure or unambiguous answers. For example, What do we mean by "naturally" differ?

Essential questions have proven to be an effective way of framing a course or an entire program of study. Indeed, some school districts have grounded their curriculum in essential questions.[3]

Experience has shown that an essential question may not always serve as a fruitful doorway into a specific topic, despite the question's overarching and provocative nature. The question may simply prove to be too global, abstract, or inaccessible for students (e.g., Is biology destiny?). Thus, more specific questions are often needed to introduce and guide the work of a particular unit of study.

We find it helpful to distinguish between two types of curriculum-framing questions: *essential* questions and *unit* questions. Unit questions are more subject- and topic-specific, and therefore better suited for framing particular content and inquiry, leading to the often more subtle essential questions. The differences in specificity are illustrated by the examples in Figure 2.3. Unit questions such as those in the figure

■ *Provide subject- and topic-specific doorways to essential questions.* Unit questions frame a specific set of lessons; they are designed to point to and uncover essential questions through the lens of particular topics and subjects. For example, Is science fiction great literature? is a unit question that guides inquiry in a specific literature course. Are "good reads" great books? is an essential question that the entire English/Language Arts faculty in a district or school would address.

■ *Have no one obvious "right" answer.* Answers to unit questions are not self-evidently true. Unit questions open up and suggest important multiple lines of research and discussion; they uncover rather than cover up the subject's controversies, puzzles, and perspectives. They serve as discussion starters and problem posers, rather than lead toward "the" answer the teacher wants.

■ *Are deliberately framed to provoke and sustain student interest.* Unit questions work best when they are designed to be thought provoking to students. Such questions often involve the counterintuitive, the thought provoking, and the controversial as a means of engaging students in sustained inquiries. They should be sufficiently open to accommodate diverse interests and learning styles and allow for unique responses and creative approaches—even ones that the teacher had not considered.[4]

It is important to note that the distinctions between essential and unit questions are not categorically pure, not black and white. Instead, they should be viewed as residing along a continuum of specificity as shades of gray. The point is not to quibble about whether a given question is an essential or a unit question, but rather to focus on its larger purposes—to frame the learning, engage the learner, link to more specific or more general

Figure 2.3 **SAMPLE ESSENTIAL AND UNIT QUESTIONS**

Essential Question	Unit Question
Must a story have a moral, heroes, and villains?	What is the moral of the story of the Holocaust? Is Huck Finn a hero?
How does an organism's structure enable it to survive in its environment?	How do the structures of amphibians and reptiles support their survival?
Who is a friend?	Are Frog and Toad true friends? Has it been true in recent U.S. history and foreign affairs that "the enemy of my enemy is my friend"?
What is light?	How do cats see in the dark? Is light a particle or a wave?
Do we always mean what we say and say what we mean?	What are sarcasm, irony, and satire? How do these genres allow us to communicate *without* saying what we mean?
Is U.S. history a history of progress?	Is the gap between rich and poor any better now than it was 100 years ago? Do new technologies always lead to progress?

questions, and guide the exploration and uncovering of important ideas.

Questions do more than serve as doorways to understanding. They can effectively establish priorities in a course of study. The following *set* of such questions, posed by two history scholars (Burns & Morris, 1986), is a way of coming to understand the U.S. Constitution. Think of an entire course in civics, government, or U.S. history designed around these questions:

■ *Is there too much—or too little—national power?* Are the limits placed on the federal government's powers by the U.S. Constitution realistic and enforceable?

■ *Does federalism work?* Is the Constitution maintaining an efficient and realistic balance between national and state power?

■ *Is the judicial branch too powerful?* Are the courts exercising their powers appropriately as interpreters of the Constitution and shapers of public policy?

■ *Can liberty and security be balanced?* How can a republican government provide for the national security without endangering civil liberties?

- *What do we mean by "All men are created equal"?* What kinds of equality are and should be protected by the Constitution and by what means?

- *Are the rights of women and minorities adequately safeguarded?*

- *Does the president possess adequate—or too much—power over war making and foreign policy?*

- *Does the U.S. Government have too many constitutional checks and balances?* Does the separation of powers among the three branches of government create a deadlock in governance?

Such questions are not just posed once orally by teachers. They are posted on blackboards, as the headings of student pages in notebooks, and on unit handouts. They frame and structure the lessons and give rise to appropriate research, note taking, and final performance.

In the absence of explicit overarching questions, students are left with rhetorical questions in a march through coverage or activities. Students then come to realize that their *real* job is to take in sanctioned views, as purveyed in authoritative teacher and textbook pronouncements. Such official opinions, especially when combined with many leading teacher questions, will eventually stifle thoughtful inquiry, as the philosopher Gadamer (1994) suggests:

> It is opinion that suppresses questions. Opinion has a curious tendency to propagate itself . . . to question means to lay open to place in the open. As against the fixity of opinions, questioning makes the object and its possibilities fluid. A person skilled in the "art" of questioning is a person who can prevent questions from being suppressed by the dominant opinion. . . . Only a person who has questions can have [understanding] (pp. 364–367).

A Cycle of Questions-Answers-Questions

Our *designs*, not just our teaching style, must ensure that students see learning as anchored in questions and requiring cycles of questions-answers-questions. The key to understanding by design is to cause rethinking through appropriate inquiry and performance. That work requires a very different curricular design than the typical scope and sequence of a march through answers, with those expert answers unmoored from the questions that gave rise to them in the first place.

When merely learning answers is the goal, too often the instruction ironically precludes students from pursuing the questions that *naturally arise* in the unfolding work—leading to less understanding as well as less engagement. That result is because a unit is too often tacitly conceived as a set of unproblematic facts and theories to be learned without interrogation.

Simple examples from mathematics can illustrate the need. It would be silly to argue that students only need to learn the theorems in geometry in the form of statements to be memorized without their also learning about the proofs that justify the theorems—learning how to come up with and recreate such proofs. There is no other way to understand except through asking: Why *is* it true a triangle always has 180 degrees? How can we say that for sure? We would think it odd or unacceptable for a geometry teacher to argue that there is no time to inquire into theorem statements because there are so many proofs to cover. Yet, this approach is now unfortunately what many teachers end up doing when they march through books and lessons as if hearing and reading facts were sufficient to understand those facts.

Questions not only focus learning, they also make all subject-knowledge possible. If students are to understand what is known, they need to simulate or recreate some of the inquiry by which the knowledge was created. Such an approach is, after all, how the pioneer came to understand the unknown: asking questions and testing ideas.[5] Think of curriculum as not just the teaching of what we know but the designing of student inquiries into what justifies calling the content that is covered genuine knowledge; into how the knowledge came to be understood (i.e., the history of what is known and the different interpretations that have occurred and are possible); and into the value or importance of the knowledge (found through applying it). As later chapters show, such explorations and performances are central to our attempts to make sense of anything we don't understand and to demonstrate that we understand it.

■ MISCONCEPTION ALERT

To say that "coursework derives from questions" might be misunderstood, however, because all teachers ask questions. We mean here the development and unfolding of content out of *itself*, not teacher probing of student answers or the asking of leading questions. Anchoring work in questions in this sense is very different from teachers' using questions to check for factual knowledge, move toward the right answer, or sharpen students' responses. Too often, students leave school never realizing that knowledge is answers to someone's prior questions, produced and refined in response to puzzles, inquiry, testing, argument, and revision. To teach from questions means rhetorically asking, If knowledge is made up of answers, then what were the questions that gave rise to textbook or teacher answers and current subject-matter knowledge answers?

Entry-Point Questions for Understanding

Essential and unit questions, though thought provoking, are typically difficult and sometimes esoteric. The questions may not initially connect with the experiences or interest of students. Or students may have a hard time seeing the relationship of an overarching question to the facts and skills they are expected to learn. How, then, do we introduce students to big-idea questions? How do we make essential or unit questions an accessible and useful foundation upon which inquiry and performance can be built? We do so by starting units with provocative and specific entry-point questions that point to the larger questions.

Students of all ages—children and adults—need concrete and meaningful experiences, problems, applications, and shifts of perspective to enable an important question to *arise*. An abstract discussion of property rights is made quickly accessible and intriguing by asking students if the saying, "Finders keepers, losers weepers," is a sound moral principle, and by building role-play around the idea. Then, when the discussion and exercise are de-briefed, the larger questions about property naturally arise. The student must come to understand each unit and its specific questions and activities as raising larger questions. *If we do our preliminary entry-point question and activity design well, the student is more likely to spontaneously ask important questions and more quickly see their importance. Such insight is a key indicator of the success of our design for understanding.*

In science, suppose the unit centers on the basic astronomy idea discussed earlier. Starting with the question, Why is the heliocentric view more justified than the geocentric view in explaining phenomena? is unlikely to capture the interest of most students. On the other hand, merely stating the truth—i.e., providing an answer to a question the student has not asked or been helped to ask—bypasses inquiry and deep understanding. We might begin instead with a dare: Can you provide a plausible argument that the earth is stationary? Or, we might begin instead with the question, Why is it warmer in summer and colder in winter? and ask students to come up with provisional answers. We might then encourage them to interview a few other people—students and adults—to ask their opinion. Larger questions naturally arise out of the debate or surveys once the correct answer is known: Why is the right answer so poorly understood? Why is the truth so counterintuitive? How was it figured out? At some point in the unit, other inquiry or essential questions may arise: Is science "common sense" or not? What did Ptolemy explain clearly, but it took thousands of years before the current theory was developed? How did Copernicus, Kepler, and Newton come up with the modern answer?

We do not mean to imply that students are never ready, willing, and able to handle important questions. On the contrary, sometimes a simple introductory talk, problem, or case study can make them ready for a headlong assault on a question occupying the greatest minds. For that matter, students sometimes ask such questions entirely on their own, and the teachable moment has arrived. Our caution is that teachers and curriculum designers should map out a likely progression of simple to complex questions to provide a framework for the unfolding of student inquiry. Often the essential or unit question cannot be immediately accessible or useful without background knowledge and investigation.

Though we discuss the practical structuring of such work in later chapters, the general point here is that plunking down a big-idea question at the beginning of a unit may not always succeed in stimulating interest and inquiry. The student typically does not know enough or care enough about the issues involved to see the need or value in addressing such a question. Rather, simple introductory questions are needed that frame the design of lessons or a unit as lead-ins to the overarching unit and essential questions.

One straightforward first approach for making essential or unit guiding questions more accessible is through selective editing. This method was used by a teacher in New York State for a Russian history unit within a global studies course. He modified the original essential question, Was Gorbachev a hero or a traitor to his country? with a simple edit to create an entry-point question linked to provocative role-play. The students were involved in a meeting-of-the-minds format involving Gorbachev, Yeltsin, Lenin, Stalin, Marx, Trotsky, and Catherine the Great. The debate question was, Who Blew It? The work culminated in a mock newspaper article and editorial, and an essay on the key unit question.

Thus, guidelines for entry-point questions involve four criteria. The questions should be framed for maximal simplicity; be worded in student-friendly language; provoke discussion and questions; and point toward the larger essential and unit questions. Heidi Hayes Jacobs cites an example of an entry-point question to use with young children: What is snow?[6] The question quickly challenges the boundaries of the concept that press the matter deeper: Is snow ice? Is ice water? Is man-made snow the same as natural snow? Here are some other examples of possible entry-point questions:

■ Start with the expression, "You know who your real friends are," then ask, Do you? (Can be used to study works such as *A Separate Peace*, *To Kill a Mockingbird*, and *Pigman*, with the same question asked in different ways.)

■ Does food that is good for you have to taste bad? (Used as a stimulus to some lessons in the nutrition unit discussed throughout this book.)

■ In what ways is a fairy-tale "true"? In what ways is any documentary "false"? (Can be used to compare myths, novels, biographies, histories, and docudramas.)

■ Was George Washington any different from Palestinian terrorists trying to protect their country?

■ Is a straight line always the shortest possible distance? (Can be used to study spherical and other non-Euclidean geometries.)

■ Was Jefferson a hypocrite? Did he really think of a slave as a sub-human while writing the Declaration of Independence?

■ What makes people act phony? (Can be used to introduce *Catcher in the Rye*.)

■ Is slang untranslatable? (Can be used to introduce colloquialisms and the problems of translating into a foreign language.)

■ Is honesty the best policy or just the right thing to do? (Can be used to study noble characters in literature and history.)

The kinds of entry-point questions we are discussing often emerge from student responses to lessons or inquiries, followed by guided reflection on their work. Here are examples of student questions:

■ Wait, yesterday you said it's colder in winter because of the sun's angle, but how does that explain cold days in summer? And why aren't the coldest days of the year in December?

■ How can that be? How could we have called ourselves a democracy but not have allowed people to directly elect their own senators for over a century?

■ But if Oedipus was really so clever, why would he be so blind to. . . ?

Indeed, if you are not getting at least occasional student questions such as these, it is likely that not enough opportunity for digging into ideas is being provided; that is, instruction is too didactic or textbook driven.

A Return to the Nutrition Unit

Setting: Bob James, our teacher from Chapter 1 who was designing a unit on nutrition, reflects on the role of essential and unit questions.

This idea of essential and unit questions has really gotten me thinking. I'm especially intrigued by this notion: If the textbook contains the answers, then what are the questions? As I reflect on my own education, I can't recall ever being in a course in which the content was framed around important, thought-provoking questions. Some of my teachers and professors asked thought-provoking questions during class, but I see these essential questions as different. I see how they provide a focus for all the work and knowledge mastery, if done right. I now feel a bit cheated since I'm beginning to realize the power of these overarching questions for pointing to the bigger ideas within a subject or topic.

Ever since I began teaching, I have tried to get my students to stretch their thinking by asking questions such as: Can you give another example of ____? How does ____ relate to ____? What

might happen if ____? Do you agree with ____, and why or why not? While I'm pretty good at posing these day-to-day questions, I realize that for the nutrition unit, I'll have to give more thought to up-front questions.

Well, I suppose a basic question for the unit should be, What is healthy eating? That gets at the essence of what I want my students to take away—the enduring understanding. It also links naturally to larger essential questions that could be used to frame the entire health curriculum: What is healthy living? What is wellness? But will that grab my kids? A more provocative entry question might be, Can food that is good for you also taste good? That might work because kids at this age are fond of junk food, and many seem to believe that if food is nutritional, it has to taste "yucky."

To see if I was on the right track, I brought up my ideas over lunch with a few of the teachers in the faculty room, and they really got into it! We had a very interesting discussion about my question that led to other questions: If left on their own, will children eat what they need nutritionally? Do tastes change as we grow up—in the direction of healthier eating? If so, why? What about others in the animal kingdom, then? Do young animals naturally eat what is good for them? What is the role of junk food advertising on the eating patterns of children and adults? We were really "cooking" when the lunch period ended and I had to leave for recess duty. I think I'll stew on this awhile.

(Later) I've decided to keep my initial question, What is healthy eating? for the overall unit, but I'll use an entry question, Can food that is good for you also taste good? to get the students involved from the start. Because I try to give my kids some say in what they'll be learning, I'll also ask them for

any questions that interest them about eating and health. A 3rd grade teacher suggested posting these overarching questions on a bulletin board. I really like this idea because the posted questions will provide a visible reminder of the focus of our work during the unit.

Now that I'm adding essential and unit questions to my teaching repertoire, I can be even more effective in framing my units of study around important ideas. In addition, these questions will provide a clearer focus for my kids and a sharper target for my own teaching.

Endnotes

1. Some of the clearer state and district documents take a slightly different formatting approach. They first state the standard, then use bulleted indicators to show the kinds of lessons, activities, and performances that are appropriate for learning and assessing such standards.

2. See Chapter 1 of Erickson (1998) for a thorough discussion of the limits of various national standards documents and the need to be clearer about the questions and understandings sought.

3. For example, Lake Washington School District in Redmond, Washington, and Pomperaug Regional School District 15 in Middlebury, Connecticut, use discipline-based essential questions to guide their development of courses, units, and accompanying performance assessment tasks. For further information, see Erickson (1998) and Educators in Connecticut's Pomperaug Regional School District 15 (1996).

4. A variant of these questions and criteria was first proposed in Wiggins (1987a). In the Harvard *Teaching for Understanding* project (Wiske, 1997) and Blythe & Associates (1998), when used as overarching course and program standards, such questions are presented under the heading of "throughlines." See pp. 69 ff. in Wiske, 1997.

5. This is not a blanket call for a discovery-based or recapitulationist approach to instruction. Rather, we note here that understanding a big idea typically requires the kind of active inquiry, discussion, and applications we describe. See Chapter 8 for a more comprehensive discussion of the problem.

6. For other ideas on how to make effective use of such questions, readers should consult Jacobs's new book on curriculum mapping (1997, pp. 26–33). It has a short but insightful chapter on essential questions as a way of curricular mapping, with other fine examples and ideas for their use.

3

UNDERSTANDING UNDERSTANDING

*Education: That which discloses
to the wise and disguises from the foolish
their lack of understanding.*
—AMBROSE BIERCE, *THE DEVIL'S DICTIONARY* (1881–1906)

UP TO NOW WE HAVE PRESENTED UNDERSTANDING AS if we understood it. The irony is that though we all claim, as teachers, to be after understanding we may not adequately understand our goal. But how can this be? Teachers aim for understanding every day, don't they? How can they not know what they are aiming for? Yet, there is plenty of evidence to suggest that "to understand" and "teach for understanding" are ambiguous and slippery terms.

This conceptual uncertainty appears in the *Taxonomy of Educational Objectives: Classification of Educational Goals* (Bloom, 1956). Bloom and his colleagues wrote the book to classify and clarify the range of possible intellectual objectives, from the cognitively easy to the difficult. They intended to classify degrees of understanding, in effect. Bloom and his coauthors said the writing of the book was driven by persistent problems in testing: Just how should educational objectives or teacher goals be measured in light of the fact that there was (and is, in our opinion) no clear meaning to or agreement about the meaning of objectives such as "critical grasp of" and "thorough knowledge of"—phrases that test developers must make operational?

In the introduction to the taxonomy, Bloom (1956) refers to "understanding" as a commonly sought but ill-defined objective:

> For example, some teachers believe their students should "really understand," others desire their students to "internalize knowledge," still others

want their students to "grasp the core or essence." Do they all mean the same thing? Specifically, what does a student do who "really understands," which he does not do when he does not understand? Through reference to the Taxonomy . . . teachers should be able to define such nebulous terms (p. 1).

To better grasp the importance of this conceptual problem and the difficulties of resolving it, let us turn to the discussion of terminology in the American Association for the Advancement of Science (AAAS) *Benchmarks for Science Literacy* (1993). The authors succinctly describe the problem they faced in framing benchmarks for science teaching and assessing:

> *Benchmarks* uses "know" and "know how" to lead into each set of benchmarks. The alternative would have been to use a finely graded series of verbs, including "recognize," "be familiar with," "appreciate," "grasp," "know," "comprehend," "understand," and others, each implying a somewhat greater degree of sophistication and completeness than the one before. The problem with the graded series is that different readers have different opinions of what the proper order is (p. 312).

The authors say they also decided against specifying action verbs or observable behaviors to clarify what kinds of evidence were required to reveal understanding, because "the choice among them is arbitrary" and using particular verbs "would be limiting and might imply a unique performance that was not intended" (pp. 312–313).

Yet the authors' resolution of the problem is unsatisfying. Without clarity about appropriate kinds of work and criteria to be met, a teacher might well be satisfied by a factual test of knowledge, even

though only a complex experiment and defense of procedure will truly do justice to the standard. The argument for backward design takes the view that we are not likely to achieve our target of understanding unless we are explicit about what counts as *evidence* of understanding. And the more we ask that nitty-gritty question, the clearer it is that we do not adequately understand understanding.

Understanding and Apparent Understanding

Knowing the facts and doing well on tests of knowledge do not mean that we understand. Bloom (1956) and his colleagues remind us to be specific about how understanding differs from merely accurate knowledge when they recount a famous John Dewey story:

> Almost everyone has had the experience of being unable to answer a question involving recall when the question is stated in one form, and then having little difficulty . . . when the question is stated in another form. This is well illustrated by John Dewey's story in which he asked a class, "What would you find if you dug a hole in the earth?" Getting no response, he repeated the question; again he obtained nothing but silence. The teacher chided Dr. Dewey, "You're asking the wrong question." Turning to the class, she asked, "What is the state of the center of the earth?" The class replied in unison, "igneous fusion" (p. 29).

Dewey's story also illustrates the rote recall nature of some knowledge learning. The emphasis on knowledge as involving little more than remembering or recall distinguishes it from conceptions of knowledge that involve understanding or

insight, or that are phrased as "really know" or "true knowledge."

A Universal Problem

While extreme, this example illustrates a universal problem. Teachers are often satisfied by signs of apparent understanding, such as when students deliver the right words, definitions, or formulas. And the problem is greatly exacerbated by a world of high-stakes testing and grading. For as long as there is a cat-and-mouse game in education that gives students an incentive to *appear* to understand what they are supposed to be learning, the challenge of teaching and assessing will be great.

The authors of the *Taxonomy of Educational Objectives* made a helpful conceptual distinction: Real knowledge involves using learning in new ways (what is often called "transfer"). They distinguish this intellectual ability from knowledge that is based on recall and scripted use. Similarly, Perkins, in the recent book *Teaching for Understanding* (Wiske, 1997), defines understanding as, "the ability to think and act flexibly with what one knows . . . a flexible performance capability as opposed to rote recall or plugging in of answers" (p. 40). Yet, this important distinction is often lost in conventional testing, in which one session of right answers is seen as sufficient evidence of competence. (Remember the Introduction's vignette about the class valedictorian who admitted a lack of understanding despite high marks on tests of recall.)

A Need for Conceptual Clarity

In short, what we call understanding is not a matter of "mere" semantics but one of conceptual clarity. We sharpen the distinction between a superficial or borrowed opinion and an in-depth, justified understanding of the same idea. It does not matter what we call understanding-related targets, but it matters greatly that we specify what types of student work and assessment evidence characterize a student as "really understanding." Without this clarification, we retain assessment habits that focus on the more superficial, rote, out-of-context, and easily tested aspects of knowledge.

But if "correct" answers may offer inadequate evidence of understanding, or if good test results can hide misunderstanding, then what *is* understanding, and how is it more effectively and reliably revealed by design? To design effective units and assessments, educators need to be grounded in a better understanding of understanding.

What Our Language Reveals About Understanding

The English language offers a challenge to *understanding* as a word, with different meanings. A closer look at everyday speech and usage also suggests that understanding is a matter of degree, symbolizes not one achievement but several, and is revealed through diverse performances and products.

Consider the adjectives we use, describing understanding as "deep" or "in depth," as opposed to "superficial." Understanding "takes time and practice." Understandings are developed, "hard won." Thus, understanding is not immediate, not a matter of "either you get it or you don't" (Perkins, 1992, p. 78), but a matter of degree. The continuum of understandings ranges from naive to sophisticated, and from simplistic to complex (as opposed to merely right or wrong). In all these connotations, the emphasis is on getting below the surface, or achieving greater nuance and discrimination in judgment. To understand means not just knowledge of more difficult things but also the ability to offer qualifications and conditionals—to say, "If . . . then . . ." and "Under these conditions yes, but under those no."

In terms of synonyms for the noun form of *understanding*, it is common for educators to talk about insight and wisdom—both clearly different from, yet somehow related to, knowledge. Yet our language also suggests that real understanding is beyond academic understanding. The expressions "egghead" and "pointy-headed intellectual" suggest that mere intellectual prowess can be sham understanding, and that too much learning can sometimes *impede* understanding, as this chapter's opening quotation from Bierce suggests.

The verbs educators use in describing understanding are equally instructive: You understand it only if you can teach it, use it, prove it, explain it, defend it, or read between the lines. Clearly, the argument for performance assessment ties into these usages: The students must perform using knowledge to convince us that they really understand material that quizzes and short-answer tests only *suggest* they understand. And, understandings can differ: To talk about seeing things from an interesting perspective is to imply that complex ideas invariably have legitimate diverse points of view.

Moreover, the verb form of *understanding* (to understand) has an interpersonal as well as an intellectual meaning. We try to understand ideas, but we also work to understand other people and situations. We talk of "coming to understand" or "reaching an understanding" in the context of social relations. We sometimes talk of "changing our mind" or

"having a change of heart" after a great effort to understand a complex matter.

The *Oxford English Dictionary* says the verb *understand* means "to apprehend the meaning or import" of an idea. Recall, as an example of this usage, the recent case of a 6-year-old boy charged with sexual harassment for kissing a girl in his class. As reported in the paper, the father's response was, "We might read him that sexual harassment [policy statement] all night, and he might be bright enough to remember it. But would he understand it?" (*New York Times,* 1996b, p. A14).

Whether we use terms like *wisdom, insight,* or *maturity* to make this sense of the term clearer, understanding implies the ability to escape a naive or inexperienced point of view. Similarly, when describing adults, we imply that to understand a difficult situation means to escape the understandable passions, inclinations, and dominant opinions of the moment to do what circumspection and reflection reveal to be best.

Sometimes, to understand another we need the opposite of distance—a conscious rapport—if we are to understand, as in "Boy, do I understand what you're going through." When one person fails to understand another, there usually is a failure to consider or imagine the possibility of different points of view, much less "walking in their shoes." It has become a cliché of gender relations that one person says to the other, "You just don't understand." Tannen's (1990) book on gender differences in conversation, *You Just Don't Understand: Women and Men in Conversation,* suggests that interpersonal understanding requires grasping unstated, but very real, differing styles and purposes for conversation.

Her observation is borne out in cross-cultural conflict, as seen in the following quotes from the

New York Times (1996a) about a flare-up of violence in the Middle East:

> Both sides were taken aback by the speed and fury with which the ancient hatreds resurfaced, however, and there were some voices predicting that the conflagration would produce a renewed sense that two peoples cannot live in such close quarters without coming to some form of understanding. . . .
>
> We will come to [the idea of peace] out of fatigue. We will come to this idea out of a very painful understanding that the way to war leads us nowhere (p. A1).

Student Misunderstanding and What It Tells Us

We also gain a crucial insight into our quarry, understanding, by considering its opposite. Somehow, well-intentioned students can take away lessons that their teachers never intended. What is our true complaint when we say students just don't seem to understand what they have learned? *The Catcher in the Rye* is a fixture of U.S. high school English courses, for example. Many students who read the book believe it is about Holden's "excellent adventure," living the life of a hooky-playing prep school student. Often, the fact that Holden is in great emotional pain, and that he tells the story from his hospital bed, gets lost, unseen—perhaps denied—by many students.

Different from Ignorance

Misunderstanding is not ignorance. It is the mapping of an idea onto a plausible but incorrect framework, as when one of our own children asked, "Dad, are Spanish and English using the same words, but just pronouncing them differently?" One has to have a fair amount of knowledge to misunderstand things. One of the authors taught a very bright and able boy who had taken advanced placement science courses but who thought "error" in science meant avoidable mistakes, as opposed to being inherent in inductive reasoning.

We get a glimmer of the deeper problem of teaching for understanding and the anxieties it raises for us when we watch other teachers lose their patience with students who don't "get" the lesson. When *attentive* students don't "get it," we are liable to question many of our methods and implied goals.

Research on Misconception

A sense of greater urgency stems from research over the past 20 years. Such research shows that even some of the best students, who appear to understand class material—as revealed by their tests and in-class discussion—later reveal significant misunderstanding of what they learned when asked to answer follow-up questions or to apply what they learned. Gardner, Perkins, and their Harvard colleagues at Project Zero have summarized these findings eloquently and thoroughly in the past six years, though the misconception research goes back to work in science in the 1970s.

As Gardner (1991) sums up the research:

> [What] an extensive research literature now documents is that an ordinary degree of understanding is routinely missing in many, perhaps most students. It is reasonable to expect a college student to be able to apply in new context a law of physics, or a proof in geometry, or the concept in history of which she has just demonstrated acceptable mastery in her class. If, when the circumstances of testing are slightly altered,

the sought-after competence can no longer be documented, then understanding—in any reasonable sense of the term—has simply not been achieved (p. 6).

Confirmed by Testing

Even conventional testing can reveal failures to understand. Consider this result in mathematics: Most U.S. teenagers study Algebra I and get passing grades. Yet National Assessment of Educational Progress (NAEP) results show that only 5 percent of U.S. adolescents perform well at tasks requiring higher-order use of Algebra I knowledge (NAEP, 1988). The recent Third International Math and Science Study (TIMSS) reached a similar conclusion for science in one of the most exhaustive studies to date (reprinted in *Trenton Times*, 1997a). And so did NAEP's most recent test, showing "a stark gap between the ability of students in general to learn basic principles, and their ability to apply knowledge or explain what they learned" (*New York Times*, 1997, p. 19). The test was a mixture of multiple-choice, constructed response, and performance task questions.

To see how easy it is to misunderstand things we all know, consider the entry-point question in the previous chapter, "Why is it warmer in summer and colder in winter?" Every student in the United States has been taught basic astronomy. We know that the earth travels around the sun, that the orbit is elliptical, and that the earth tilts at about 20 degrees off its north-south axis. But even when graduating Harvard seniors were asked the question (as documented in a video on the misunderstanding phenomenon), we discover that few can correctly explain why it is colder in winter than in summer (Schneps, 1994). They either have no adequate explanation for what they

claim to know, or they provide a plausible but erroneous view (i.e., the weather changes are due to the earth being closer or farther from the sun). Similar findings occur when we ask adults to explain the phases of the moon: Many well-educated people describe the phases as lunar eclipses.

Teachers who take a proactive approach to design can combat the likelihood of deeply rooted misconceptions and the potential for misunderstanding. To successfully engineer understanding, educators have to be able to describe what it looks like, how it manifests itself, and how apparent understanding (or misunderstanding) differs from genuine understanding.

A Need for Circumspection

As educators, we need to cultivate circumspection. Understanding is multidimensional and complicated. There are different types of understanding and different methods of understanding, as well as conceptual overlap with other intellectual targets. Sometimes understanding requires disinterest, while at other times, it requires heartfelt solidarity with others. Sometimes we think of understanding as highly theoretical; at other times, we see it revealed in effective real-world application. Sometimes we think of it as dispassionate critical analysis; at other times, as empathetic response. Sometimes we think of it as dependent upon direct experience; at other times, as gained through detached reflection.

It makes sense, therefore, to identify different aspects of understanding, even if they overlap and ideally would be integrated. We now turn to a more thorough and precise theory of understanding.

THE SIX FACETS OF UNDERSTANDING

*There are many different ways of
understanding, overlapping but not reducible
to one another and, correspondingly,
many different ways of teaching to understand.*
—PASSMORE, 1982, P. 210

WE HAVE DEVELOPED A MULTIFACETED VIEW OF WHAT makes up a mature understanding, a six-sided view of the concept. The six facets are most easily summarized by specifying the particular achievement each facet reflects. When we truly understand, we

■ Can *explain*: provide thorough, supported, and justifiable accounts of phenomena, facts, and data.

■ Can *interpret*: tell meaningful stories; offer apt translations; provide a revealing historical or personal dimension to ideas and events; make it personal or accessible through images, anecdotes, analogies, and models.

■ Can *apply*: effectively use and adapt what we know in diverse contexts.

■ Have *perspective*: see and hear points of view through critical eyes and ears; see the big picture.

■ Can *empathize:* find value in what others might find odd, alien, or implausible; perceive sensitively on the basis of prior direct experience.

■ Have *self-knowledge:* perceive the personal style, prejudices, projections, and habits of mind that both shape and impede our own understanding; we are aware of what we do not understand and why understanding is so hard.

These facets are different but related, in the same way that different criteria are used in judging the quality of a performance. For example, "good essay writing" is composed of persuasive, organized, and clear prose. All three criteria need to be met, yet each is different from and somewhat independent of the other two. The writing might be clear but unpersuasive; it might be well organized but unclear and somewhat persuasive.

Similarly, a student may have a thorough and sophisticated explanation but not be able to apply it, or see things from a critical distance but lack empathy. The facets reflect the different connotations of *understanding* we considered in the previous chapter, yet a complete and mature understanding ideally involves the full development of all six kinds of understanding.

■ MISCONCEPTION ALERT

We caution readers to treat these divisions as somewhat artificial and not the only possible take on the subject. The analytic framework we offer makes teaching and assessing for subject-matter mastery more manageable. Further analysis might yield different conceptual distinctions and hierarchies, and we are open to what our readers might say on this subject.

The important point is that understanding is a family of related abilities. We trust that readers will see that "understanding by design" is made more likely through the kinds of distinctions we are making here.

Overview of the Facets

Understanding is always a matter of degree, typically furthered by questions and lines of inquiry that arise from reflection, discussion, and use of ideas—including our attempts to understand understanding. Our explanation of each facet involves three different takes on the concept:

■ Introduce each facet with a brief definition, followed by an apt quote and questions that might be typical of someone wishing to understand.

■ Offer two examples for each facet, one from daily public life and one from the classroom, as well as an example of what a lack of understanding looks like.

■ Provide an analysis of each facet, offering a brief look at the instructional and assessment implications to be explored later in this book.

- -

Facet 1: Explanation
Explanation: sophisticated and apt explanations and theories, which provide knowledgeable and justified accounts of events, actions, and ideas.

> We see something moving, hear a sound unexpectedly, smell an unusual odor, and we ask: What is it? . . . When we have found out what it signifies, a squirrel running, two persons conversing, an explosion of gunpowder, we say that we understand
> —Dewey, 1933, pp. 137, 146

Why is that so? What explains such events? What accounts for such action? How can we prove it? To what is this connected? How does this work? What is implied?

✓ A cook explains why adding a little mustard to oil and vinegar enables them to mix. The mustard acts as an emulsifier.

✓ A 10th grade history student provides a well-supported view of the economic and political causes of the American Revolution.

✗ A 10th grade student knows the facts of the Boston Tea Party and the Stamp Act but not why they happened and what they led to.

Facet 1 involves the kind of understanding that emerges from a well-developed and supported theory, an explanation that makes sense of puzzling or opaque phenomena, data, feelings, or ideas. It is understanding revealed through performances and products that clearly, thoroughly, and instructively explain how things work, what they imply, where they connect, and why they happened.

Knowledge of Why and How

Understanding is thus not mere knowledge of facts but knowledge of why and how. Here are some examples:

■ We know that the Civil War happened, and we can perhaps cite a full chronology. But why did it happen?

■ We may know that different objects fall to the ground with apparent uniformity of acceleration. But how is that so? Why does mass not make a difference in acceleration? To understand in this sense is to connect facts and ideas—often seemingly odd, counterintuitive, or contradictory facts and ideas—into a theory that works.

As Dewey (1933) explained, to understand something "is to see it in its *relations* to other things: to note how it operates or functions, what consequences follow from it, what causes it" (p. 137) (emphasis in original). We go beyond the information given to make inferences, connections, and associations—a theory that works. Powerful and insightful models are the results of this understanding. We can bind together seemingly disparate facts into a coherent, comprehensive, and illuminating account. We can predict heretofore unsought for or unexamined results, and we can illuminate strange or unexamined experiences.

What do we mean by a theory that works? Let us first consider a successful adult theory, the example of modern physics. Galileo, Kepler, and finally Newton and Einstein developed a theory capable of explaining the movement of all physical objects, from falling apples to comets. The theory predicts tides, the location of planets and comets, and how to put the nine ball in the corner pocket.

The theory was not obvious or due to mere cataloging of facts: The authors had to imagine a frictionless world, with movement on earth a special case. Of course, their critics had a field day with the idea that there was a force—gravity—everywhere on earth, acting at a distance, but by no discernible means—and (contrary to the ancient Greek view and common sense) acting in such a way that the weight of an object had no effect on its rate of descent to earth. The theory eventually won over competing theories because, despite its counterintuitive elements, it did a better job than any competing theory of explaining, ordering, and predicting phenomena.

Similarly, a student who can explain why steam, water, and ice, though superficially different, are the same chemical substance has a better understanding of H_2O than someone who cannot. A student reveals an understanding of things—perhaps an experience, a lesson by the teacher, a concept, or her own performance—when she can give good reasons and provide relevant and telling evidence to support her claims. More thorough understandings involve more thorough and systematic explanations, typically when an event is subsumed under general and powerful principles. Merely learning and giving back on tests the official theory of the textbook or teacher are not evidence of understanding. Facet 1 calls for a student to be given assignments and assessments requiring an explanation of what the student knows and good reasons in support of it before we can conclude that the student understands what was taught.

Warranted Opinions

Understandings in this sense thus go beyond true or borrowed opinions (mere right answers) to *warranted* opinions—a student's ability to explain an answer so that he can justify how he arrived at that answer and why it is right. We call upon students to reveal their understanding by using such verbs as *explain, justify, generalize, predict support, verify, prove,* and *substantiate.*

Regardless of the subject content or the age or sophistication of the student, when the student understands in the sense of Facet 1, that student has the ability to "show her work": explain why an answer is right or wrong, give valid evidence and argument for a view, and defend that view against other views, if needed. We are also implying for assessment that the student must be confronted with a *new* phenomenon, fact, or problem to see if she can, on her own, subsume it under the correct principle and explain away apparent counterarguments and counterexamples.

The student with the most in-depth understanding in this sense both sees and explains diverse data more precisely and grasps the more subtle aspects of the ideas or experience in question. Those understandings are invariably described by teachers as thorough, nuanced, or thoughtfully qualified (as opposed to merely glib, sweeping, or grandiose theorizing). The student has an understanding of guiding principles that explain and give value to the facts. An explanation or theory without such understanding is typically not so much wrong as it is incomplete or naive. It is not wrong to say that the Civil War was fought over slavery, or that literature often involves good versus evil, however naive or simplistic those answers might appear.

Instructional Implications

What are the instructional implications for developing the type of understanding described in Facet 1? This facet suggests that we deliberately seek a better balance between knowledge transmission (through the teacher and text) and student theory building and testing. A simple strategy to accomplish this goal is to focus on the 5 "W" questions at the heart of journalism—who, what, where, when, and why—in instruction and assessment.

From a design point of view, Facet 1 calls for building units around overarching (essential and unit) questions, issues, and problems that demand student theories and explanations, such as those found in problem-based learning and effective hands-on and minds-on science programs. The implications for assessment are straightforward— use assessments (e.g., performance tasks, projects, prompts, and tests) that ask students to explain, not simply recall; to link specific facts with larger ideas and justify the connections; to show their work, not just give an answer; and to support their conclusions.

Facet 2: Interpretation
Interpretation: interpretations, narratives, and translations that provide meaning.

> Juzo Itami's films revealed truths to the Japanese they never knew existed—even though they were right there in their daily life. "He could express the inside story about things people think they understand but really don't," said film critic Jun Ishiko
> —*Washington Post*, 1997, p. A1

The object of interpretation is understanding, not explanation. Understanding occurs when we organize essentially contestable but "incompletely verifiable propositions in a disciplined way" (Bruner, 1996, p. 90). A principal means for doing that organizing is through narrative: by telling a story of what something is about. But as Kierkegaard had made clear many years before, telling stories in order to understand is no mere enrichment of the mind; without them we are, to use his phrase, reduced to fear and trembling (Kierkegaard, in Bruner, 1996, p. 90).

What does it mean? Why does it matter? What of it? What does it illustrate or illuminate in human experience? How does it relate to me? What makes sense?

✓ A grandfather tells stories about the Depression to illustrate the importance of saving for a rainy day.

✓ An 11th grader shows how *Gulliver's Travels* can be read as a satire on British intellectual life; it's not just a fairy tale.

✗ A middle school student can translate all the words but does not grasp the meaning of a Spanish sentence.

We value good storytellers with reason: A good story both enlightens and engages. A clear and compelling narrative helps us find meaning, not just scattered facts and abstract ideas. Stories help us remember and make sense of our lives and the lives around us. The deepest, most transcendent meanings are found, of course, in the stories, parables, and myths that anchor all religions. A story is not a diversion; the best stories make our lives more understandable and focused.

Meanings Transform Understanding

The meanings we ascribe to all events, big and small, transform our understanding and perception of particular facts. The student possessing this understanding can show an event's significance, reveal an idea's importance, or provide an interpretation that strikes a deep chord of recognition and resonance. Consider how memorable Martin Luther King Jr.'s March on Washington speech ("I have a dream") and imagery crystallized the many complex ideas and feelings behind the Civil Rights movement. Or, think of how the best newspaper editorials make sense of complex political currents and ideas.

Meaning, of course, is in the eye of the beholder. Think of how much November 22, 1963 (the day of President Kennedy's assassination), means as a watershed event to those of us who came of age in the '60s. Or, consider how differently a mother, a police officer, or an adolescent in a foster home might perceive the same newspaper account of severe child abuse. Social workers and psychologists might well have an accepted theory of child abuse in the sense of Facet 1. But the meaning of the event, hence an understanding of it, may have little to do with the theory; the theory may be only a scientific account, with no bearing, for example, on the abused person's view of the event and the world.

Making sense—of the stories of others and of discrete data on facts—involves translation and interpretation. Whether we think of a struggling student taking German 1, a 12th grader reading *King Lear*, a 6th grade student pondering the curve implied in a data set, or a scholar poring over the Dead Sea Scrolls, the challenge is the same: understanding words rooted in an author's intent but a puzzle to the reader, or understanding facts that tell no self-evident or single story. Similarly, in fields like history and archaeology, we must reconstruct the meaning of events and artifacts from clues provided by the historical record. With this type of understanding, teachers ask learners to interpret, translate, make sense of, show the significance of, decode, and make a story meaningful.

The Challenge: Bringing Text to Life

In classrooms, this facet—interpretation—manifests itself in every discussion of books and experiences. The challenge in teaching is to bring the text to life by revealing, through study and discussion, that the text speaks to our concerns. For example, we all struggle in our relationships with our parents, and Shakespeare offers us great insights if we can only decode the language in *King Lear*. Students move between the text and their own experience to find legitimate but varying interpretations and further insights.

All understandings of a text, person, or event are not equal in depth and breadth of insight. Some readings, histories, or psychological cases are stronger than others by virtue of their coherence, thoroughness, and documentation. But all interpretations are bound by the personal, social, cultural,

and historical contexts in which they arise.

This truth holds in mathematics, as Henri Poincaré (1913/1982), famous turn-of-the-century French mathematician, reminds us:

> What is it to understand? Has this word the same meaning for all the world? To understand the demonstration of a theorem, is that to examine successively each of the syllogisms composing it and to ascertain its correctness, its conformity to the rules of the game? . . . For some, yes; when they have done this, they will say they understand.
>
> For the majority, no. Almost all are more exacting; they wish to know not merely why the syllogisms . . . are correct, but why they link together in this order rather than another. In so far as to them they seem engendered by caprice and not by an intelligence always conscious of the end to be attained, they do not believe they understand (p. 431).

The act of interpretation is clearly more fraught with ambiguity than the act of theory building and testing. A text or a speaker's words will always have different valid readings; as Bruner (1996) puts it: "Narratives and their interpretations traffic in meanings, and meanings are intransigently multiple" (p. 90). Indeed, modern literary criticism has been enlivened by the view that not even the author's view is privileged, that regardless of author intent, texts can have unintended meanings and significance.

Explanation and interpretation are thus related but different. A jury trying to understand a case of child abuse seeks significance and intent, not generalizations from theoretical science. The theorist builds objective and general knowledge about the phenomenon called abuse, but the novelist or journalist may offer as much or more insight into the

"why?" We may know the relevant facts and theoretical principles, but we can and must still always ask, What does it all mean? What is its importance—to me, to us?

Overlap of Theory and Story

Clearly, though, a theory and a story have some overlap. As Bruner points out, a scientific notion persists or is overthrown by virtue of the meaning it provides—even when supportive facts are missing or data are anomalous. And just as our view of the characters in a novel shifts with each episode so, too, does the scientist's view of the meaning of phenomena, as Thomas Kuhn's (1970) history of scientific revolution reveals.

Sulloway (1996), citing Kuhn, underscores the point that the revolutionary aspect of Darwin's work was not in the facts but in its picture of evolution as arising out of no larger purpose—an idea without meaning to Victorian thinkers—in a way that scientists today take for granted. The theory itself was not complex, but its acceptance was slow and hard-won because of the habits of thought it threatened.

And yet, there are vital differences between theories on the one hand and stories, explanations, and interpretations on the other, especially relating to their truth value and the different criteria by which we judge them. A theory needs to be true to work; a story need only illuminate, engage, and have verisimilitude. The existence of three different theories for the same physical phenomenon is intellectually unacceptable, but the existence of many different plausible and illuminating interpretations of the same stories and human events is acceptable. Indeed, the view that human intentions provide key meaning to human events is a "theory" at the heart of all narrative and history, but it is a view contradicted by a good deal of modern psychological and biological theory.

The differences in theories and stories were well summarized by Jerome Bruner in his most recent book, *The Culture of Education* (1996), in discussing a narrative view of understanding: "Understanding is the outcome of organizing and contextualizing essentially contestable, incompletely verifiable propositions in a disciplined way" (p. 90).[1] This view raises the stakes considerably in teaching and especially in assessment. Bruner goes on to say, "Since no one narrative rules out all alternatives, narratives pose a very special issue of criteria. By what standards can narratives or competing interpretations be adjudged as 'right' or 'acceptable'?" (p. 90). He thinks we especially need to avoid two errors that educators sometimes succumb to in testing: We must not try to test and find a single "preemptive story" or to "push a partisan point of view" (p. 90).

This narrative building (as well as the theory building of Facet 1) is the true meaning of constructivism. When we say that students must make their own meaning, we mean that it is counterproductive to hand students prepackaged "significance" or "interpretations" without letting them work through the problem to where they see these explanations and interpretations as valid. This practice promotes sham understanding.

A purely didactic teaching of *the* interpretation is likely to lead to misunderstanding and forgotten knowledge and will mislead students about the arguable nature of interpretation. This didacticism has clear implications for our teaching if we over-rely on textbooks that tend to offer *the* version of history or science (a point to which we devote greater detail in Chapter 5).

Developing Interpretations

The inherently problematic nature of certain ideas, texts, and experiences mandates an education that requires students, not just teachers and textbook writers, to develop interpretations and stories, as well as ensures that student ideas receive the feedback necessary to force continual testing and revision of those accounts.

The implications for instruction parallel those for the previous facet of understanding. Learning cannot be primarily or exclusively the process of learning what someone else says is the meaning of something, except as a way to model meaning making or overcome basic decoding inability, or as a prelude to testing the interpretation so as to better understand the possibilities.

To educate students for autonomous intellectual performance as adults, we must teach them to build stories and interpretations, not just passively take in official ones. They need to see how knowledge is built "from the inside." Examples are inviting students to fashion an oral history out of disparate interviews, a mathematical conclusion out of discrete data, or a story interpretation based on a careful reading. In short, students must have firsthand knowledge of the history of knowledge creation and refinement if they later are to create and refine knowledge.

Facet 3: Application
Application: ability to use knowledge effectively in new situations and diverse contexts.

> [By understanding] I mean simply a sufficient grasp of concepts, principles, or skills so that one can bring them to bear on new problems and situations, deciding in which ways one's present competencies can suffice and in which ways one may require new skills or knowledge
> —Gardner, 1991, p. 18

How and where can we use this knowledge, skill, or process? How should my thinking and action be modified to meet the demands of this particular situation?

✓ A young couple uses their knowledge of economics (e.g., the power of compounded interest and the high cost of credit cards) to develop an effective financial plan for saving and investing.

✓ 7th grade students use their knowledge of statistics to accurately project next year's costs and needs for the student-run candy and supply store.

✗ A physics professor cannot diagnose and fix a broken lamp.

To understand is to be able to use knowledge. This is an old idea in U.S. education—indeed, an old idea in the long tradition of our U.S. pragmatism and cultural disdain for ivory-tower, academic thinking. We say to young and old alike, "You need to walk the walk, not just talk the talk."

Bloom (1956) and his colleagues saw *application* as central to understanding and quite different from the kind of plugging-in and fill-in-the-blanks pseudoapplication found in so many classrooms:

> Teachers frequently say: "If a student really comprehends something, he can apply it. . . ." Application is different in two ways from knowledge and simple comprehension: The student is not prompted to give specific knowledge, nor is the problem old-hat (p. 120).

Matching an Idea to a Context

Understanding involves matching one's idea or action to context. Also, it involves tact in the sense William James (1899/1958) referred to the tact needed for teaching, namely "knowledge of the concrete situation" (as opposed to theoretical—Facet 1—knowledge of child psychology).

The implications for teaching and assessment are straightforward and at the heart of the performance-based reforms the authors have been a part of for the last decade. We show our understanding of something by using it, adapting it, and customizing it. When we must negotiate different constraints, social contexts, purposes, and audiences, understanding is revealed as performance know-how, the ability to accomplish tasks successfully, with grace under pressure, and with tact.

Application of understanding is thus a context-dependent skill, requiring the use of new problems and diverse situations in assessment, as Bloom (1956) and his colleagues long ago argued:

> If the situations . . . are to involve application as we are defining it here, then they must either be situations new to the student or situations containing new elements as compared to the situation in which the abstraction was learned. . . . Ideally we are seeking a problem which will test the extent to which an individual has learned to apply the abstraction in a practical way (p. 125).

Similarly, in describing synthesis, the authors of the taxonomy research argue that the student must apply knowledge by developing a complete unique product or performance, noting, "It is obvious that the student must have considerable freedom in defining the task for himself/herself, or in redefining the problem or task."

Real-World Problems

The problems that we develop for students should be as close as possible to the situation in which a scholar, artist, engineer, or other professional attacks such problems. The time allowed and conditions of work, for example, should be as far away as possible from the typical controlled exam situation. Bloom, Madaus, and Hastings (1981) take this view:

> The adequacy of the final product may be judged in terms of:
> a. the effect it has on the reader, observer, or audience,
> b. the adequacy with which it has accomplished the task, and/or
> c. evidence on the adequacy of the process by which it was developed (p. 268).

Or, as Gardner (1991) recently argued:

> The test of understanding involves neither repetition of information learned nor performance of practices mastered. Rather it involves the appropriate application of concepts and principles to questions or problems that are newly posed. . . . Whereas short-answer tests and oral responses in classes can provide clues to student understanding, it is generally necessary to look more deeply. . . . For these purposes, new and unfamiliar problems, followed by open-ended clinical interviews or careful observations, provide the best way of establishing the degree of understanding . . . attained (pp. 117, 145).

Swiss child psychologist Jean Piaget (1973/1977) argued more radically that student understanding reveals itself by student innovation in application. He said that many so-called application problems, especially in mathematics, were not truly novel and hence not indicative of understanding:

Real comprehension of a notion or a theory [which] implies the reinvention of this theory by the student. Once the child is capable of repeating certain notions and using some applications of these in learning situations he often gives the impression of understanding; however, this does not fulfill the condition of reinvention. True understanding manifests itself by new spontaneous applications (pp. 726–732).

Thus, the instructional and assessment implications of Facet 3 call for an emphasis on performance-based learning: work that focuses on and culminates in more authentic tasks, supplemented by more conventional tests (see Wiggins, 1998; McTighe, 1996–1997).

Facet 4: Perspective
Perspective: critical and insightful points of view.

The profit of education is the ability it gives to make distinctions that penetrate below the surface . . . . One knows that there is a difference between sound and sense, between what is emphatic and what is distinctive, between what is conspicuous and what is important
— Dewey, in Johnson, 1949, p. 104

An important symptom of an emerging understanding is the capacity to represent a problem in a number of different ways and to approach its solution from varied vantage points; a single, rigid representation is unlikely to suffice
— Gardner, 1991, p. 13

From whose point of view? From which vantage point? What is assumed or tacit that needs to be made explicit and considered? What is justified or warranted? Is there adequate evidence? Is it reasonable? What are the strengths and weaknesses of the idea? Is it plausible?

What are its limits? So what?

✔ A 10-year-old girl recognizes in TV advertising the fallacy of using popular figures to promote products.

✔ A student explains the Israeli and Palestinian arguments for and against new settlements on the Gaza Strip.

✘ A bright but rigid student refuses to consider that there is another way to look at gun control.

To understand in this sense is to see things from a dispassionate and disinterested perspective. This type of understanding is not about any student's particular point of view but about the mature recognition that *any* answer to a complex question typically involves a point of view; hence, an answer is often one of many possible plausible accounts. A student with perspective is alert to what is taken for granted, assumed, overlooked, or glossed over in an inquiry or theory.

Perspective involves making tacit assumptions and implications explicit. It is often revealed through an ability to ask, What of it? and to see an answer—even a teacher's or textbook's answer—as a point of view. This type of perspective is a powerful form of insight, because by shifting perspective and casting familiar ideas in a new light, one can create new theories, stories, and applications.

The Advantage of Perspective

In the critical-thinking sense of the term, students with perspective expose questionable and unexamined assumptions, conclusions, and implications. When a student has or can gain perspective, she can gain a critical distance from the habitual or knee-jerk beliefs, feelings, theories, and appeals that characterize less careful and circumspect thinkers.

Perspective involves the *discipline* of asking, How does it look from another point of view? How, for example, would my critics see things? In his autobiography, Darwin (1958) noted that this critical stance was key to his success in defending his controversial theory:

> I . . . followed a golden rule that whenever a published fact, a new observation or thought came across me, which was opposed to my general results, to make a memorandum of it without fail and at once; for I had found by experience that such facts and thoughts were far more apt to escape from memory than favorable ones. Owing to this habit, very few objections were raised against my views that I had not at least noticed and attempted to answer (p. 123).

Thus, perspective as an aspect of understanding is a mature achievement, an earned understanding of how ideas look from different vantage points. Novice learners, those just setting out on the road to mastery, may have a revealing point of view, even when they lack a thorough explanation of things. Consider the child who speaks out in *The Emperor's New Clothes*. But novices, by definition, lack the ability to take *multiple* perspectives, as Gardner pointed out earlier.

Clear Performance Goals

To develop fluency and flexibility in perspective taking—if understanding is to blossom—a student needs to have a clear performance goal and to keep that goal in constant view as different points of view emerge. The case method in law and the problem-based learning method in medicine exemplify this point.

Therefore, students learn they are not "done" with a project or lesson simply because they worked hard, followed directions, and turned in a piece of work from a single point of view—their own. Instruction and performance standards must require students to see things from the perspective of the ultimate standards, the various players, and the primary audience—not their own intentions—as they doggedly try to solve a particular problem.

A more subtle and sophisticated perspective involves grasping the points of view behind teacher and textbook pronouncements. What is the point of view of the authors of the U.S. history and physics textbooks concerning what is true, verified, and important? Do other authors share those views? Do different experts, teachers, and authors establish different priorities? If so, with what justification and advantages or disadvantages? That this line of questioning seems too esoteric shows how far we are from giving students needed perspective.

Everyone recognizes the problem of achieving perspective in newspaper reporting, so why isn't it addressed in textbook writing? Everyone knows that authors' views shape choice of content, emphasis, and style, so why aren't educators helping students to use these language arts skills in understanding textbooks and theories in them? What questions and assumptions informed the text's authors? What were Euclid, Newton, Jefferson, Lavoisier, and Darwin trying to accomplish? Based on what assumptions? Students cannot be said to have perspective, hence understanding, of the *Elements* of Euclid, Newton's *Principia*, the *Declaration of Independence,* or Darwin's *Origin of Species* unless they have some insight into point of view.

Thus, an essential perspective on perspective involves encouraging not only students but also their coursework to ask and answer, What of it? What is assumed? What follows? These questions need to be asked for all core knowledge and texts in the students' experience. Our instructional and assessment strategies need to better highlight the means and ends of a liberal education, namely, greater control over essential questions and ideas so the student can see both intrinsic and extrinsic value in intellectual life.

The *Oxford English Dictionary* offers one definition of the verb *understand* as "to know the import" of something. By this criterion, our educational system is not very successful in causing understanding. Few students leave school with an understanding of the value of their schoolwork—and of the value of the discipline required to learn the disciplines. Few can successfully ask and answer, What of it? Such a critical stance toward knowledge underlies what we mean by a liberal education. Thus, it is a sad commentary when we reduce liberal education to a few courses in the humanities, organized around some old texts—as if the content, not the critical point of view, defined a liberal education. But why should we be surprised? Few courses are taught and assessed from the vantage point of a guiding question—one that implies multiple points of view and intellectual criteria focusing on justification as opposed to mere correctness.

Facet 4 promotes the idea that instruction should include explicit opportunities for students to confront alternative theories and diverse points of view regarding the big ideas. In an earlier era, Joseph Schwab (1978) at the college level came closest to envisioning an education for perspective. He developed what he called the art of "eclectic": the deliberate design of coursework that compelled students to see the same important ideas (e.g., free will versus determinism, the development of personality) from very different theoretical perspectives.

Facet 5: Empathy
Empathy: the ability to get inside another person's feelings and worldview.

To understand is to forgive.
—French proverb

"Do women ever come up to you and say 'How did you know that? How did you feel that?'" I ask, and for the first time, he turns and looks at me evenly: "Yeah, that's the normal response," he says in a voice that suddenly isn't so shy. "It's not that I understand women any better than anyone else, but I do understand feelings. . . . All you have to do is imagine what that girl is going through, just turn it around and put yourself in those same shoes. . . . We're all the same people."
—The singer Babyface *New York Times Sunday Magazine,* 1997, Sec. 6, p. 22

How does it seem to you? What do they see that I don't? What do I need to experience if I am to understand? What was the artist or performer feeling, seeing, and trying to make me feel and see?

✓ An Israeli adolescent empathizes with the restrictive, constrained lifestyle of his Palestinian contemporaries.

✓ From a recent British national exam: "*Romeo and Juliet,* act 4. Imagine you are Juliet. Write your thoughts and feelings explaining why you have to take this desperate action."

✗ An accomplished basketball player-turned-coach berates his young players often because he cannot relate to their struggles to learn the game.

Empathy, the ability to walk in another's shoes, to escape one's own emotional reactions to grasp another's, is central to the most common colloquial use of the term *understanding*. When we try to understand another person, people, or culture we strive for empathy. It is not simply an affective response or sympathy.

Empathy is a *learned* ability to grasp the world from someone else's point of view. It is the discipline of using one's imagination to see and feel as others see and feel. It is different from seeing in perspective, which is to see from a critical distance, to detach ourselves to see more objectively. With empathy, we see from inside the person's worldview; we embrace the insights that can be found in the subjective or aesthetic realm.

A German scholar, Theodor Lipps, coined the term *empathy* at the turn of the 20th century to describe what the audience must do to understand a work or performance of art. Empathy is the deliberate act of finding what is plausible, sensible, or meaningful in the ideas and actions of others, even if they are puzzling or off-putting. Empathy can lead us not only to rethink a situation but to have a change of heart as we come to understand what formerly seemed odd or alien.

This kind of understanding implies an existential or experiential prerequisite. If someone were to refer to experiences like poverty, abuse, racism, or high-profile competitive sports and say, "You cannot possibly understand without having been there," the implication would be that insight from experience is necessary for understanding.

A recent controversy involving the songwriter Paul Simon echoed the same theme (*USA Today*, 1997). Some Puerto Ricans contended a Jew cannot possibly understand the experience of Puerto Ricans. The subject was a new musical, *Capeman*, cowritten and produced by Simon and Reuben Blades. Though we might disagree with that particular sentiment, as teachers, we regularly acknowledge that students need to directly or indirectly experience the ideas they study.

A Form of Insight

Empathy is a form of insight because it involves the ability to get beyond odd, alien, seemingly weird opinions or people to find what is meaningful in them. Students have to *learn* how to open-mindedly embrace ideas, experiences, and texts that might seem strange, off-putting, or just difficult to access if they are to understand them and their connection to what is more familiar. They need to see how weird or dumb ideas can seem insightful or sophisticated once we overcome habitual responses, and they need to see how habit can block our understanding of another person's understanding.

All great interpreters and historians of ideas need empathy. "If we laugh with derision" at the theories of our predecessors, as anthropologist Stephen Jay Gould (1980) says, we will fail "in our understanding of their world" (p. 149).

From his own experience in reading Aristotle, Kuhn (cited in Bernstein, 1983) suggests:

> When reading the works of an important thinker, look first for the apparent absurdities in the text and ask yourself how a sensible person could have written them. When you find an answer, when those passages make sense, then you may find that more central passages, ones you previously thought you understood, have changed their meaning.

A simple example of the need for empathy can be found in our own system of government. Few students know that U.S. senators were appointed, not popularly elected, for more than 100 years. Fewer still understand why such a practice seemed like a good idea then. It is easy to imagine that our forefathers were misguided or hypocrites. We can think of assignments and assessments that ask students to role-play the writers of the Constitution. The challenge would be to make a case to a group of citizens that appointed offices are in the citizens' best interest. As a postscript, we could ask students to write an essay or journal entry on the pros and cons of our current popular vote system and to consider the value, if any, of the electoral college.

A Change of Heart

As we noted in our earlier discussion of language, understanding in the interpersonal sense suggests not merely an intellectual change of mind but a significant change of heart. Empathy requires respect for people different from ourselves. Our respect for them causes us to be open-minded, to carefully consider their views when they are different from ours.

It becomes easier, then, to imagine schoolwork that deliberately confronts students with strange or alien texts, experiences, and ideas to see if they can get beyond what is off-putting about the work. This is, in fact, a common activity in foreign language classes that stress cultural issues. The Bradley Commission on the Teaching of History argued that a primary aim of history is to help students escape their ethnocentric and present-centered views (Gagnon, 1989).

More Experiences in Learning

To ensure greater understanding of abstract ideas, students must have far more direct or simulated experiences of them than most current textbook-driven courses now allow. We refer in this book to the idea of an intellectual Outward Bound to ensure the needed changes: Learning needs to be more experiential, more geared toward making students directly confront the effects—and *affect*—of decisions, ideas, theories, and problems. The absence of experience in learning may explain why so many important ideas are misunderstood and learnings so fragile, as the misconception literature reveals. Assessment also must pay greater attention to whether students have overcome egocentrism, ethnocentrism, and present-centeredness in their answers and explanations.

Facet 6: Self-Knowledge
Self-knowledge: the wisdom to know one's ignorance and how one's patterns of thought and action inform as well as prejudice understanding.

> All understanding is ultimately self-understanding. . . . A person who understands, understands himself. . . . Understanding begins when something addresses us. This requires . . . the fundamental suspension of our own prejudices.
> —Gadamer, 1994, p. 266

> It is the duty of the human understanding to understand that there are things which it cannot understand, and what those things are.
> —Kierkegaard, 1959

How does who I am shape my views? What are the limits of my understanding? What are my blind spots? What am I prone to misunderstand because of prejudice, habit, or style?

✓ A mother realizes that her frustration with her daughter's shyness is rooted in issues from her own childhood.

✓ Mindful of the fact that many students are visual learners, a middle school teacher deliberately includes visual organizers and images.

✗ "When all you have is a hammer, every problem looks like a nail."

Deep understanding is ultimately related to what we mean by wisdom. To understand the world we must first understand ourselves. Through self-knowledge we also understand what we do *not* understand; "know thyself" is the maxim of those who would *really* understand, as the Greek philosophers often said. In a sense, Socrates is the patron saint of understanding. He knew he was ignorant, whereas most men did not realize they were.

In daily life, our capacity to accurately self-assess and self-regulate reflects understanding. Metacognition refers to self-knowledge about how we think and why, and the relation between our preferred methods of learning and our understanding (or lack of it). The immature mind is thus not merely ignorant or unskilled but unreflective. A naive student, no matter how bright and learned, is lacking in self-knowledge to know when an idea is "out there" or a projection; to know when an idea seems objectively true but really only fits the student's beliefs; or to know how templates or frames for perception shape how and what the student understands.

Intellectual Rationalization

Our intellectual blind spots predispose us toward *intellectual rationalization*: the ability to unendingly assimilate experience to beliefs, and categories that seem not merely plausible ideas but objective truths. Too easily, we keep verifying our favored and unexamined models, theories, analogies, and viewpoints.

For example, thinking in either-or terms is a common example of such a natural habit, one that we see rampant in education reform and one that Dewey viewed as the curse of immature thought. Students often think in dichotomies without seeing those categories as narrow projections. She's cool. He's a jerk. They're in the jock crowd, not the nerd crowd. That teacher likes me and hates you. Math isn't for girls. Football is for animals. This is a fact; that's wrong.

Salinger (1951) made brilliant use of this propensity in *The Catcher in the Rye*. Holden is prone to viewing other adolescent boys and adults as "phonies," and his prejudice conceals more than it reveals. We learn a good deal about Holden's alienation, in fact, when by his own admission his categorization of people as either phony or not breaks down when he considers such interesting and competent adults as the Lunts, the blues piano player, and his teacher. Maturity is evident when we look beyond simplistic categories to see shades of perhaps unexpected differences, idiosyncrasies, or surprises in people and ideas.

We educators, too, are often unthinkingly reliant on and satisfied by neat categories and striking metaphors, seeing their limits and subjectivity only long after the fact. Is the brain really like a computer? Are children really like natural objects or phenomena to be treated as equal, so that a standardized test can be modeled on the procedures of scientific experiments? To talk of education as "delivery of instructional services" (an economic metaphor and a more modern variant of the older factory model) or as entailing "behavioral objectives" (language rooted in Skinnerian animal training) is to use metaphors, and not necessarily helpful ones.

A Paradox

The paradox is that our language and grammar are the stuff of all new explanation, but they can impede progress as much as promote it, as Wittgenstein (1953) argued in describing philosophy as conceptual and linguistic analysis:

> The fundamental fact is that we lay down rules, . . . and then when we follow the rules, things do not turn out as we assumed. That we are therefore, as it were, entangled in our own rules. This entanglement in our rules is what we want to understand (Aphorism 125).

More than 300 years ago, Francis Bacon (1620/1960) provided a thorough account of the misunderstandings introduced by our own habits of thought and the cultural context in which we find ourselves:

> The human understanding is of its own nature prone to suppose the existence of more order and regularity in the world than it finds . . . [and] when it has once adopted an opinion draws all things else to support and agree with it. . . . It is the peculiar and perpetual error of the intellect to be more moved and excited by affirmatives than by negatives. . . . Numberless, in short, are the ways, and sometimes imperceptible, in which the affections color and infect the understanding (Book I, Nos. 45–49).

Yet seeing prejudice as always wrong or harmful is also prejudice. Gadamer and Heidegger, for example, see human prejudice as inseparable from human understanding. And Woolf (1929) noted

that a self-conscious explanation of our prejudices may be the best knowledge we can offer:

> Perhaps if I lay bare the ideas, the prejudices that lie behind this statement ["A woman must have money and a room of her own to write fiction"], you will find that they have some bearing upon women and fiction. At any rate, when a subject is highly controversial—and any question about sex is that—one cannot hope to tell the truth. One can only show how one came to hold whatever opinion one does hold. One can only give one's audience the chance of drawing their own conclusions as they observe the limitations, the prejudices, the idiosyncrasies of the speaker. Fiction here is likely to contain more truth than fact (p. 4).

In talking about open-mindedly interpreting texts, Gadamer (1994) says that the right stance

> Supposes only that we self-consciously designate our opinions and prejudices and qualify them as such. . . . In keeping to this attitude, we grant the text the opportunity to appear as an authentically different being and to manifest its own truth, over and against our preconceived notions (pp. 238–239).

What Self-Knowledge Demands

Self-knowledge is a key facet of understanding because it demands that we self-consciously question our understandings to advance them. It asks us to have the discipline to seek and find the *inevitable* blind spots or oversights in our thinking and to have the courage to face the uncertainty and inconsistencies lurking underneath effective habits, naive confidence, strong beliefs, and worldviews that only seem complete and final. When we talk of subject-matter "disciplines," such courage and persistence is

the essential source of rational understanding as opposed to dogmatic belief.

Practically speaking, a greater attention to self-knowledge means that we must do a better job of teaching and assessing self-reflection in the broadest sense. In one sense, we do that quite well: Many programs and strategies help students develop greater metacognition and awareness of their own learning style. But the ideas we express here suggest that greater attention is needed to self-assess performance and the philosophical abilities that fall under the heading "epistemology"—the branch of

---

■ MISCONCEPTION ALERT

We have noted that any robust teaching of understanding must grapple with the phenomenon of misunderstanding. And throughout this book, we alert readers to potential misunderstandings. Now we direct that concern to the facets themselves. The following list is not intended to be exhaustive, merely suggestive and cautionary.

Facet 1: Explanation

Misconception 1: If the student gives a correct answer to a complex and demanding question, he must have an in-depth understanding.

Misconception 2: If the student cannot write an explanation of her views, she lacks understanding.

Both these misconceptions involve the plausible but incorrect view that a student who can provide an accurate answer and explanation on a test understands the answer. But we have all seen students who could correctly give back what they learned without understanding why the answer or

explanation is correct. This concern is one reason that at the doctoral level a dissertation and its defense are required. Right answers, with documentation, could be merely borrowed and not understood.

The second misconception is the reverse view, a common problem in assessment: A performance test can be an invalid way to assess knowledge when the performance ability (or lack of it, in this case) determines the quality of the answer. For example, a student may write a beautiful and flowing essay but have little of substance or novelty to say; another student is a poor writer but filled with insights. Often in such assessments, the writing quality counts for more than the understanding being assessed—improperly, if our aim is to assess understanding as opposed to writing ability.

Facet 2: Interpretation

Misconception: If the student offers an engaged and rich response to literature, he understands that work of literature.

This is a common misconception in language arts. Reader response becomes equated or confused with understanding the text. For example, a student might have a thoughtful, engaged, and fluent response to a text, but the teacher's assessment of that response might erroneously suggest that he also has provided a substantiated and subtle interpretation of the text. But some highly responsive and engaged readers get the meaning all wrong, whereas some seemingly detached or bored readers can penetrate to the core of a book's most important ideas and meanings without being engaged by them.

Facet 3: Application

Misconception 1: Any effective performance with knowledge indicates understanding of that knowledge.

Misconception 2: Any ineffective performance with knowledge indicates a lack of understanding of that knowledge.

In activity-based teaching and performance-based assessment, we all too easily can assume that if the student performs well then he understands; that if she has learned the skills of persuasive writing or soccer then she must understand them. But the two are not synonymous. We can make this assessment clearer by asking such questions as, Does the student understand persuasion? Does the student understand the purpose of the game and act on an explicit strategy? In other words, is there a deliberate purposefulness and reflectiveness to performance?

In fact, persuasion and the point of the game can and must be taught, learned, and assessed using additional performances from the targeted skills. We will likely need to hear or read Facet 1 answers, namely, explanations of what the student did and why.

The reverse is true. Students who do poorly on a specific performance task do not necessarily misunderstand the topic. As with explanation, they may be unskilled at the performance but understand it. Consider, for example, sports commentators who cannot play a sport but reveal through analysis their deep understanding of the game. Here, too, we must be wary of making invalid inferences on the basis of performance results. To put the matter more precisely, we need to make sure that we have built in the most appropriate and varied performances of understanding.

Misconception 3: Application means that the student can correctly answer teacher-assigned problems based on what was taught.

This is a long-standing misconception abetted by textbook end-of-chapter problems and standard-

ized tests. As we noted in Chapter 3, Bloom's (1956) taxonomy does not support such a view. Authentic application involves novel problems, realistically messy situations, and required adaptations and adjustments to theoretical knowledge and skill. Algorithmic or mechanical application is rarely adequate in authentic contexts that require judgment, heuristics, problem solving, and adjustment based on feedback.

Facet 4: Perspective
Misconception 1: Having an opinion equals having perspective.

Misconception 2: Perspective implies relativism.

Both views represent an ancient misunderstanding, one that many thinkers have tried to expose and eradicate. Just because we find a view plausible or well argued does not mean that it is correct. Just because we can find criticisms in all complex theories and arguments does not mean that all theories are equal. On the contrary, criticism is the only way to get beyond relativism. Such perspective is, of course, threatening to those who prosper and retain authority based on an orthodoxy.

Facet 5: Empathy
Misconception 1: Empathy is affect, synonymous with sympathy or heartfelt rapport.

Misconception 2: Empathy requires agreement with the point of view in question.

Empathy is not sympathy. It is a disciplined effort to understand what is different, not a question of feeling what other people feel. Similarly, just because we work to understand what is different doesn't mean we agree with it. Rather, we come to understand it as plausible or meaningful.

Facet 6: Self-Knowledge

Misconception: Self-knowledge equals self-centeredness.

Self-knowledge is the opposite of self-centeredness. When we know ourselves, we know our limits and are far less likely to confuse our views with those of others or our knowledge with our prejudices.

philosophy that addresses what it means to know and understand knowledge and understanding, and how knowledge differs from belief and opinion— what we are striving for in this book.

If understanding is composed of the six facets, what do they look like in practice? How can we more accurately distinguish between those students with and without understanding? If understanding can be described as naive and sophisticated, how can we use rubrics to assess it? What problems in assessment are peculiar to understanding, and how can we become better at assessing for it? To those questions we now turn.

Endnote

1. Bruner contrasts human science "interpretations" with scientific "explanations." The latter are "preemptive," according to Bruner. Two explanations or theories of phenomena cannot both be correct. In history, sociology, or textural analysis, multiple accounts can be valid.

5

THINKING LIKE AN ASSESSOR

HAVING CLARIFIED UNDERSTANDING—THE DESIRED result of teaching, in this case—we now move to the second stage of backward design. Here, we consider the assessment implications by asking the assessor's questions:

■ Given our account of the facets, what follows for assessment?

■ What is evidence of in-depth understanding as opposed to superficial or naive understanding?

■ Where should we look and what should we look for to determine the extent of student understanding?

■ What kinds of assessment tasks and evidence needs will anchor our curricular units and thus guide our instruction?

Our chart of the three stages of backward design (see Figure 5.1 on p. 64) presents the considerations and design standards that apply. The Stage 2 section (in boldface) summarizes the elements to consider when planning for the collection of evidence from assessments.

Nowhere does the backward design process depart more from conventional practice than at this stage. Because instead of moving from target to teaching, we ask, What would count as evidence of successful teaching? Before we plan specific learning activities, our question must first be, What counts as evidence of understanding?

The six facets (see Chapter 4)—explanation, interpretation, application, perspective, empathy,

Figure 5.1 **A Focus on Stage 2 of Backward Design**

Key Design Question	Design Considerations	Filters (Design Criteria)	What the Final Design Accomplishes
Stage 1. What is worthy and requiring of understanding?	National standards. State standards. District standards. Regional topic opportunities. Teacher expertise and interest.	Enduring ideas. Opportunities for authentic, discipline-based work. Uncoverage. Engaging.	Unit framed around enduring understandings and essential questions.
Stage 2. What is evidence of understanding?	**Six facets of under-standing. Continuum of assessment types.**	**Valid. Reliable. Sufficient. Authentic work. Feasible. Student friendly.**	**Unit anchored in credible and educationally vital evidence of the desired understandings.**
Stage 3. What learning experiences and teaching promote understanding, interest, and excellence?	Research-based repertoire of learning and teaching strategies. Essential and enabling knowledge and skill.	WHERE Where is it going? Hook the students. Explore and equip. Rethink and revise. Exhibit and evaluate.	Coherent learning experiences and teaching that will evoke and develop the desired understandings, promote interest, and make excellent performance more likely.

and self-knowledge—provide the first consideration. Teaching for understanding aims at having students explain, interpret, and apply, while showing insight from perspective, empathy, and self-knowledge. The facets also suggest where to look for evidence of understanding: to the various performances and products central to each facet—explanations, interpretations, and applications. For example, Facet 1 involves the ability to explain, verify, or justify a position. We need similar specificity for all the facets. Thus, it will be useful to start with the stem, "A student who *really* understands . . . " to suggest other kinds of assessment tasks (see Figure 5.2 on p. 66).

The bulleted list for each facet provides the start of a blueprint for assessing understanding. Regardless of our topic or the age of our students, the verbs suggest the kinds of assessments needed to determine whether the students understand.

In addition to the six facets, a second design consideration suggests the use of a range of methods of assessment noted in Chapter 1. Too often as teachers, we rely on only one or two types of assessment, then compound that error by concentrating on those aspects of the curriculum that are most easily tested by multiple-choice or short-answer items. And frequently, we fail to consider the differences between tests and other forms of assessment that are particularly well-suited for gathering evidence of understanding or its absence.

In fact, in aiming for understanding, we err in assuming that formal testing is the main vehicle for evidence gathering. On the contrary, as the phrase "check for understanding" implies and as Bloom's work reveals, ongoing formative and informal assessment is vital if students are to achieve understanding and avoid misunderstanding.

Without pressing the point too much, we urge teachers to think of students as juries think of the accused: innocent (of understanding) until proven guilty by a preponderance of evidence that is more than circumstantial. That's why it is vital for teachers to learn to think like assessors and not just activity designers.

The following true stories suggest the extent of the problem:

■ A 5th grade teacher proposes to center the major project of her Civil War unit around a student diorama of a great battle of the war, with supporting exhibit materials. But the stated standards for the unit require students to understand the causes and effects of the Civil War. Here, then, is a basic validity problem: Excellent or poor performance on the proposed project is unrelated to the content standard. In other words, a student could produce a wonderful diorama while having only limited understanding of the war's causes and effects.

■ A 7th grade general science teacher captures the energy and imagination of his students by announcing that they will have to eat the results of their next science experiment. But what is engaging is not always what is most effective or appropriate, given the time available. In this instance, making peanut brittle offers little in the way of big ideas and enduring understanding for the week of experimentation allotted.

Both of these unit assessments have merit, but each could be made more valid and tied more closely to the core curriculum. Our point is that a more rigorous backward design—from the key ideas to the assessments they imply—would have provided that tie.

Not a Natural Process

To think like an assessor prior to designing lessons—what backward design demands—does not come naturally or easily to many teachers. We are far more used to thinking like an activity designer once we have a target. That is to say, we easily and unconsciously jump to Stage 3 of design, the design of lessons, without asking ourselves whether we have the necessary evidence to assess for the core knowledge and are aiming for it.

Backward design demands that we short-circuit this natural instinct. Otherwise, our design is likely to be less coherent and focused on understanding— and more the result of chance and able students.[1] Consider a summary of the differences in approaches, shown in Figure 5.3 (see p. 68).

Figure 5.2. **A STUDENT WHO *REALLY* UNDERSTANDS . . .**

Each of the six facets of understanding lends itself to certain assessment tasks. Here are some examples.

Facet 1. A student who really understands *can explain*.
She demonstrates sophisticated explanatory power and insight. She can

■ Provide complex, insightful, and credible reasons—theories and principles, based on good evidence and argument—to explain or illuminate an event, fact, text, or idea; provide a systematic account, using helpful and vivid mental models.

❑ Make fine, subtle distinctions; aptly qualify her opinions.

❑ See and argue for what is central— the big ideas, pivotal moments, decisive evidence, key questions, and so on.

❑ Make good predictions.

■ Avoid or overcome common misunderstandings and superficial or simplistic views— shown, for example, by avoiding overly simplistic, hackneyed, or imprecise theories or explanations.

■ Reveal a personalized, thoughtful, and coherent grasp of a subject—indicated, for example, by developing a reflective and systematic integration of what she knows effectively and cognitively. This integration would therefore be based in part upon significant and apt *direct or simulated* experience of specific ideas or feelings. Substantiate or justify her views with sound argument and evidence.

Facet 2. A student who really understands *can interpret*.
He offers powerful, meaningful interpretations, translations, and narratives. He can

■ Effectively and sensitively interpret texts, language, and situations—shown, for example, by the ability to "read between the lines" and offer plausible accounts of the many possible purposes and meanings of any "text" (e.g., book, situation, or human behavior).

■ Offer a meaningful and illuminating account of complex situations and people. He has the ability, for example, to provide historical and biographical background, thereby helping to make ideas more accessible and relevant.

Facet 3. A student who really understands *can apply*.
She uses knowledge in context, has know-how. She can

■ Employ her knowledge effectively in diverse, authentic, and realistically messy contexts.

■ Extend or apply what she knows in a novel and effective way—that is, invent in the sense of innovate, as Piaget (1973) discusses in *To Understand Is to Invent.*

■ Effectively self-adjust as she performs.

Facet 4. A student who really understands *sees in perspective*.
He can

■ Critique and justify a position to see it as a point of view; to use skills and dispositions that embody disciplined skepticism and the testing of theories.

■ Know the history of an idea to place discussion and theory in context; know the questions

(Figure continues on next page.)

Figure 5.2. (continued)

or problem to which the knowledge or theory studied is an answer or solution.

■ Infer the assumptions upon which an idea or theory is based.

■ Know the limits as well as the power of an idea.

■ See through argument or language that is biased, partisan, or ideological.

■ See and explain the importance or worth of an idea.

■ Wisely employ *both* criticism and belief, an ability summarized by Peter Elbow's (1973) maxim that we are likely to better understand when we methodically "believe when others doubt and doubt when others believe."

Facet 5. **A student who really understands** ***demonstrates empathy.* She has the ability to sensitively perceive.** She can

■ Project herself into, feel, and appreciate another's situation, affect, or point of view.

■ Operate on the assumption that even an apparently odd or obscure comment, text, person, or set of ideas may contain insights that justify

working to understand it.

■ See when incomplete or flawed views are plausible, even insightful, though perhaps somewhat incorrect or outdated.

■ See and explain how an idea or theory can be all too easily misunderstood by others.

■ Listen—and hear what others often do not.

Facet 6. **A student who really understands** ***reveals self-knowledge.* He can**

■ Recognize his own prejudices and style, and how they color understanding; see and get beyond egocentrism, ethnocentrism, present-centeredness, nostalgia, and either-or thinking.

■ Engage in effective metacognition; recognize intellectual style, strengths, and weaknesses.

■ Question his own convictions; like Socrates, able to sort out mere strong belief and habit from warranted knowledge, be intellectually honest, and admit ignorance.

■ Accurately self-assess and effectively self-regulate.

■ Accept feedback and criticism without defensiveness.

Source: Based on material in Wiggins (1998), pp. 86–88.

Two Basic Questions

Thinking like an assessor boils down to two basic questions. *Where should we look* to find hallmarks of understanding, and *What should we look for* in determining and distinguishing degrees of under-

standing? The first question asks us to consider the necessary evidence in general—the *kinds of performance or behavior* indicative of understanding; the second question asks us to focus on the most salient and revealing criteria for identifying and *differentiating* levels or degrees of understanding—

using criteria and rubrics to sort work by quality along a continuum.

The first set of questions in Figure 5.3 ensures that the eventual activities and instructional strategies simultaneously derive from and point toward the appropriate final assessments. The second set of questions, though logical from the perspective of activity design, makes it far less likely that the work will culminate in understanding or that we will have the evidence we need to judge whether such understanding has occurred. In effect, when we only think like an activity designer, we end up with the apples unit described in the Introduction. Even though some students may develop important understandings through the various activities comprising the unit, the teacher did not consider, at the design stage, how to build the activities around the need for evidence of understanding.

Criteria and Indicators

Having clarified the kinds of evidence needed to assess for understanding, we turn to the second phase of thinking like an assessor, asking, Against what criteria will we judge such evidence? What are the kinds of things to look for? These questions challenge us to

Figure 5.3. **TWO DIFFERENT APPROACHES**

Thinking Like an Assessor	Thinking Like an Activity Designer
What would be sufficient and revealing evidence of understanding?	What would be interesting and engaging activities on this topic?
What performance tasks must anchor the unit and focus the instructional work?	What resources and materials are available on this topic?
How will I be able to distinguish between those who really understand and those who don't (though they may seem to)?	What will students be doing in and out of class? What assignments will be given?
Against what criteria will I distinguish work?	How will I give students a grade (and justify it to their parents)?
What misunderstandings are likely? How will I check for those?	Did the activities work? Why or why not?

clarify the criteria for judging performance. We ask, Given the right kinds of evidence, what is the difference between successful and unsuccessful explanations, interpretations, and applications?

Presumably, for example, an in-depth understanding requires a "systematic" and "justified" explanation—two criteria seemingly central to the first facet, explanation. And what will distinguish understanding from its absence or lesser degrees of understanding? Our rubrics must eventually flesh out all the relevant criteria as well as help differentiate levels of understanding. Figure 5.4 provides a partial list of applicable criteria.

Naive Versus Sophisticated Understandings

Sophistication: Of a person: free of naiveté, experienced, worldly-wise; subtle, discriminating, refined, cultured; aware of, versed in the complex-

ities of a subject or pursuit. Of equipment, techniques, theories, etc.: employing advanced or refined methods or concepts; highly developed or complicated.

—*Oxford English Dictionary*, CD-ROM version

This definition of *sophistication* is good as far as it goes. But to develop a sound and comprehensive assessment of understanding, we need more than this picture of what people with understanding do and look like. We need some way to more precisely, validly, and reliably distinguish between degrees of understanding.

Oddly enough, assessment is always about discrimination. We get into the business of judging relative strengths and weaknesses with increasing precision. How, then, can we learn to distinguish a deep understanding from a more superficial understanding? Which actions, responses, or performances are most characteristic of—indicators of—understanding, some understanding, or little understanding?

Figure 5.4 **CRITERIA FOR EACH FACET**

Facet 1 Explanation	Facet 2 Interpretation	Facet 3 Application	Facet 4 Perspective	Facet 5 Empathy	Facet 6 Self-Knowledge
Accurate	Meaningful	Effective	Credible	Sensitive	Self-aware
Coherent	Insightful	Efficient	Revealing	Open	Meta-cognitive
Justified	Significant	Fluent	Insightful	Receptive	Self-adjusting
Systematic	Illustrative	Adaptive	Plausible	Perceptive	Reflective
Predictive	Illuminating	Graceful	Unusual	Tactful	Wise

Clearly, understanding is a matter of degree on a continuum. It is not a matter of right versus wrong but *more or less* naive or sophisticated; *more or less* superficial or in-depth. What does a range of explanations look like, for example, from the most naive or simplistic to the most complex and sophisticated? Whatever the response, rubrics provide useful guidance in assessment.

Many rubrics describe a progression of *skills* from novice to expert. Our quest, however, is not for a rubric of skill development but for a rubric that combines insight and performance related to understanding of ideas and meaning. What does a novice's understanding of the Cold War look like compared with an expert's? What characterizes a more in-depth but still not expert view?

These are the types of questions we need to ask for any specific understanding, but they apply to more general understandings as well. What are the key characteristics of an elementary theory versus an advanced theory for the same phenomenon in science? What is the difference between a simple and a sophisticated proof in mathematics? What is the difference between a complex and simple analysis of a literary text or historical event?

Some Excerpts from Rubrics

Consider excerpts from a few rubrics to suggest some preliminary answers.

A U.S. History Rubric

This rubric is from the advanced placement (AP) exam in U.S. history:

■ Clear, well-developed thesis that deals in a sophisticated fashion with [key] components . . . .

■ Clear, developed thesis that deals with [key issues] . . . .

■ General thesis responding to all components superficially . . . .

■ Little or no analysis . . . . (Educational Testing Service/College Board, 1992, p. 25).

The rubric explicitly warns judges, first, to assess the degree of student understanding (sophisticated analysis versus mere retelling), and second, to not confuse either the number of factual errors or the quality of the writing with the student's understanding of the time period.

A Mathematics Rubric

In mathematics, too, we need to better distinguish between more and less sophisticated understandings. Consider two answers to the same problem, shown in Figure 5.5. Note that although both answers are correct and well-explained, the second answer reflects a somewhat deeper understanding of the problem.

The following rubric shows how we might distinguish levels of understanding in mathematics:

■ Shows a sophisticated understanding of the subject matter involved. The concepts, evidence, arguments, qualifications made, questions posed, or methods used are expertly insightful, going well beyond the grasp of the subject typically found at this level of experience. Grasps the essence of the idea or problem and applies the most powerful tools for solving it. The work shows that the student is able to make subtle distinctions and to relate the

Figure 5.5. **MORE AND LESS SOPHISTICATED UNDERSTANDINGS**

Consider an ice cream sugar cone, 8 cm in diameter (d) and 12 cm high (h), capped with an 8 cm in diameter sphere of luscious rich triple chocolate ice cream. If the ice cream melts completely, will the cone overflow or not? How do you know?

v = volume   r = radius π = 3.1416

Answer 1

We must first find the volume of the cone and ice cream scoop:

$$v \text{ cone} = 1/3 \pi r^2 h$$
$$= 1/3 \pi 50.26 \times 12$$
$$= 201.06 \text{ cm}^3$$

$$v \text{ scoop} = 4/3 \pi r^3$$
$$= 4/3 \pi (4)^3$$
$$= 4/3 \times 201.6 \text{ cm}^3$$
$$= 268.08 \text{ cm}^3$$

We now see that the scoop of ice cream has a volume that is well over 50 cm more than the cone's volume. Therefore, it is unlikely that the melted ice cream could fit completely inside the cone. However, as all ice cream lovers like myself know, there is a certain amount of air within ice cream. (Therefore, experiments would have to be done.)

Answer 2

We first need to plug in the values in the equations for the volume of a cone and sphere. (The student performs the same calculations as above.) From this calculation, we can see that the ice cream will not fit in the cone.

Now compare the two formulas:

$$1/3 \pi r^2 h = 4/3 \pi r^3$$
$$\pi r^2 h = 4 \pi r^3$$
$$\pi h = 4 \pi r$$
$$h = 4r$$

From this final comparison, we can see that if the height of the cone is exactly 4 times the radius, the volumes will be equal. . . . (The student goes on to explain why there are numerous questions about ice cream in real life that will affect the answer. For example, Will the ice cream's volume change as it melts? Is it possible to compress ice cream?)

The second explanation is a more penetrating one because it subsumes the problem under a broader one, one of our criteria for "depth": Under what conditions are the volumes equal? In the first case, all the student has done is calculate the areas based on the formula and the given numbers. In terms of the *knowledge* tested, the answers were equally acceptable. Indeed, the teacher gave the same grade to both.

In assessing understanding, however, we are more interested in judging the sophistication (depth and breadth) of the students' approach and the quality of their reasoning. That judgment calls for assessments that evoke and require student initiative and explicit reasoning.

particular challenge to more significant, complex, or comprehensive principles.

■ Shows a mature understanding of the subject matter involved. The ideas, evidence, arguments, and methods used are advanced and revealing. Grasps the essence of the idea or problem and applies powerful tools to address or solve it. The student makes important distinctions and qualifications as needed.

■ Shows a good understanding of the subject matter involved. The concepts, evidence, arguments, and methods used involve an advanced degree of difficulty and power. Frames the matter appropriately for someone at this level of experience. There may be limits to the understanding or some naiveté or glibness in the response, but there are no misunderstandings in or overly simplistic aspects to their work.

■ Shows an adequate understanding of the issues involved. Work reveals control of knowledge, concepts, or methods that enable the problem to be solved at the intended level of difficulty. There is less subtlety/discrimination/nuance than found in the more sophisticated work, and there may be evidence of some misunderstanding of key ideas. The work may yield correct answers, but the approach/concepts/methods used are more simplistic than we would expect at this level of experience.

■ Shows a naive or limited understanding of the ideas and issues involved. Simple rules/formulae/approaches/concepts are used where more sophisticated ones are called for and available from previous learning. Important ideas may be misunderstood or misapplied. The student's work *may* be adequate to address all or most aspects of the problem, but the concepts and methods used are simplistic.

■ Shows no apparent understanding of the underlying ideas and issues involved in the problem. Brings to bear inappropriate or inadequate knowledge of the problem.

■ Insufficient evidence in the response to judge the student's knowledge of subject matter involved in this problem (typically due to a failure to complete the work).

Longitudinal Rubrics

In the discussion up until now, we have assumed that an assessment of understanding involves judging singular performances or products. But, given the nature of our topic and the iterative nature of the development of understanding, our assessment needs to be longitudinal—over time. Understanding develops slowly and reveals itself as a progression along a continuum for any single idea; our assessments must better reflect this fact. We need to use more recurring tasks than we now do, and we need rubrics to better help us see the student's ability to make increasing sense and use of big ideas. In other words, we need to be asking for all key ideas and overarching questions: What does a progression from naive to sophisticated understanding look like for the same complex idea or question?

Some such rubrics already exist, especially in other countries. Consider the following science rubric from Great Britain (School Curriculum and Assessment Authority, 1995):

■ Pupils use scientific knowledge and understanding to identify the key factors they need to consider and, where appropriate, to make predictions. They make observations and measure with precision a variety of quantities, using instruments with fine divisions. They make enough measurements and observations for the task. They choose scales for graphs that enable them to show appropriate data effectively. They identify measurements and observations that do not fit the main pattern or trend shown. They draw conclusions that are consistent with the evidence and explain these using scientific knowledge and understanding.

■ Pupils identify the key factors they need to consider in contexts that involve only a few factors. Where appropriate, they make predictions based on their scientific knowledge and understanding. They select apparatus for a long range of tasks and use it with care. They make a series of observations or measurements with precision appropriate to the task. They begin to repeat observations and measurements and to offer simple explanations for any differences they encounter. They record observations and measurements systematically and present data as line graphs. They draw conclusions that are consistent with the evidence and begin to relate these to scientific knowledge and understanding.

■ Pupils recognize the need for fair tests, describing or showing in the way they perform their task how to vary one factor while keeping others the same. Where appropriate, they make predictions. They select suitable equipment to use and make a series of observations and measurements that are adequate for the task. They present their observations and measurements clearly, using tables and bar charts. They begin to plot points to form simple graphs and use these graphs to point out and interpret patterns or trends in their data. They take account of these patterns when they draw conclusions, and begin to relate their conclusions to scientific knowledge and understanding.

■ Pupils respond to suggestions, put forward their own ideas, and, where appropriate, make simple predictions. They make relevant observations and measure quantities, such as length or mass, using a range of simple equipment. With some help, they carry out a fair test, recognizing and explaining why it is fair. They record their observations in a variety of ways. They provide explanations for observations and, where they occur, for simple patterns in recorded measurements. They say what they have found out from their work.

■ Pupils respond to suggestions of how to find things out and, with help, make their own suggestions. They use simple equipment provided and make observations related to their task. They compare objects, living things, and events they observe. They describe their observations and record them, using simple tables where it is appropriate to do so. They say whether what happened was what was expected.

■ Pupils describe simple features of objects, living things and events they observe, communicating their findings in simple ways, such as by talking about their work or through drawings or simple charts.

In the benchmarks in science developed by the American Association for the Advancement of Science (1993), the authors used the all-encompassing verb *to know* in part to concentrate their efforts on describing how the "same" important understandings should be revealed in increasingly sophisticated ways. Consider how an understanding of evolution is described developmentally:

By the end of the 2nd grade, students should know that

■ Different plants and animals have external features that help them thrive in different kinds of places.

■ Some kinds of organisms that once lived on earth have completely disappeared, although they were something like others that are alive today. . . .

By the end of the 5th grade, students should know that

■ Individuals of the same kind differ in their characteristics, and sometimes differences give individuals an advantage in surviving and reproducing.

■ Fossils can be compared to one another and

to living organisms according to their similarities and differences. . . .

By the end of the 8th grade, students should know that

■ Small differences between parents and off-spring can accumulate (through selective breeding) in successive generations so that descendants are very different from their ancestors.

■ Individual organisms with certain traits are more likely than others to survive and have off-spring. Changes in environmental conditions can affect the survival of individual organisms and entire species. . . .

By the end of the 12th grade, students should know that

■ The basic idea of biological evolution is that the earth's present-day species developed from earlier, distinctly different species.

■ Molecular evidence substantiates the anatomical evidence for evolution. . . .

■ Natural selection provides the following mechanism for evolution: Some variation in heritable characteristics exists within every species, some of these characteristics give individuals an advantage over others in surviving and reproducing, and the advantaged offspring, in turn, are more likely than others to survive and reproduce. The proportion of individuals that have advantageous characteristics will increase (pp. 123–125).[2]

This phrasing indicates that the student will have to gain not merely more knowledge of detail but increased understanding of complex function and interrelatedness—knowledge that can only be gained through some inquiry, argument, and verification (in addition to summary accounts by teacher and text).

Noteworthy here is that sophistication involves not only greater depth and breadth of formal knowledge but also greater awareness of how the discipline really operates, as well as greater personal control over and flexibility with knowledge.

A Set of Rubrics for the Facets of Understanding

How, then, should we assess for the facets of understanding, as described in the previous two chapters? The rubric shown in Figure 5.6 (see pp. 76–77) provides a general framework for making distinctions and judgments in accordance with the six facets of understanding. The rubric reflects a continuum of performance—from naive understanding (at the bottom) to sophisticated understanding (at the top)—for each of the facets.

As the rubric makes clear, understanding is a matter of degree. In even the most capable or mature person, understanding is a mixture of insight and misconception, knowledge and ignorance, skill and awkwardness. This observation about understanding is true within and across the six facets, complicating assessment further.

Moreover, individuals can have diverse but valid understandings of the same ideas and experiences. In other words, one person's profile might look very different from another's even as we describe them both, in general, as "sophisticated" (in the same way we give holistic scores to writing performances consisting of different patterns of the analytic traits involved). To make the rubric useful within a specific course of study, add bulleted indicators under each descriptor.

Standards for Assessment

Having clarified the considerations in designing assessments for understanding, we move to the next phase of Stage 2 to ask, Against what criteria should our assessment be judged? Any assessment must be *valid* (evidence that will let us draw accurate inferences about specific student understandings, not muddied by other variables) and *reliable* (evidence that gives us confidence, where we see a pattern that gives us a picture of the students' "true" abilities). By implication, the overall evidence must be *sufficient*.

As we noted earlier in our judicial analogy (student is innocent of understanding until proven guilty by a preponderance of evidence), we want more than just circumstantial evidence to convict the student of understanding. We need to be concerned with whether we have seen the student's understanding in different contexts, at different times, and on different types of assessments, before we render a confident judgment.

Three other criteria need to be added if our work is going to yield understanding by design. Any thorough and revealing assessment of understanding should be *grounded in an authentic performance* application. In addition, the plan for assessment needs to be *feasible* and *student friendly*.

Is "Sufficient" Redundant?

Some readers might argue that "sufficient" as a standard is redundant, given the standards of "valid" and "reliable." We think it is necessary to call attention to the need for more diverse and balanced assessment.[3] Educators in the United States are highly accustomed to thinking of assessment as "out-of-context tests using discrete items" and seeing complex targets as assessable in one test. Thus, before moving on, we want to emphasize *likely diversity and amount of evidence needed.*

In addition, our constant reference to possible performance tasks in this chapter might lead some readers to conclude that more traditional forms of

testing have little value. Not so. We believe in the value of a balanced use of assessment as the continuum of methods (observation/quiz/test, prompt/task/project) illustrated in Chapter 1.

Figure 5.7 (see p. 78) shows how we might balance assessment methods in the overall evidence requirements for the nutrition unit introduced in Chapter 1.

Although we have thus far concentrated on more formal and *summative* assessments of understanding (given the nature of backward design), it is through the informal day-in and day-out teacher checks that we are able to monitor whether or not students understand. The iterative nature of understanding, the likelihood of confusions or misconceptions, and the need for interactive evidence make it imperative, in fact, that teachers know how to teach through assessment of understanding. (See Chapter 10 for more on checks for understanding.)

All these formative strategies have the advantage of offering alternatives to formal and complex performance—an essential need if we are to make legitimate distinctions between good performance ability, such as writing and speaking, and the understanding itself.[4]

Critical Implications for Grading

The regular use of multiple checks for understanding also has critical implications for grading and affects the practice of many teachers, especially at the secondary level. Secondary school teachers have a long-standing habit of putting a grade in the gradebook for each assessment given and then averaging those grades to come up with a final grade. This practice makes less sense when using checks for understanding. The aim of this type of diagnostic assessment is to teach more than it is to test. And

Figure 5.6 **RUBRIC FOR THE SIX FACETS OF UNDERSTANDING**

Explanation	Interpretation	Application
Sophisticated: an unusually thorough, elegant, and inventive account (model, theory, or explanation); fully supported, verified, and justified; deep and broad: goes well beyond the information given.	*Profound:* a powerful and illuminating interpretation and analysis of the importance/meaning/significance; tells a rich and insightful story; provides a rich history or context; sees deeply and incisively any ironies in the different interpretations.	*Masterful:* fluent, flexible, and efficient; able to use knowledge and skill and adjust understandings well in novel, diverse, and difficult contexts.
In-depth: an atypical and revealing account, going beyond what is obvious or what was explicitly taught; makes subtle connections; well supported by argument and evidence; novel thinking displayed.	*Revealing:* a nuanced interpretation and analysis of the importance/meaning/significance; tells an insightful story; provides a telling history or context; sees subtle differences, levels, and ironies in diverse interpretations.	*Skilled:* competent in using knowledge and skill and adapting understandings in a variety of appropriate and demanding contexts.
Developed: an account that reflects some in-depth and personalized ideas; the student is making the work her own, going beyond the given—there is supported theory here, but insufficient or inadequate evidence and argument.	*Perceptive:* a helpful interpretation or analysis of the importance/meaning/significance; tells a clear and instructive story; provides a useful history or context; sees different levels of interpretation.	*Able:* able to perform well with knowledge and skill in a few key contexts, with a limited repertoire, flexibility, or adaptability to diverse contexts.
Intuitive: an incomplete account but with apt and insightful ideas; extends and deepens some of what was learned; some "reading between the lines"; account has limited support/argument/data or sweeping generalizations. There is a theory, but one with limited testing and evidence.	*Interpreted:* a plausible interpretation or analysis of the importance/meaning/significance; makes sense of a story; provides a history or context.	*Apprentice:* relies on a limited repertoire of routines; able to perform well in familiar or simple contexts, with perhaps some needed coaching; limited use of personal judgment and responsiveness to specifics of feedback/situation.
Naive: a superficial account; more descriptive than analytical or creative; a fragmentary or sketchy account of facts/ideas or glib generalizations; a black-and-white account; less a theory than an unexamined hunch or borrowed idea.	*Literal:* a simplistic or superficial reading; mechanical translation; a decoding with little or no interpretation; no sense of wider importance or significance; a restatement of what was taught or read.	*Novice:* can perform only with coaching or relies on highly scripted, singular "plug-in" (algorithmic and mechanical) skills, procedures, or approaches

Perspective	Empathy	Self-Knowledge
Insightful: a penetrating and novel viewpoint; effectively critiques and encompasses other plausible perspectives; takes a long and dispassionate, critical view of the issues involved.	*Mature:* disposed and able to see and feel what others see and feel; unusually open to and willing to seek out the odd, alien, or different.	*Wise:* deeply aware of the boundaries of one's own and others' understanding; able to recognize his prejudices and projections; has integrity—able and willing to act on what one understands.
Thorough: a revealing and coordinated critical view; makes own view more plausible by considering the plausibility of other perspectives; makes apt criticisms, discriminations, and qualifications.	*Sensitive:* disposed to see and feel what others see and feel; open to the unfamiliar or different.	*Circumspect:* aware of one's ignorance and that of others; aware of one's prejudices; knows the strengths and limits of one's understanding.
Considered: a reasonably critical and comprehensive look at all points of view in the context of one's own; makes clear that there is plausibility to other points of view.	*Aware:* knows and feels that others see and feel differently; somewhat able to empathize with others; has difficulty making sense of odd or alien views.	*Thoughtful:* generally aware of what is and is not understood; aware of how prejudice and projection can occur without awareness and shape one's views.
Aware: knows of different points of view and somewhat able to place own view in perspective, but weakness in considering worth of each perspective or critiquing each perspective, especially one's own; uncritical about tacit assumptions.	*Developing:* has some capacity and self-discipline to "walk in another's shoes," but is still primarily limited to one's own reactions and attitudes; puzzled or put off by different feelings or attitudes.	*Unreflective:* generally unaware of one's specific ignorance; generally unaware of how subjective prejudgments color understandings.
Uncritical: unaware of differing points of view; prone to overlook or ignore other perspectives; has difficulty imagining other ways of seeing things; prone to egocentric argument and personal criticisms.	*Egocentric:* has little or no empathy beyond intellectual awareness of others; sees things through own ideas and feelings; ignores or is threatened or puzzled by different feelings, attitudes, or views.	*Innocent:* completely unaware of the bounds of one's understanding and of the role of projection and prejudice in opinions and attempts to understand.

Figure 5.7 **EVIDENCE (NUTRITION UNIT)**

DETERMINE ACCEPTABLE EVIDENCE

What evidence will show that students understand _elements of good nutrition_ **?**

Performance Tasks, Projects

- _Family Meals._ Students analyze a hypothetical family's diet for one week and make recommendations for improving its nutritional value.
- _You Are What You Eat._ Students create an illustrated brochure to teach younger children about healthy eating.
- _Chow Down._ Students develop a three-day menu for meals and snacks for an upcoming Outdoor Education camp experience. Their menu must be tasty while meeting the USDA food pyramid recommendations.

Quizzes, Tests, Academic Prompts

Quiz 1: The food groups	**Prompt:** Describe two health problems that could arise as a result of poor nutrition and explain how these could be avoided.
Quiz 2: The USDA food pyramid	

Other Evidence _(e.g., observations, work samples, dialogues)_

Informal observations/discussions during work on the performance tasks and the camp menu project.

Student Self-Assessment

1. Self-assess your brochure.
2. Self-assess the camp menu.
3. Self-assess the extent to which you "eat healthy" two times: at the start and at the end of the unit.

averaging one's initial versus one's final understanding of a complex idea would be a questionable measurement.[5]

The Problem of Insight

Whether our methods are formal or informal, formative or summative, it is difficult to assess validly and reliably for understanding. We cannot mince words or shirk duties here. As we previously noted, to aim for understanding is to aim for something more slippery and ambiguous than other objectives.

Understanding falls through the cracks of testing and grading quite easily. It happens when we pay much attention to *knowledge* (and thus the easy right-wrong dichotomy in scoring that makes assessment so much easier) and too little attention to the *quality* of an understanding (clearly a somewhat subjective act). This challenge comes to the fore when we have to justify the grade we have assigned a student to suspicious parents or faraway college admissions officers.

But the thorniest problem we face in assessing for understanding is differentiating between the student's insights and the student's performance. How do we identify a sophisticated understanding buried in weak performance or incorrect facts? By contrast, how do we avoid overrewarding students for being articulate and dutiful?

If we typically assess students primarily for technical knowledge and ability to explain what they know, we risk both overlooking genuine insights that students of limited expression may have and continuing to assign more value to merely correct and well-articulated answers.

One common meaning of the word *understand* involves the idea of having an insight or intuition that may not be expressible clearly in words. To speak of *an* understanding suggests a certain mental grasp of specific important ideas; that there are "nouns," not just "verbs" of understanding.

Look at common language use and classroom experience. We talk about some kids "getting it" or others "not seeing" the point or drawing appropriate inferences. We detect a pearl of wisdom inside a halting and incomplete comment. A student offers a novel angle in a class discussion about a possible solution to the math problem at hand, but she cannot prove it. She may even preface her remarks with, "I know this sounds stupid, but ____." And vice versa: We hear students deliver articulate, thorough explanations, but on trivial or obvious points.

Consider the following simple examples:

■ A 9th grader reading Plato's account of Socrates's trial comes into class and asks: "Mr. Wiggins, why is it called the *Apology*? Socrates doesn't seem very sorry."

■ After hearing the term *malicious*, Jay's 8-year-old daughter asks, "Does that mean something tastes bad?"

■ Grant's 5-year-old son, during a family flight to California, turns and asks, "If the plane keeps flying, will we be upside down on the other side of the world?"

In these examples, the learner has an insight without necessarily being able to fully or effectively articulate it. We have all seen this as teachers: A student is onto something but cannot get the words out quite right to explain it, get others to appreciate it,

or say where the idea came from. Indeed, the student's inarticulateness can easily lead others to ignore or dismiss his good idea. Sometimes, sophisticated *understandings* lurk beneath weakly executed *performances.*

Earlier we noted that certain kinds of knowledge make up a genuine understanding: control over linchpin ideas, the overcoming of common misconceptions, and a grasp of the key questions at the heart of a subject. Thus, we need to stress in our assessment of "explanation" that the quality of the insights is important and distinct from the quality of the arguments and articulation. Practically speaking, we will sometimes want to use at least two distinct criteria in assessing: the quality of the performances (such as the explanations), and the quality of the ideas.

Deep Understanding: Perceiving the Essence

Sometimes deep understanding is best revealed by a simple yet profound insight, phrased modestly. In our work in assessment reform, we (the authors) have occasionally seen younger students outperform older ones on writing or mathematics tasks, even though the older students had more knowledge and skill at their command. The younger students' success usually was a function of their ability to perceive the essence of the problem, in spite of their limited tools.

The caution against making assumptions about understanding or lack of it also pertains to our knowledge about multiple intelligences. Penetrating insights can manifest themselves in facets other than explanation (such as in application or silent empa-

thy), as the following remark about the codiscoverer of the transistor suggests:

> Conyers Herring, now an emeritus professor of physics at Stanford, said that [John] Bardeen's gift for physics was magisterial, in the realm of Beethoven's gift for music. Bardeen had "an intuition" for the way nature worked in a given situation, says Herring. But Bardeen had trouble expressing himself. He would ponder so long before replying to a question that people would wonder whether he had a hearing problem, says his son William (*Trenton Times,* 1997b, pp. B1–2).

Assessment must reflect this caution: Understanding could be sophisticated in the absence of a good explanation. The quality of the insight may be less *or* more than the quality of the explanation or performance in general. The theory may be poorly expressed, but insightful.

To judge an understanding of how someone makes sense of something, we typically need the person to explain it to us. The quality of an explanation depends in part upon its clarity and in part upon the quality of the evidence and the reasoning. Is the evidence believable? Does it bear on the matter at hand? Reasoning should be logical, naturally. Adequate evidence and reasons then culminate in proof, verification, justification—a thorough and convincing explanation.

But if we think less in terms of explanation and more in terms of theory, we see a third criterion at work: Is the explanation powerful? In other words, does it explain many heretofore unexplained facts? Does it predict heretofore unpredicted results? Does it enable us to see order where before there were only random or inexplicable phenomena? Good explanations are not just words and logic but insight

into essentials. The best explanations involve inferences made from often limited evidence for fundamental principles or patterns. A good explanation,
in Bruner's well-known phrasing, takes us "beyond
the information given," and toward ideas that define
and structure ideas, even a whole discipline. In
other words, we as assessors need to distinguish
between the adequacy of the explanation and the
power of the ideas.

What, then, *are* we perceiving when we claim to
see student insight inside poor explanations—e.g.,
great physics despite inarticulate responses?
Naturally, to assess such a grasp the student has to
perform well in some way; there is clearly something tangible in what was said or revealed in the
Bell Labs 50 years ago about transistors, or his colleagues would not have described Bardeen as having
great insight.

We thus find it unsatisfying to say (as the
Harvard Project Zero researchers say in *Teaching for
Understanding* [Wiske, 1997]) that understanding *is*
a set of performances. We believe understanding
reveals itself best through certain kinds of performances, and performance assessment is made more
precise and helpful by distinguishing the sophistication and power of the ideas from their expression or
other performance.

A practical effect on assessment is that our intuition may be ahead of or behind our ability to prove
it and explain it—a typical contradiction in the world
of science—and our assessment needs to reflect this
complexity. As Bruner (1996) expressed it:

> As every historian of science in the last hun-
> dred years has pointed out, scientists use all sorts
> of aids and intuitions and stories and metaphors to
> help them in their quest of getting their speculative
> model to fit "nature". . . . My physicist friends are

fond of the remark that physics is 95 percent spec-
ulation and 5 percent observation. And they are
very attached to the expression "physical intuition"
as something that "real" physicists have: They are
not just tied to observation and measurement but
know how to get around in the theory even without them (p. 123).

How Discovery Works

Discovery works this way: Our imagination and
hunches precede our proof and teaching of them.[6]
In judging understanding, therefore, we must
beware of *overvaluing* the articulateness and accuracy of formalized knowledge, a deep-seated teacher
habit—of *conflating* knowledge with understanding.
At stake in assessment of understanding is something different from determining the accuracy and
breadth of the student's technical knowledge.
People with limited explanatory powers and technical vocabulary may have a deep insight into things.
Highly learned people may be unable to draw powerful inferences and meaning from what they know.

We are after the student's grasp of key ideas. So,
a student's technical knowledge may sometimes be
limited or even mistaken, but we could still conclude that he understands important things.
Sometimes, a wrong answer can hide a great deal of
understanding and vice versa; our assessments must
make room for this difficult reality.

On the other hand, unless we fully explicate
and justify our idea, it remains only a potential
explanation, interpretation, or application—a limited understanding. A good idea is only that—it is not
yet a theory. Our fledgling theory only makes objective sense if we test and explicate it. Our hunch
about the interpretation of a text only yields under-

standing if it illuminates more text. Our skillfulness becomes more fluid and fluent only if we show that we can use our ideas in appropriate settings.

Intuition often yields imaginative and promising theories and is, therefore, not a *criterion* of understanding. Indeed, the "Eureka!" feeling can mislead us into thinking that insight is immediate ("You either get it or you don't"), or mislead us into thinking that teaching for understanding is chancy and not at all possible "by design." Our instructional design and teaching challenge is then clear: We must set up conditions and design work that foster, develop, test, and refine intuitions.

The practical upshot of this problem for assessment is that the *latter three facets of understanding— perspective, empathy, and self-knowledge—often play a key role in revealing insight or its absence.* Indeed, a useful way to describe the problem of insight and imagination outpacing performance ability is that a student's perception, empathy, and self-knowledge are more sophisticated than his current ability to explain, interpret, and apply. That is yet another reason to use a six-faceted rubric, despite the complexity of doing so and the understandable desire to reduce things to a single rubric.

Here are some "look-fors" for insight derived from what we have said above about the three latter facets. Insight is revealed by ability to grasp and show

■ Other ways to look at and define the problem.

■ A potentially more powerful principle than the one taught or on the table.

■ The tacit assumptions at work that need to be made explicit.

■ Inconsistency in current versus past discussion.

■ Author intent, style, and bias.

■ Comparison and contrast, not just description.

■ Novel implications.

■ How custom and habit are influencing the views, discussion, or approach to the problem to date.

The following writing rubric is from a provincial exam in Alberta, Canada. It offers a revealing, though not entirely successful, way to attack the problem. Four separate criteria (and rubrics for them) are used to assess writing that responded to a reading in literature. The criteria are thought and detail, matters of choice, organization, and matters of convention. Clearly the first criterion, thought and detail, is intended to separate the quality of the understanding from the other qualities of writing performance. Here is the rubric:

5-PROFICIENT: An insightful understanding of the reading selection(s) is effectively established. The student's opinion, whether directly stated or implied, is perceptive and appropriately supported by specific details. Support is precise and thoughtfully selected.

4-CAPABLE: A well-considered understanding . . . Opinion is thoughtful. . . . Support is well defined and appropriate.

3-ADEQUATE: A plausible understanding is established and sustained. The student's opinion is conventional but plausibly supported. Support is general but functional.

2-LIMITED: Some understanding is evidenced, but the understanding is not always defensible or sustained. Opinion may be superficial and support scant and/or vague.

1-POOR: An implausible conjecture . . . The student's opinion, if present, is inappropriate or incomprehensible. Support is inappropriate or absent.

The evaluation of the answer should be in terms of the amount of evidence that the student has actually read something and thought about it, not a question of whether he/she has thought about it in the way an adult would, or in line with an adult's "correct" answer.

Note especially the comment to judges at the bottom, which clarifies their intent, even though it complicates matters further.

The problem we alluded to in this rubric involves the supposedly tight link between the quality of the insight and the quality of the support: Couldn't someone have an insightful understanding (5-Proficient) with only well-defined and appropriate support (4-Capable)? As in many complex rubrics, difficulties arise when we combine independent variables in the same descriptor: Should we give the writing a "5" or a "4," then? The criteria of insight and support should become separate rubrics, as our approach to the facets suggests. But criticisms aside, the rubric reveals how we *can* assess the quality of insight—even within the context of a provincial exam—despite the subjectivity involved.[7]

An overall strategy for addressing this complexity, therefore, is to frame multiple rubrics in light of the distinctions made in the facets generally and the previously mentioned point about insight versus performance. For instance, here is an example from each of five rubrics (edited to just the top score for each), which can be used to assess the various dimensions of mathematical understanding and performance. The "sophistication" criterion is a variant of the one given above, adapted for use in mathematics:

The criteria: insight, reasoning, effectiveness, accuracy, and quality of presentation.

■ **Mathematical Insight**

Shows a sophisticated understanding of the subject matter involved. The concepts, evidence, arguments, qualifications made, questions posed, and methods used are expertly insightful, going well beyond the grasp of the topic typically found at this level of experience. Grasps the essence of the problem and applies the most powerful tools for solving it. The work shows that the student is able to make subtle distinctions, and to relate the particular problem to more significant, complex, or comprehensive mathematical principles, formulas, or models.

■ **Mathematical Reasoning**

Shows a methodical, logical, and thorough plan for solving the problem. The approach and answers are explicitly detailed and reasonable throughout (whether or not the knowledge used is always sophisticated or accurate). The student justifies all claims with thorough argument: Counterarguments, questionable data, and implicit premises are fully explicated.

■ **Effectiveness of Mathematical Solution**

The solution to the problem is effective and often inventive. All essential details of the problem, and audience, purpose, and other contextual matters are fully addressed in a graceful and effective way. The solution may be creative in many possible ways: an unorthodox approach, unusually clever juggling of conflicting variables, the bringing in of unobvious mathematics, or imaginative evidence.

■ **Accuracy of Written Mathematical Work**

The work is accurate throughout. All calculations are correct, provided to the proper degree of precision and measurement error, and properly labeled.

■ **Quality of Mathematical Presentation**

The student's performance is persuasive and

unusually well presented. The essence of the research and the problems to be solved are summed up in a highly engaging and efficient manner, mindful of the audience and the purpose of the presentation. Craftsmanship in the final product is obvious. Effective use is made of supporting material (e.g., visuals, models, overheads, and videos) and of team members (where appropriate). The audience shows enthusiasm and confidence that the presenter understands what she is talking about and understands the listeners' interests.

Appreciating the Debate

In closing, we note that this discussion of assessing insight does not settle a long-standing controversy among philosophers and psychologists: Whether the act of understanding primarily involves a mental representation independent of action or a performance capacity. To frame it as a question, the debate involves asking, Is performance ability necessarily *preceded* by a mental model or picture? Or is understanding more like successful jazz improvisation— something that is inherently a performance ability and sensitivity in which prior mental perceptions play no determining role?

Although we are not officially taking sides here, the problem clearly bears on the argument. Indeed, readers might want to head back to Gilbert Ryle's *The Concept of Mind* (1949) and Perkins's chapter in *Teaching for Understanding* (Wiske, 1997). These sources enhance appreciation of this debate and the light each author sheds on the view that understanding is a performance achievement as opposed to primarily a mental representation to be acted upon.

Even though we tend to side with the performance view, we are really proposing a practical solution to an assessment need. Two independent variables need to be assessed—the quality of the idea and the quality of the performance—and our rubrics must reflect these variables for the sake of validity and better feedback to students.

Having clarified in general terms what kinds of evidence we need, let us now take a closer look at the implications of the six facets of understanding for assessment.

Endnotes

1. Readers interested in a more thorough account of assessment and this part of the logic of design are referred to Wiggins (1998).
2. Compare this rubric to those for the Harvard Teaching for Understanding project. See Wiske (1997).
3. See Wiggins (1998), Chapters 5 and 6, for further information on ensuring diversity and adequacy of evidence in assessment.
4. White & Gunstone (1992) provide numerous such strategies, with helpful guidance on how to implement such probes. See also Hunter (1982, pp. 59–62) and Saphier & Gower (1997).
5. See Wiggins (1998), Chapter 10, for more information on performance assessment and grading.
6. For a comprehensive set of recent studies of intuition, see Sternberg & Davidson (1995).
7. See Wiggins (1998), Chapters 3 and 6, on the so-called problem of subjectivity. All assessment is subjective because it involves a human subject who designs the test, scores it, or both. We know from the advanced placement program and from such sports as diving, figure skating, and dressage that high interrater reliability is possible if clear models and standards, good training, and good oversight in the judging are present.

6

HOW IS UNDERSTANDING ASSESSED IN LIGHT OF THE SIX FACETS?

GIVEN AN INITIAL BLUEPRINT, A DEVELOPMENTAL RUBRIC, and the peculiar problems in assessing our achievement target, what further guidelines can be provided to make sure teachers can effect sound assessments of understanding?

In this chapter, we probe into how the six facets of understanding inform and guide our assessment of understanding.[1] For each facet, we give suggestions or strategies for getting at the heart of the topic, the reasoning behind those suggestions, and assessment tasks to take class lessons beyond mere activity-based work.

Facet 1: Explanation

1. *Use dialogue or interaction to assess.* Mere answers or student products, even in response to demanding questions and performance tasks, will not tell us the "theory" the student has in her head—the reasons behind why she answered or performed a certain way. To ensure that students understand why an answer or approach is the right one, Facet 1 demands that we have students explain or justify their responses or justify their course of action.

Consider the requirements for a doctoral degree, the key exit task of formal education. The doctoral candidate not only must write a thorough dissertation (typically buttressed by many footnotes)

but also *defend* it in an oral exam. That is, the written thesis alone is not considered sufficient evidence of mastery. The candidate is confronted with challenges, counterarguments, and requests for commentary and critiques on other points of view.

The importance of dialogue in assessment is recognized in many countries outside the United States, where oral exams play a significant part in secondary-level programs. Piaget taught us the vital importance of the clinical interview in ascertaining what the child really knows. In fact, the hallmark of the clinical interview (as opposed to the standardized test) is that we may legitimately deviate from a standardized script, as needed, to find out what lies behind a student response that seems unclear or undeveloped (Wiggins, 1993). Similarly, a spontaneous question-and-answer session after a speaker's polished presentation often reveals more about that person's understanding than the talk itself. Gardner (1991) argues:

> Whereas short-answer tests and oral responses in classes can provide clues to student understanding, it is generally necessary to look more deeply. . . . For these purposes, new and unfamiliar problems, followed by open-ended clinical interviews or careful observations, provide the best way of establishing the degree of understanding . . . attained (p. 145).

While Gardner's approach does not seem feasible given the large class sizes and student loads many teachers face, it may be possible if we require students to self-assess all products and performances, and if we interview students as they work on complex projects.

2. Use reiterative core performance tasks to assess whether understanding is becoming more sophisticated.

If we desire a clear sense of the student's developing explanations, we need to use *recurring* tasks and questions to assess sophistication of understanding—not just one-shot, secure test questions. The tasks should be designed specifically to assess for core ideas or questions that are at the heart of a subject.

We as educators should identify at the local and national levels *touchstone tasks:* the most important performances that can fruitfully be used over time to assess enduring understandings and core processes, or abilities such as effective writing, research, problem solving, and oral communication. Using these reiterative tasks provides educators, parents, and students with rich and credible evidence that key understandings and proficiencies are being developed over time.

One approach to meeting this need for evidence is to use the same writing prompt across many or all grades, as has been done in South Brunswick, New Jersey, and Edmonton, Alberta. Here is a prompt used in Edmonton across grades 1–8:

> Imagine that your uncle is a Hollywood film producer and has asked for your ideas for a possible new movie. Because many movies are based on books, he has asked you to tell him about a book you've read that you think would make a good movie. Write a letter to your uncle and describe a book that you enjoyed and explain why you think it would make a good movie.

The tasks and prompts we are suggesting would be effectively used to assess mature understanding of the core ideas of each subject. Then teachers at all grade levels could scaffold or modify the task as needed to allow novice and advanced students to answer the same question in a developmentally appropriate way, as the Edmonton, Alberta, public schools have also done in mathematics K–8 for the last few years.

3. *In light of the likelihood of misconception, use assessment tasks that will best evoke such misunderstandings.* Misunderstandings are likely, and overcoming them takes active and constructive work on the student's part. Therefore, we need to ask questions that are ambiguous enough to elicit the dominant misunderstanding. These questions or tasks resemble test distracters (i.e., answers that might sound right but are not) that traditional test designers use, but our goal is to see whether the student can recognize and *overcome* a misconception. This self-assessment and self-adjustment should be part of any assessment. (This goal was at the heart of all Piagetian interviews and tasks. It was no accident that the original misconception research in physics drew directly from Piaget's experiments.)

For instance, the *Benchmarks for Science Literacy* produced by the American Association for the Advancement of Science (1993) for its "Project 2061: Science for All Americans," offer examples of potential misconceptions. Here is Benchmark 4G:

> By the end of the 12th grade, students should know that . . . gravitational force is an attraction between masses. The strength of the force is proportional to the masses and weakens rapidly with increasing distance between them.
>
> The "inversely proportional to the square root" is not a high priority for literacy. Much more important is escaping the common adult misconceptions that the earth's gravity does not extend beyond its atmosphere.

We need to agree in each subject area on the most important, frequent, and persistent misconceptions in learning. Then we must build tasks and

test questions that deliberately assess for these misunderstandings. Finally, we must design teaching and learning experiences for explicitly confronting and overcoming them. (These challenges are discussed in the next two chapters.)

4. *Assess student theories along a novice-expert continuum, not merely through task-specific rubrics.* When we use reiterative tasks in hopes of gauging sophistication, we need conceptually developmental rubrics. What is a naive view of the American Revolution? What is a sophisticated view?

From novice learners, we expect answers that oversimplify or misconceive. We can predict, for example, that a naive thinker will view the Bill of Rights as either a set of clear, unambiguous rules or as an unrestricted license. A more sophisticated account will make clear the difference between the spirit and the letter of the law. A still more sophisticated view will be based on an awareness that in judging the spirit and the letter, conflict over meaning is inevitable; nevertheless, some opinions can be better supported by analysis and precedent than others.

5. *Design curriculums and build tests around* recurring *essential questions that give rise to important theories and stories.* To judge growth in the relative sophistication of a student's model, story, or explanation, we need to ask similar questions over and over: Does a particular book necessarily have a moral? Is history only the winners' story? What is a proof? How do scientific and mathematical proofs differ?[2] In other words, an assessment of understanding invariably involves an assessment of a student's concepts. This type of assessment is one reason that *concept webs* or *maps* have become such a relevant and interesting tool for assessing as well as instructing (White & Gunstone, 1992).

We need to know how the student sees the interrelation of ideas and the depth of his conceptual grasp. Moreover, the student can learn definitions and statements about complex theories as mere verbal formulas without really understanding them. *Indeed, a major goal of assessment for understanding is to find out whether a student's definitions or statements are simply a memorized rehashing of the teacher's words or text or a formulaic "plug-in."*

An assessment for understanding must demand thoughtful and qualified responses to sometimes *unanswerable* questions. This approach is the opposite of an assessment using unambiguous and non-problematic questions to test uncontroversial and discrete knowledge.

A positive example is a course titled "Art and Artifacts," in which students receive the following prompt: "Given our work during the last semester, revisit our essential question, 'Does art reflect a society's culture or help shape it?' and respond, citing examples from both historical and contemporary cultures."

6. *Assess student control of the big picture.* Can students see the connections between lessons, units, and courses? Do they understand the bearing of current work on past work? We must ask them. A simple device is the one-minute paper. At the end of each lecture, students are asked to answer two questions: What is the big point you learned in class today? And, What is the main unanswered question you leave class with today? Harvard professors have called this technique one of the most effective innovations in their teaching (Light, 1990).

In our teaching, we have required students to bring at least two written questions to class each day. We typically begin class by having the students discuss their questions in groups of three, bringing their most important question to the entire class for consideration. Then we look for patterns through a concept web of questions and proposed answers. With a few minutes to go at the end, we ask a few students to summarize the conversation and ask everyone to write some notes. All these materials can be assessed, for control over both process and content. Perkins (1992) proposes many other strategies, and we also suggest numerous checks for understanding in Chapter 10.

7. *Assess the student's questions.* We require an assessment system that knows how to judge understanding based on the thoughtful questions a *student* (as opposed to a testmaker) asks. We seek tasks that show whether students can derive and make increasingly better meaning with (and of) limited knowledge.

For example, from a completed unit of study, ask students to generate big-idea questions related to the important content.

8. *Assess breadth independently of depth of understanding.* As we emphasized earlier, extensive control over factual knowledge is insufficient evidence of understanding. Nor is deep insight into a few key ideas sufficient evidence of breadth. Looking at, say, the opium wars or the fundamental theorem of calculus, a student could have a deep insight—subtle, refined views—yet have some or even many of the details wrong. (We concede it is unlikely that someone could be said to have a sophisticated understanding of complex ideas if she were ignorant—as opposed to forgetful—of key facts, arguments, or points of view.) We should, therefore, deliberately and explicitly seek a balance of depth and breadth in our assessment strategies and instruments.

Although we should take points off for inaccuracies, some errors might be judged as minor compared to others in an assessment for understanding. Therefore, we use multiple rubrics for better control over content, process, work quality, and sophistication of understanding—all separate and often *independent* traits of performance. The next chapter discusses the meaning of depth and breadth, with examples of the kinds of performances corresponding to each.

Facet 2: Interpretation

1. *Assess the student's ability to weave together a coherent, illuminating, and substantiated story.* As Bruner (1996) notes, multiple interpretations are the norm:

> Understanding, unlike explaining, is not pre-emptive; for example, one way of construing the fall of Rome narratively does not preclude other ways. Nor does the interpretation of any particular narrative rule out other interpretations. For narratives and their interpretations traffic in meaning, and meanings are intransigently multiple. . . . Since no one narrative construal rules out alternatives, narratives pose a very special issue of criteria (p. 90).

The challenge, then, in assessing for Facet 2 is to avoid arbitrary dogmatism—the "one right answer" and thought-ending relativism of "All stories are equally meaningful." The teacher avoids this dogmatism by demanding interpretations that are principled (i.e., able to encompass as many salient facts and points of view as possible):

> In a word, narrative accounts can be principled or not but do not rest on stark verification

alone, as with scientific explanations. Any constitutional lawyer worth his salt can tell you how Justice Taney's way of construing history in the Dred Scott decision was excruciatingly tunnel-visioned, unmindful of competing perspective, and therefore lethal in its consequences (Bruner, 1996, p. 91).

We need clear and consistent scoring rubrics, work samples, and training to help all students understand that some meanings are better than others—in the sense that they provide greater meaning, make more sense of more facts, and make more sense of many different stories. But we also need more examples of assessment tasks that avoid the errors of activity-based work. We need tasks that can be done only if the student has the requisite understanding, as opposed to only having engaged in interesting activities. The following two tasks show how the work can be both engaging and valid:

News Hounds at the Tabard

You are part of a group of journalists in England during the Middle Ages. You are responsible for the full broadcast of the daily "Good Morning, Canterbury" show. While hanging out at the Tabard Tavern, you notice a very diverse and noisy group of pilgrims and decide to feature them on your next available show. In journeying with them, you learn their stories and work the themes into a news show that gives viewers a good understanding of the temperament of the times.

This show will include national news of England, the local news, job opportunities, fashion, entertainment, and editorial comment. After watching your show, a viewer should understand what it was like to live in England during that time.

Songs of Allegiance

While working for the Smithsonian Institution, you are asked to develop a museum exhibit and accompanying CD on songs about the United States from the Civil War to the present. How have we seen ourselves as a nation, as reflected in popular songs? Which attitudes have changed and which have not? You will present your draft exhibit and a tape of your songs to the directors of the National Museum of American History.

2. *Assess the student's understanding of the story behind an idea.* Is the student aware of the history of the idea or theory? Self-assessment and portfolios make a student document and think about the history of "biography" of a piece of writing. Similarly, if the focus is on an education for understanding, students should learn that each key text or idea they study in a discipline has a history—one that too often gets hidden behind the imposing veneer of proofs and formal exposition. This approach helps students learn that they do not have to be experts to develop an understanding. Knowledge is a hard-won *result,* the end point of disciplined thinking; it is not a static, ex cathedra pronouncement made by intuitive geniuses.

Facet 3: Application

1. *Use simulations or real applications that require students to use knowledge with an overarching purpose, audience, and setting (context) in mind.* If understanding reveals itself through use of knowledge in context, then we should require far more contextualized performance tasks. That is the core idea in "authentic assessment."[3] Authenticity requires a real

or simulated audience, purpose, setting, options for personalizing the work, realistic constraints, and "background noise." Here are two sample tasks that try to ground fairly straightforward content into such situational tasks:

Puppy Pen

Students display their understanding of area and perimeter by designing the shape of a fenced-in section of a yard, given a specified length of fencing material. Their goal is to maximize the play area for a new puppy.

Towering Trees

Students must determine a linear function relating height and another appropriate variable. Using the given equation, they must use the most appropriate and cost-effective size of plywood to construct some props for the Summer Theater Arts Guild productions. They must support their findings both orally and in a written report to their boss, using appropriate graphics and other visuals.

Even within the context of traditional exams, we can improve questions by creating situations that simulate authentic inquiries and uses of knowledge. The following exam question from a Harvard core curriculum course in science (asked as part of a traditional blue-book exam) illustrates this application:

Snail Harvest

Your government wants to harvest the rare and commercially important snail *Helix memoresus* for its memory-enhancing mucus. The government decides to adopt a fixed-quota harvesting policy.

As an expert naturalist, explain to the myopic politicians the potential problems of such a policy:

What advice would you give about how to set the harvest and why?

2. *Use tasks and rubrics that determine whether students have mastered the goals of skills, knowledge, and performance, not just isolated techniques or formats.* Regardless of whether students write effective, persuasive essays using the usual criteria of ideas, organization, and mechanics, we too rarely ask: Does the student understand what it means to persuade? Too few students understand *persuasiveness* and are taught merely to follow certain recipes for writing essays that are labeled "persuasive." We need to more explicitly assess student understanding of the key concepts that focus such performance—what it is, when it happens, when it does not happen, and why. Here is such a task:

Hazards Consultant

Sulfuric acid, lead nitrate, barium chloride dihydrate, and benzene represent common industrial waste materials—and environmental hazards. Propose a treatment for each in writing and demonstrate the success of that treatment in the lab. Your treatment must yield products at or below the lowest rating allowed by the government on each of the four criteria rated: reactivity, flammability, health, and the specific hazards of each material. Your final write-up should state the degree of the danger of the waste, effectiveness of the solution, and approximate cost per use of the treatment.

3. *Assess student self-adjustment in response to feedback.* Only when students can respond intelligently and effectively to unanticipated effects of their work or errors they have made can we conclude that they understand the nature, purpose, and

quality expected of their work. A regular inability to accurately self-assess personal performance indicates that a student—regardless of how well she does on conventional tests—lacks understanding of both the task and the standards that best evaluate that kind of task.

Feedback need not come from humans. Genuine performance in science and other fields often involves the process of trial and error (i.e., revealing one's understanding by adjusting performance in light of results). This task requires that ability to adjust:

Are Brine Shrimp Worth Their Salt?

Students are interested in sending brine shrimp to their friend for his aquarium. However, they have a problem: They do not know the best salinity level for the water in which they would send the shrimp. Thus, the teacher asks the students to design and carry out an experiment to determine the best salinity for brine shrimp survivability (Baron, 1993).[4]

4. *Ensure that we assess the understanding, not just the performance.* As we noted in concluding the last chapter, a constant danger in performance assessment is paying too much attention to performance competence and not enough to the ideas. A student can perform well without understanding exactly what she does. For example, try to explain how a bicycle works even if you can ride one well. Consider the following task in which understanding is revealed only through the building of an object:

Old Bessie

Because Farmer Jones is having problems with his new tractor, he has decided to try out "Old Bessie," his original tractor. Old Bessie has been in

storage with all her oil drained out. But the farmer cannot recall which of the four vats in the barn contains the right oil—the oil with the highest density. You have a sample from each of the vats.

First, determine which oil is right for Old Bessie. (Student is given four unknown liquids and a commercial hydrometer.) Then, using the equipment listed below, construct and calibrate a hydrometer:

Straws	Plasticine	Lead shot
Wax pencil	Ziplock bags	Ruler
Cylinder of water density = 1g/ml	Cylinder of glycerol density = 1.3g/ml	Masking tape

Often we need certain kinds of explanation performances so we can distinguish blind luck from thoughtful understanding in application. Asking the student only to exhibit understanding can provide insufficient evidence—we need to know why the student performed the way she did, what she thinks it means, and what justifies her moves or approach, not just that she did it. In performance-based assessment, in other words, the key performances are conscious and explicit reflection, self-assessment, and self-adjustment, with reasoning made evident.

Facet 4: Perspective

1. *Require the students to answer the question, What of it?* Many dictionaries offer as a core meaning of *understand* "to know the importance or significance of something." To grasp the importance (or unimportance) of an idea is key to understanding. Yet we rarely encourage students to step back and ask, Of what value is this knowledge? How important is this idea? What does this idea enable us to do that is important?

2. *Assess the degree of sufficiency and circumspection of answers, not simply their correctness.* The student can know the right answer and even defend it without understanding why it is the right answer. Consider, for example, the student who recalls a geometry proof while at the blackboard, but who is stumped when we ask him to consider an alternative proof. We would not attribute a high level of understanding in such a case. But in conventional testing, the student would be judged to have understood.

We seek evidence of critical distance. The focus in assessing for understanding, then, must turn to the *adequacy* (effectiveness, plausibility, thoroughness, and aptness) of evidence, argument, approach, or style—not merely whether an answer is right or wrong. And it must move between different points of view, commenting and critiquing on each one as part of a larger understanding.

In scoring students' answers, these questions emerge: In what ways do these different answers work in this context? To what extent are they reasonable? Substantiated? Unlike questions and tasks related to knowledge recall or plugging-in skills, these questions and tasks assess more for the critical thinking they reflect than for accuracy.

Here is a simple idea for a task that is adaptable to any subject area:

Flinty-Eyed Editor

You are an editor at a major publishing house, and the following short story has been submitted to you. [The students do not know it is a story written by one of the authors they have studied this year.]

The story reads very well—maybe a little too well. You suspect plagiarism. Check out your suspicion and write a tactful but firm letter back to the "author" on the likely source of this manuscript.

3. *Assess students' ability to adopt a critical perspective.* Perspective taking invariably leads to more justified and coherent theories, psychologically astute and engaging stories, and effective problem solving. As we discussed earlier, students should be able to look at ideas, approaches, and systems learned from new, unanticipated, or odd but revealing points of view.

We assess students' use of perspective by asking these questions: Is the student aware of different ways of knowing, seeing, or proving a specific idea? Students with understanding know that invariably there are alternate proofs, powerful analogies, and other ways of making meaning of a phenomenon. They are more inclined to ask (and answer): Are both views compatible? Isn't there another way to look at this? Can this plausible view really be justified? Here is a history task that points in such a direction:

The Trouble with Textbooks

You are an attorney in a trial brought by a parent group that does not want the high school to use a particular U.S. history textbook (excerpted below). The book will be used as a required supplement to the current text—not as a substitute. You will present a five-minute oral case, in pairs, to a jury, taking either side of the question, "Is the book appropriate for school adoption and required reading?"

An angry parent group says the book in question is propaganda. However, the high school teacher who wants the book says it "provides an important perspective on our history and how history gets made."

What is your view? You will be assessed on how well you support your claim about the presentation of history in the text. Are the accounts biased, inaccurate, or merely different from our usual viewpoint?

[Excerpt from "odd" U.S. history textbook]
On the American Revolution

As a result of the ceaseless struggle of the colonial people for their political rights, the 13 colonies practiced bourgeois representative government by setting up their own local legislatures. As electoral rights were restricted in many ways in every colony, those elected to the colonial legislatures were mostly landlords, gentry, and agents of the bourgeoisie, without any representation whatsoever from the working people. There were struggles between the governors and the legislatures. These struggles reflected the contradictions between the colonies and their suzerain state. . . .

The British administration of the colonies was completely in the interests of the bourgeoisie in Britain. . . . The British colonial rule impeded development of the national economy in North America. It forced certain businesses into bankruptcy. As a consequence, contradictions became increasingly acute between the ruling clique in Britain and the rising bourgeoisie and broad masses of the people in the colonies. . . .

Heretofore [prior to the Boston Massacre], the struggle of the colonial people had been scattered and regional. In the course of the struggle, however, they summed up their experience and came to feel it necessary to stand together for united action. Thus in November 1772, a town meeting held in Boston adopted a proposal made by Samuel Adams to create a Committee of Correspondence to exchange information with other areas, act in

unison, and propagate revolutionary ideas. . . . In less than 2 months, a Committee of Correspondence was formed by more than 80 cities and towns in Massachusetts, and later became the organs of revolutionary power. . . .

The Declaration of Independence was a declaration of the bourgeois revolution. The political principles enunciated in it were aimed at protecting the system of capitalist exploitation, legitimizing the interests of the bourgeoisie. In practice, the "people" referred to in the Declaration only meant the bourgeoisie, and the "right of the pursuit of happiness" was deduced from the "right of property" and intended to stamp the mark of legitimacy on the system of bourgeois exploitation. The Declaration was signed by 56 persons, of whom 28 were bourgeois lawyers, 13 were big merchants, 8 were plantation slave owners, and 7 were members of the free professions, but there was not one representative of the working people.

During the time of the war, America began its westward expansion on a large scale. From the first, the colonies had been founded on the corpses of the Indians. . . . In 1779 George Washington sent John Sullivan with a force of soldiers to "annihilate" the Iroquois tribe settled in northern New York. In his instructions he wrote: "The present aim is to completely smash and flatten their settlement, take as many prisoners as possible, the more the better, whether they are men or women. . . . You must not only mop up their settlement but destroy it." Thus at the time of its founding, America had already nakedly exposed its aggressive character. . . .

During the war, patriotic women also played a big role. While men went to the front, they took over the tasks of production. They tilled fields and wove cloth, and sent food, garments, and other articles to the front. When Washington was in a precarious situation retreating into Pennsylvania with his army, the women of Philadelphia raised a huge fund to procure winter clothes for the revolutionary army. This event deeply moved the fighters. Under fire on the battlefields, women risked their lives to bring ammunition, transmit intelligence, and rescue the wounded. Some even served as artillery gunners. . . .

After the outbreak of the war, America not only failed to organize the enslaved Negroes but guarded them even more closely, thus intensifying their oppression. This seriously impeded their participation in the war and was one reason why the war for Independence was slow in achieving victory. . . .

The American people are a great people. They have a revolutionary tradition. At present [1970], they are in a period of new awakening. We believe that the American people will make still greater contributions to the cause of human progress in the future (U. S. Department of Health, Education, and Welfare, 1976).

Note: This excerpt is translated from a Chinese textbook.

Questions to consider in your research and presentation:

■ What can you infer about the text's author? From what clues do you infer this? What can be said to be the most likely political influences on the author's point of view? What evidence is there of that influence? How does it affect the author's choice of language? Does the language reflect bias or an acceptable (but different) point of view? Explain your reasoning.

■ Why does it make sense, given the authors' perspective, that they pay particular attention to the Committee of Correspondence? The contribution of women? The plight of Indians and Negroes? Are the facts accurate? Do they warrant that much attention in your view, or does such selective emphasis reveal bias?

You will be judged on the historical accuracy, apt and convincing documentation, and rhetorical effectiveness of *your* case. Be fair, but be an effective speaker and writer! A 6-point scoring scale will be used for each dimension to be assessed.

Mathematics tasks might focus on inquiries like these:

- Compare the distance formula in Euclidean space and Cartesian coordinates with the geometry of city streets ("taxicab geometry").

- Ask students whether the Pythagorean theorem ($A^2 + B^2 = C^2$) holds for *differently shaped* figures on the triangle legs—namely, figures other than squares. Does the theorem work on a spherical shape, such as the earth?

A simple science or social science task might involve asking students to sketch a map of the world with Australia at the center, survey people about its accuracy or usefulness, and research the problems of orientation and projection in map making.

4. *Assess the student's grasp of the author's intent.* Is the student aware of an author's, scientist's, or historian's particular perspective and intent? We may not be able to adequately judge a student's understanding of a text unless we know the author's intent because the judgment involves knowing whether that particular intent was realized. This limitation is perhaps more obvious in fiction and history; true in science; and true in mathematics. We would guess that algebra students are never asked, What was Descartes's purpose in inventing the Cartesian coordinate system? What problems did it solve? Yet these questions can engender vital inquiry and deeper understanding into mathematics.[5]

The following English task takes author intent to another level. As part of an exam a few years back that involved short-answer questions about *A Midsummer Night's Dream,* students throughout Pittsburgh were asked:

Having watched three different video versions of the Pyramis and Thisby scene, choose the interpretation in which you feel the director has made the most effective staging choices. In a multiparagraph essay, explain, using details, why the interpretation you chose is effective.

Having a thorough technical mastery of a subject is not necessarily the same as having perspective on the subject. Students may be able to solve every algebra problem they encounter and document their work but still not understand the meaning of what they do. For example, a student may prove that a set of data points yields the apparent shape of a parabola. But it doesn't follow that the student can "stand outside" her work to grasp the importance of parabolic data.

In history, we might ask students to explain the difference, if any, between a sound generalization and a stereotype about a group of people. The students could use their textbook and some much older textbooks as sources for the generalizations and stereotypes.[6]

Facet 5: Empathy

1. *Assess the student's ability to walk in someone else's shoes.* Teachers have often employed this approach as a learning activity. The challenge is to design assessment and scoring mechanisms for judging the ability to empathize. Here is a brief sample from the rubric for the recent British national exam question on *Romeo and Juliet* (also mentioned in Chapter 4):

Romeo and Juliet, act 4

Imagine that you are Juliet. Write your thoughts and feelings explaining why you have to

take this desperate action [of killing yourself].

Top score: Pupils give a confident and sustained response that shows insight into Juliet's character and the different pressures she is facing. They sustain the role very convincingly, and there is awareness of the linguistic features of the scenes and how they build toward Juliet's soliloquy. A sense of tragic irony illuminates their answers (School Curriculum and Assessment Authority, 1997).

Here are two sample tasks that involve empathy issues as well as perspective, application, and explanation:

Get a Mythic Job

Select an epic hero from the literature we have read. Write him a letter in which you apply for a job as a member of his expedition team. Be specific about the position you want, your qualifications for the job, and why you would be an asset to the team.

Make your letter persuasive, emphasizing that you understand the particular struggles and adventures the team has already been through and how you might be of value to it in handling future situations and difficulties. Write in business letter form and include a résumé.

Federation or Confederation

This task, reflecting the Civil War period, has three parts. First, the teacher asks each student to assume the role of a resident of North Carolina on the eve of secession and deliver a speech from that person's perspective on whether or not North Carolina should secede from the Union. Second, each student then synthesizes the points from all the speeches given by other students and writes a letter to the editor of the local newspaper reflecting whether or not this North Carolinian changed his or her point of view regarding secession. Third, each student examines the situation from her historical figure's perspective 15 years after secession and then writes a reflective piece in that figure's journal, reexamining the wisdom of her earlier positions.

2. *Assess the student's ability to empathize with a villain, oddball, or outcast.* Intellectual imagination is essential to understanding through not only art and literature but also people who think differently from each other. We need to assess students' ability to see the world from different viewpoints. The point is not to make students accept those ways but to help them better understand the diversity of thought and feeling in the world. In this way, students can avoid stereotyping and broad-brush characterizations and learn how yesterday's weird idea can become commonplace today.

In the sciences, we teach empathy to make students realize the plausibility of once-accepted but now overthrown ideas. In physics or astronomy, do students know the decisive experiments and data that overthrew the heliocentric perspective—despite its obvious plausibility? We might use a question from Ptolemy about why the earth doesn't move and ask students to write a response from Copernicus's perspective.

3. *Require the student to teach.* Teaching someone else something you understand is not only a vital application but also a key to further developing intellectual empathy. We come to understand how hard it is to make something that is obvious to us equally obvious to a novice in a given area. This insight into the irony of perspective and empathy was beautifully illustrated in Plato's dialogues.[7]

Those who really understand can easily and patiently enter the worldview of the novice. We might ask students to teach novices what the students themselves now claim to understand, as Einstein tested his ideas by imagining how the ideas would have to be presented to audiences with a different perspective and knowledge (Gardner, 1991).

Facet 6: Self-Knowledge

1. *Require students to self-assess their past as well as their present work.* It is only through student self-assessment that we gain the most complete insight into how sophisticated and accurate a student's view is of the tasks, criteria, and standards he is to master.

A simple strategy is to make the first and last written assignments for any course *the same question*, and require students to write a self-assessment postscript describing their sense of progress in understanding. (This strategy has ties to Strategy 5 in Facet 1, relating to recurring tasks and questions.)

A related approach is frequently used by teachers who have their students collect their work samples in portfolios. Periodically, students are asked to review their portfolios and respond to reflective questions such as, How does your work show how you have improved? What task or assignment was the most challenging and why? Which selection are you most proud of and why?

Here is another example: Near the end of the school year, elementary and middle school teachers ask their students to write a letter describing themselves as learners to their next teacher. In the letters, the students talk about their academic strengths and set learning goals based on self-assessment of their performance during the year that is ending.

2. *Assess for self-knowledge.* Experts who are also wise individuals are quick to state that there is much they do not understand about a subject. (They have Socratic wisdom.) Enrico Fermi, the great physicist, argued for always assessing doctoral candidates in physics on the accuracy of their self-assessments concerning how much they knew about physics. He thought it was a flaw to be wrong *either* way (i.e., to be either more cocky or more unsure than was warranted).

We turn next to the third phase of backward design and the question, What is implied for instructional design and teaching, given the desired twin outcomes of understanding and greater clarity about how to assess for it?

Endnotes

1. Many of these implications were originally presented in Wiggins (1998), pp. 91–99.
2. See Wiggins (1987a) and Wiggins (1989) for more on teaching with essential questions.
3. See Wiggins (1998), Chapters 2 and 3.
4. The nature of feedback and the important role of situational feedback and adjustment to it in assessing performance are described at length in Wiggins (1998), Chapters 2 and 3.
5. Focusing on the purposes of knowledge generation and use is one of four key dimensions of the Harvard *Teaching for Understanding* project (Wiske, 1997, p. 63).
6. Examples of performance tasks that get at the same problems can be found throughout Wiggins (1993); Marzano, Pickering, and McTighe (1993); and Wiggins (1998).
7. See Perry (1970) for an elegant theory of the intellectual development levels that can be found in college students' responses to questions about their studies. This approach is also reflected, although somewhat differently, in the work of moral psychologists such as Kohlberg and Gilligan.

7

WHAT IS UNCOVERAGE?

WE HAVE CLARIFIED WHAT WE MEAN BY THE *DESIRED result* of learning—understanding—through our discussion of the six facets of understanding. We have offered a generalized rubric for *assessing* understanding as well as methods for assessing each facet. The logic of design now requires that we consider the beginning of Stage 3, the *curricular activities and teachings*—the design work at the heart of everyday teaching.

What does a curriculum for understanding look like? How do we make student understanding more likely (as opposed to resorting to the hit-or-miss "teach, test, hope for the best" approach seen in coverage-driven teaching)?

The third stage of design encompasses both curriculum and instruction, as Figure 7.1 shows.

The key point to be developed in this chapter is that any curriculum aiming for student understanding requires uncoverage of the material—inquiring into, around, and underneath content instead of simply covering it. We lay out some essential design considerations for curriculum, pursuing the twin goals of depth and breadth. The next two chapters spell out more specific strategies for unit design and curricular logic. Then in Chapter 10, we consider some specific teaching implications when the goal is understanding.

Now that we have clarified the understandings we seek, put them in essential and unit question form, and devised appropriate assessment strategies,

FIGURE 7.1 **A FOCUS ON STAGE 3 OF BACKWARD DESIGN**

Key Design Question	Design Considerations	Filters (Design Criteria)	What the Final Design Accomplishes
Stage 1. What is worthy and requiring of understanding?	National standards. State standards. District standards. Regional topic opportunities. Teacher expertise and interest.	Enduring ideas. Opportunities for authentic, discipline-based work. Uncoverage. Engaging.	Unit framed around enduring understandings and essential questions.
Stage 2. What is evidence of understanding?	Six facets of under-standing. Continuum of assessment types.	Valid. Reliable. Sufficient. Authentic work. Feasible. Student friendly.	Unit anchored in credible and educa-tionally vital evidence of the desired understandings.
Stage 3. What learning experiences and teaching promote understanding, interest, and excellence?	**Research-based repertoire of learning and teaching strategies. Essential and enabling knowl-edge and skill.**	**WHERE Where is it going? Hook the students. Explore and equip. Rethink and revise. Exhibit and evaluate.**	**Coherent learning experiences and teaching that will evoke and develop the desired under-standings, promote interest, and make excellent perfor-mance more likely.**

let us consider what kinds of lessons are needed to make big ideas understood. Our overall goal as designers can be summed up in the phrase "uncov-erage as opposed to coverage." Beyond learning *about* a subject, students will need lessons that enable them to experience directly the inquiries, arguments, applications, and points of view under-neath the facts and opinions they learn if they are to understand them. Students have to *do* the subject, not just learn its results.

The lesson-design challenge is to bring abstract ideas and far-away facts to life. The student must come to see knowledge and skill as helpful and revealing building blocks for larger inquiries and important performances, not as isolated lessons. As the facets of understanding suggest, uncoverage asks teachers and students to pay more attention to explaining, interpreting, and applying knowledge to better grasp what makes knowledge knowledge (as opposed to sanctioned belief only), and what

questions remain unanswered by current knowledge.

Uncoverage is vital because all big ideas are subtle and unobvious. Without lessons designed to bring them to life, concepts such as manifest destiny or the water cycle remain empty phrases to be memorized, not understood. The facets of understanding show us that students need to explain, interpret, apply, and so on what they learn if teachers are to have evidence that students understand. So, too, in learning, unless students are provided with lessons that give rise to a *need* to theorize, interpret, use, or see in perspective what they are asked to learn (instead of having someone reduce it to a predigested lesson for them), they will not likely understand it or grasp that their job is more than recall.

We thus uncover for students what is interesting and vital by revealing it for what it is: a shorthand phrase for the *results* of inquiries, problems, and arguments, not a self-evident fact. A course design based on textbook coverage only will likely leave students with inert phrases and an erroneous view of how arguable and hard-won knowledge has been. Rather, students need to experience what scholars know if they are to understand their work: how key facts and principles are the revealing and powerful fruit of pondering, testing, shaping, and rethinking of experience. Here, we describe what curricular design must do to develop such understandings.

Depth and Breadth

No experience is educative that does not tend both to knowledge of more facts and entertaining of more ideas and to a better, a more orderly arrangement of them. . . . Experiences, in order to be educative, must lead out into an expanding world of subject matter. . . . This condition is satis-

fied only as the educator views teaching and learning as a continuous process of reconstruction of experience.

—Dewey, 1938, pp. 82, 87

To better design for uncoverage, we first must clarify two familiar but largely unexamined terms: depth and breadth.

We talk, for example, of "going into greater depth" about a subject, but what does that really mean? In what sense must we go below the surface and dig deeper to get beyond merely covering a topic? As for breadth, what does it really mean to extend our knowledge? Is breadth, then, the same as coverage—or different? Just what *is* coverage? When we as educators say, "I would love to do more in-depth projects, but there just isn't time; I have to cover the content," what do we really mean? Any hope we have of designing instruction for better understanding rests on our ability to make practical design sense of these words.

Depth

To "go into depth" on a topic suggests getting below its surface. In what sense is getting below the surface a key to understanding? A simple analogy reveals what we mean: We may sit in a car and we may know how to drive it, but that doesn't mean we understand how it works. For that we need to look under the hood, literally and figuratively. To be a mechanic, one must know how to drive—but also know how a car works, why it works, and how to diagnose and fix it.

By analogy, solving math problems using the algorithm for simultaneous equations may enable a student to pass a test, but it may hide a lack of deeper understanding. To get beyond superficial and somewhat rigid understanding, the student must know what kind of problem it is, why the formula works in this case, how to derive the formula, and how this problem is like or unlike other kinds of problems. Without this ability, the student cannot hope to solve novel problems or problems that are cast in different language or murky real-world guise. Without fluid and flexible knowledge of how and why things work, one cannot accomplish real-world goals.

"In-depth" is opposed to "superficial," and a superficial account is shallow or insignificant. The student's viewpoint, then, may be accurate but simplistic or naive, focused only on the surface, with its more obvious details. Reporters and prosecutors dig deeper into the stories of crime suspects because often what they first discover through friends, neighbors, or relatives of the victim turns out to be wrong or misleading. We have all seen reports in the paper about "what a nice, friendly neighbor" Mr. X was—even though we later learn that indeed Mr. X *did* murder his wife and had a past history of abuse.

Similarly, in mathematics, science, and history, many of the linchpin ideas that define a modern field of study are neither obvious nor easily comprehended. Misunderstanding comes easily because important ideas are difficult to grasp and easy to get wrong. Both intellectual pioneers and naive students need to know how to get beyond appearances, which can be deceiving. Unfortunately, for all their merit when it comes to organizing and summarizing knowledge, textbooks often leave students with glib summaries and premature closure on important ideas.

Breadth

But depth alone on a topic is insufficient; we need breadth, too. Breadth implies the extensions, variety, and connections needed to relate disparate facts and ideas. Indeed, breadth brings power and relates to Facet 4: perspective. The dictionary defines *breadth of knowledge* as "freedom from narrowness, as of viewpoint."

To continue our analogy, the successful mechanic needs broad experience with many different kinds of cars, customers, and diagnostic tools. Excessive and exclusive depth is no better than excessive coverage; that is, it isn't effective to focus on a single idea, digging deeper in the same hole. Any good course of study should provide interesting and helpful detail as well as bridges to related topics.

We might think of the challenge of design for greater breadth in terms of the connect-the-dots puzzles of our youth. Conventional coverage teaching often leaves students with a number of mentally unconnected dots—no clear picture of how facts, ideas, and skills come together or create meaning. Breadth of experience provides those links. Figure 7.2 (see p. 102) summarizes these ideas in a list of verbs.

The Challenge

The challenge in blending depth and breadth in design of curriculum and instruction is to ensure that the ratio is properly balanced for the topic and time allotted. This effort naturally involves choices, compromises, and sacrifices that play off the overarching priorities, standards, and student abilities and interests.

The Need to Uncover

The need to uncover for greater depth and breadth stems in part from a blind spot many teachers exhibit when they, as experts, teach a subject to novices. What appears connected and meaningful

FIGURE 7.2. **DESCRIBING DEPTH AND BREADTH**

For Depth	For Breadth
Unearth it ■ Make assumptions explicit. ■ Make points of view clear. ■ Bring to the surface and bring to light the misunderstood, the subtle, the nonobvious, the problematic, the controversial, the obscure, the missing, and the lost. *Analyze it* ■ Inspect and examine. ■ Dissect, refine, and qualify. *Question it* ■ Test. ■ Challenge. ■ Doubt. ■ Critique. *Prove it* ■ Argue. ■ Support. ■ Verify. ■ Justify. *Generalize it* ■ Subsume it under a more encompassing idea. ■ Compare and contrast.	*Connect it* ■ Link discrete and diverse ideas, facts, and experiences. *Picture it* ■ Make it concrete and simple. ■ Represent or model the idea in different ways. *Extend it* ■ Go beyond the given to implications. ■ Imagine "what if?"

to the teacher can appear disconnected and meaningless to the student. The challenge is to uncover not more facts and ideas but nonobvious *meanings*.

Our connect-the-dots analogy applies to a common teacher error: to assume that because we or the authors of a work have connected the dots, the student now sees the picture. The student, however, often sees either many more unconnected dots or not enough lines to produce the picture the teacher is describing. We typically fail to see how *the* picture is a function of unconscious selection and emphasis from among the dots. Students may *accept* the teacher's or textbook author's view without actually understanding it. But through their own inquiries and performance, they can see for themselves—that is, develop or verify a connective meaning.

Making Ideas Real

Meanings often emerge when facts and abstract concepts cohere into a performance strategy—when they become useful, in other words. Dewey (1933) illustrates the problem when he contrasts what he calls the objective *fact* of the sphericity of the earth and the student's meaningful *idea* of it:

> Ideas, then, are not genuine ideas unless they are tools with which to search for material to solve a problem. . . . He may be shown (or reminded of) a ball or globe and be told that the earth is round like those things; he may then be made to repeat that statement day after day till the shape of the earth and the shape of the ball are welded together in his mind. But he has not thereby acquired an idea of the earth's sphericity. . . . To grasp "sphericity" as an idea, the pupil must first have realized certain confusing features in observed facts and have had the idea of spherical shape suggested to him as a possible way of accounting for such phenomena as tops of masts being seen at sea after the hulls have disappeared, the shape of shadows of the earth in an eclipse, etc. *Only by use as a method of interpreting data so as to give them fuller meaning does sphericity become a genuine idea* (pp. 133–134) (emphasis in original).

The best instructional designs uncover meanings by releasing the power and importance of ideas from within what first appears static and abstract. The work of bringing knowledge to life is made more difficult by textbook-driven instruction. A constant challenge is to uncover interesting and important meanings in relatively flat, seemingly straightforward, and invariably condensed presentations of ideas:

> No thought, no idea, can possibly be conveyed as an idea from one person to another. When it is

told, it is, to the one to whom it is told, another given fact, not an idea. The communication may stimulate the person to realize the question for himself and to think out a like idea, or it may smother his intellectual interest and suppress his dawning effort at thought. But what he directly gets cannot be an idea. Only by wrestling with the conditions of the problem at first hand, seeking and finding his own way out, does he think (Dewey, 1916, pp. 159–160).

Uncovering Ideas and Issues Underneath "Coverage"

To better uncover what lies beneath the text, we need to find the pregnant statements in it concerning key issues, and develop inquiries that help the student bring the idea to life as a solution to a problem.

Here is a simple example of the problem and the possibilities. The following sentence is provided in passing—unexplained and unpursued—as part of a U.S. history account of the Revolutionary War:

> Washington had the daring to put [his Patriots] to good use, too, as he broke the rules of war by ordering a surprise attack on the enemy in its winter quarters (Cayton, Perry, & Winkler, 1998, pp. 111–112).

Any thoughtful student should think: "Huh—*rules* of war? How can there be rules for an all-out battle to the death? And if surprise attacks were wrong, how did they normally fight—and why that way?" Using our analysis of depth and breadth, here is how we might begin to uncover the phrase "broke the rules of war":

For depth
  ■ Unearth it. What *were* the rules of war in the 1700s?

■ Analyze it. In what ways did General Washington's surprise attack violate the rules of war? Are there really rules? If so, how did they come to be?

■ Question it. Who most benefited from the rules of war?

■ Prove it. Can it be argued that the colonists regularly "fought dirty," routinely breaking the rules in their war with Great Britain?

■ Generalize it. What are the rules of war today, and how do they compare to those of the 17th century?

For breadth

■ Connect it. Does the end justify the means? Is breaking rules ever moral?

■ Picture it. Are rules of contact sports similar to rules of war? Why or why not?

■ Extend it. Are there economic rules of war today?

Linking Inquiries to Questions

Of course, not every sentence in a textbook will undergo that type of scrutiny. But once we have clarified the enduring understandings we desire for students to leave with, we are surer to uncover questions, issues, and implications because of our focus on depth and breadth. To make the task more manageable, we link particular inquiries to essential and unit questions; for example, does the end justify the means?

The following two perspectives on science and mathematics education make clear that the need for uncoverage—and the typical shortcomings of textbooks—does not affect only the humanities:

I suggest that the introductory courses in science at all levels be radically revised. Leave the fundamental, the so-called basics, aside for awhile, and concentrate the attention of students on the things that are not known. . . . Let it be known, early on, that there are deep mysteries and profound paradoxes. . . . Let it be known that these can be approached more closely and puzzled over once the language of mathematics has been sufficiently mastered. Teach at the outset, before any of the fundamentals, the still imponderable puzzles of cosmology (Thomas, 1983, pp. 151–152).

The traditional approaches treat mathematics as a cumulative logical development. . . . The new approach would present what is interesting, enlightening, and culturally significant. . . . Every topic must be motivated. Mathematics proper does not appeal to most students and [their] question, "Why do I have to learn this material?" is thoroughly justified (Kline, 1973, pp. 178–179).

Similar analysis is due state and district curricular documents, which contain global but intellectually flat statements. Here are examples:

Identify how an author's use of words creates tone and mood, and analyze how the choice of words advances the theme or purpose of the work (Massachusetts Department of Education, 1997a, p. 47).

Students will develop an understanding of the personal and cultural forces that shape artistic communication and how the arts in turn shape diverse cultures of past and present society (New York State Department of Education, 1996, p. 29).

Students understand past ideas as they were thought, and past events as they were lived, by people at different times and places (Massachusetts Department of Education, 1997b, p. 82).

The design challenge is to uncover the usefulness and significance of ideas by meaning making work—activities through which seemingly inert statements become the fruitful summation of inquiry.

Depth, Breadth, and the Six Facets

The six facets of understanding, recapped below, provide helpful direction as we develop a blueprint for uncoverage—depth and breadth—to ensure meaningful understanding of what is studied.

Facet 1: Explanation

Students have opportunities to build, test, and verify theories or explanations. The textbook and teacher theories become uncovered as we tease out and test the assumptions, questions, arguments, and evidence that lie beneath them. Problem-based learning is a vehicle for this process.

Facet 2: Interpretation

Students have opportunities to build their own interpretations, translations, and narratives from primary source texts, events, and experiences. The work will need to make clear that interpretation is always problematic, and that multiple interpretations can and do exist. Oral histories, literary analyses, the case method, and Socratic seminars are useful.

Facet 3: Application

Students have opportunities to apply what they have learned in the classroom to real or realistic situations. Such activities provide students with experience in planning and troubleshooting. Diverse contexts for these tasks or activities help students realize that theory is not simply plugged in—the particular demands of the situation must be taken into account. Examples include real or simulated tasks, such as those found in Odyssey of the Mind, Junior Achievement, engineering courses, 4-H, and work to achieve scouting merit badges.

Facet 4: Perspective

Students have opportunities to take multiple points of view on the same issue. They must develop and use critical thinking skills to determine, on their own, the strengths and weaknesses of the theories, explanations, proofs, and arguments they confront. Thus, the student should regularly confront plausible but incorrect historical narratives, false mathematical proofs, and plausible but outdated scientific theories. Examples include studying the same event through different texts; challenging assumptions, laws, or postulates; and role-play.

Facet 5: Empathy

Students are confronted with types of direct experience designed to develop greater openness and empathy for experiences and worldviews other than their own. To broaden student horizons, teachers place students in real or simulated situations, ask them to walk in other people's shoes (or at least take on their views in role-play), and challenge their assumptions. Examples include giving students direct experiences with the ideas in question, and having them re-create different characters as a way of simulating past events and attitudes.

Facet 6: Self-Knowledge

The development of self-understanding requires students both to engage in ongoing self-assessment about what they know and how they

know it and to make their thinking explicit as they examine the underlying assumptions for their ideas. Making self-assessment and self-adjustment a key part of assessment—not just of instruction—is vital.

How Coverage and Breadth Differ

> From the standpoint of the educator . . . the various studies represent working resources, available capital. Their remoteness from the experience of the young . . . is real. The subject matter of the learner . . . cannot be identical with the formulated, crystallized, and systematized subject matter of the adult. . . . Failure to bear in mind the difference . . . is responsible for most of the mistakes made in the use of texts and other expressions of pre-existing knowledge
> —Dewey, 1916, pp. 182–183

If depth and breadth make up uncoverage for understanding, how does coverage differ from breadth? How is coverage a source of misunderstanding rather than a helpful breadth?

"To travel over" is one common definition of *coverage*. We talk about covering a lot of ground, whether we are referring to travel or teaching, but here is the problem: We may have gone far, geographically or figuratively—through lots of textbook pages—but that doesn't mean we have derived great meaning or insight from our travels. The movie title *If It's Tuesday, This Must Be Belgium* supplies the analogy: too much travel, too little meaningful experience.

But *cover* has a more revealing and ominous definition: "to protect or conceal, to hide from view." In contrast, to *uncover* may be to find value in what is hidden. When we uncover something, we unearth it, examine it, ponder it, and thus reveal

something unseen. The term suggests investigative reporting, as we have already noted: A reporter uncovers facts or situations that otherwise might remain hidden or ignored.

Textbook Coverage

Invariably, textbook coverage runs the risk of covering up important ideas and understanding. When we dig deeper into "packaged" knowledge (e.g., in a textbook), we start thinking about how we know it or how it came to be known. Only then do we appreciate that knowledge itself is messier, more complicated, and more contentious than we expected.

In his famous book on scientific revolution (in which the whole idea of "paradigm shifts" was first developed to explain the nonlinear history of science), Thomas Kuhn (1970) alerts us to the misleading character of the textbook teaching of science:

> The textbook-driven tradition in which scientists come to sense their participation is one that, in fact, never existed. . . . Science textbooks refer only to that part of the work of past scientists that can easily be viewed as contributions to the statement and solution of the text's paradigm problems. Partly by selection and partly by distortion, the scientists of earlier ages are implicitly represented as having worked upon the same set of fixed canons that the most recent revolution has made seem scientific. And no wonder that, as they are rewritten, science once again comes to seem largely cumulative. . . . The result is a persistent tendency to make the history of science look linear and cumulative (p. 138).

Bruner (1996) reminds us that much objective knowledge begins as subjectively perceived hunches, analogies, and puzzle solutions:

The process of science making is narrative. It consists of spinning hypotheses about nature, testing them, correcting hypotheses, and getting one's head straight. En route to producing testable hypotheses, we play with ideas, try to create anomalies, try to find neat puzzle forms that we can apply. . . . Our instruction in science from start to finish should be mindful of the lively processes of science making, rather than being an account only of "finished science" as represented in a textbook (p. 127).

The same thinking about objective knowledge applies to the textbook-driven approach to history, as outlined in the national standards for history:

Interpretation of Narrative. One of the most common questions students ask as they embark on history papers is "Am I on the right track?" or "Is this what you want?" They feel compelled to find the one right answer, and the teacher's urging that they think about the difference between an answer and an argument is met with confusion. Their problem is deeply rooted in the conventional ways in which textbooks have presented history as a succession of facts marching straight to a single, settled outcome or resolution, whose significance one can neatly evaluate. But once students have learned the fundamental importance of keeping their facts straight, they need to realize that historians may disagree widely on how those facts are to be interpreted (National Center for History in the Schools, 1996, p. 26).

Digging Deeper

We need to help students see that blanket statements in textbooks hide controversies and difficulties. We need to uncover the history of knowledge itself to see how inert statements in textbooks are the tidied-up residue of adult attempts to understand, just as rubrics are the residue of samples of work, discussion, and analytic mucking around to find the

right language, boiled down to a neat paragraph.

When the student does get underneath or inside knowledge production, he learns something shocking. Much of what we call knowledge is the result of trial and error, inquiry, and arguments among experts. But when students are taught only from textbooks and receive only the agreed-upon residue of inquiry, they mistakenly believe that technical subject-matter knowledge is simply "there"—obvious and unproblematic, if they just look real hard or concentrate.

Without more revealing classwork, what is most likely to remain covered up is the student's naive beliefs about knowledge: that it is not hard won, that it was somehow "discovered" by apprehension and needs only to be learned (as opposed to pondered, imagined, analogized, tested, argued, and hammered out).[1]

Uncovering occurs when instructional design focuses on finding problems or questions in what may have first seemed obvious and unproblematic. Ideally, the nature of the work itself (not teacher command or student inquisitiveness) should make students want to dig deeper into past lessons.

The great teachers know precisely what their students will gloss over and misunderstand in textbooks. Thus, they design subsequent lessons to deliberately and explicitly require their students to see and find problems, gaps, perplexing questions, and inconsistencies that were hidden in the initial account.

One of us recently watched a group of mainstreamed special education students work to make sense of Macbeth. The two teachers kept deftly going back and forth between the play—reading out loud in chunks to ensure literacy issues didn't get in the way of understanding issues—and students' experience with issues of honor—using a rich set of

unit and essential questions. For example, What is the difference between things that happen to us and things that we make happen? What is honor? Is there a cost or price for honor? Is it worth it? What is loyalty? Is there tension between loyalty and honor in *Macbeth*? In our own lives? Students were asked to find answers from the play and their own lives for each question. "Why is defending your honor so hard?" one of the teachers asked, causing a student to sit bolt upright, show a kind of focus in his eyes that had been absent until then, and answer poignantly about the sacrifice of friends that had happened to him. What happened in *Macbeth* suddenly seemed more appropriately important, complex, and human to him.

In Mark Williams's U.S. history class, students constantly role-play each major period to ensure that glib characterizations and stereotypes of an era are avoided, such as in the role-play of the Kerner Commission on racial strife in the '60s:

(1) After students have studied some information about the 1950s and early 1960s, they should understand that there was a strong consensus in the U.S. in the mid-1960s for social justice. At this point, students should read the background reading on the race riots in Connecticut in 1968. Ask the students what questions come to mind. They should be puzzled about how the nationwide consensus fell apart and violence broke out in the cities. They might be encouraged to wonder about relationships—to the Vietnam War, for example, or to more militant separatist African American groups. Eventually they should define the questions President Johnson defined for the Kerner Commission: What happened? Why did it happen? What can be done to prevent it from happening again?

(2) Divide the students into role-players (with role information sheets) and commission members. Send the commission members to the "archives" (your collection of documents on the history of racial relationships in the 20th century), and show the role-players the segments of the movie *Eyes on the Prize* that deal with Elijah Mohammed, Malcolm X, the Black Power Movement, Martin Luther King's northern strategy (and his assassination), Chicago, and Detroit. This movie will help them visualize the environment in which their characters lived, and also understand the tension that erupted at the time. They will then be better able to convey the emotional side of their role, which is important for the commission to experience. The commission members need to be coached to develop questions based on the documents they read to test out hypotheses they might have, given what they learned about patterns of discrimination, racism, or any changes for the better in the first part of the century. Give them a list of the people who will come to "testify" (with their occupations or positions), so that they can prepare appropriate questions.

(3) Appoint a chairman and have the commission begin its hearings. It may take a few days to get through all the "witnesses," but if the questioning is good and the witnesses are able to develop good answers on the spot, the exercise will be well worth the time.

(4) Allow the commission time to discuss their findings and to develop a report. Perhaps members could make an outline of the report for duplication, and then present the report orally. While they are doing their work, the role-players could do some journal writing to develop their own ideas, using what they have heard about what caused the riots as a basis.

[A final essay is required on what actually happened and how the role-play did or did not shed light on the history.]

Or, consider this vignette from high school (Boyer, 1983):

> Today the discussion is on *Death of a Salesman*; the focus is on Willie's decision to commit suicide.... When the conversation begins to lose direction, the teacher breaks in.... "I have heard at least 15 explanations for Willie's suicide.... See if you can remember Cynthia's question. It was a turning point in the discussion...." When the exchanges become heated and confused, the teacher intervenes with a tentative and thoughtful voice, "Let me ask you a very hard question. What happens when a dream you've lived turns out to be a lie? How do you feel about that? Or are you too young? ..."
>
> One girl speaks with passion: "People shouldn't circle their lives around one idea."
>
> Another disagrees: "It's not one idea, it's their whole reason for living...." The teacher does not direct them toward a tidy conclusion. They are struggling with unanswerable questions, profound dilemmas.... She wants them to recognize Willie's pain. Class is over. Students leave troubled, reflective, and inspired (p. 153).

Note that in all three instances, the key is to have questions that uncover nuance and connections to personal experience, where before only dry abstractions and inert facts to learn were apparent. Such constant uncovering does more than reveal complexity; it reveals to students that uncoverage, not coverage, is the students' and teacher's real job.

By contrast, textbook-driven teaching and coverage send a message to students that the need for professional inquiry and understanding is over—that the students' job is merely to apprehend what is known. Here is an example from a history textbook (Cayton, Perry, & Winkler, 1998):

> Jefferson, like most members of the Continental Congress, had no intention of surrendering power to people who were not like him. Though he condemned slavery in theory, he was a slaveholder himself, and he could not have imagined a society in which African Americans were treated as his equals....
>
> Jefferson had a passionate commitment to human rights—and yet he owned slaves. Jefferson well knew that slavery was wrong. Few white planters wrote more eloquently about it as a moral evil; and yet he could never bring himself to free more than a few slaves. As a planter, his livelihood depended upon their labor. He would not discard his prejudices and risk losing the personal comfort that slave labor brought him, even for the principles of democratic equality (p. 149).

Politically correct thinking aside, is this the best we can say—that Jefferson stood out from among present-day white farmers? More alarming for understanding is the finality of the text. Authorities have spoken; there is no argument; this is what Jefferson believed. But we need only invoke Facets 1 (explanation), 2 (interpretation), and 5 (empathy) to say, Where is the evidence for this theory? What primary sources justify this view? How do they really know what Jefferson felt and thought? The irony in such questions is that they are what history is about, and yet the typical history course rarely allows the student to act like a historian. The loss is student engagement and understanding.

Compare the misleading and premature closure in the above passage with the invitation issued in Hakim's book (1993), *A History of Us: From Colonies to Country*, on the same topic:

> Just what does "equal" mean? Are we all the same? Look around you. Of course we aren't. Some

of us are smarter than others, and others are better athletes. . . . But none of that matters, said Jefferson. We are all equal in the eyes of God, and we are all entitled to equal rights. . . . He said, "All men are created equal." He didn't mention women. Did he mean to include women? No one knows. Perhaps not. We do know that in the 18th century the words "men" and "mankind" included men and women. . . . Did Thomas Jefferson mean to include black men when he said "all men"? Historians sometimes argue about that. You'll have to decide for yourself (p. 101).

Though Hakim simplifies the argument for young students, she doesn't make a simplistic claim. She leaves a debatable historical question open for budding historians to research and argue. Teachers need to ensure that all big ideas receive similar treatment—that they are accessible in preliminary accounts but not construed as impenetrable, unpackable, or unworthy of further thought.

The same hidden messiness occurs in the sciences. As noted earlier, Kuhn (1970) showed how the nonlinear and contentious history of science is invariably covered up in science textbooks:

> A concept of science drawn from [textbooks] is no more likely to fit the enterprise that produced them than an image of a natural culture drawn from a tourist brochure. . . .
>
> Those texts have, for example, often seemed to imply that the content of science is uniquely exemplified by the observations, laws, and theories described in their pages. . . .
>
> The textbook-driven tradition in which scientists come to sense their participation is one that, in fact, never existed. . . . Partly by selection and partly by distortion, the scientists of earlier ages are implicitly represented as having worked upon the same set of fixed canons that the most recent revolution has made seem scientific. . . . The result is a persistent tendency to make the history of science look linear and cumulative (pp. 1–3; 138–139).

Covering Up: An Example from Geometry

The same covering up can be seen in subjects as seemingly staid as geometry. In geometry textbooks, little is said about the historical *controversies* surrounding Euclid's key postulates from the moment they were written, leading to the revolution unleashed by the development of non-Euclidean geometries. For example, the following account in a highly regarded geometry text appears 600 pages after the idea of postulates was first introduced, as a seemingly unproblematic need for starting with "givens":

> You can see that the fifth postulate [Euclid's parallel postulate] is much longer and more complex than the others. This bothered mathematicians, who felt that such a complicated statement should not be assumed true. For 2000 years they tried to prove the fifth postulate from Euclid's other assumptions. . . . The works of these mathematicians greatly influenced *all* later mathematics. For the first time, postulates were viewed as statements assumed true instead of statements definitely true (Coxford, Usiskin, & Hirschhorn, 1993).

Why weren't students alerted to these controversies in the beginning? In fact, this idea about postulates is never uncovered for them. Why were postulates introduced as "assumptions" needed to avoid logical circularity, with no further inquiry or discussion of that assumption? What does it mean to try to prove a postulate? "You told us they were *assumptions*, Mr. Smith!" So what is a student to think about the postulates now? Are they arbitrary? True? Self-evident?

These questions, however unaddressed, are basic to an understanding of geometry and the transformation of its meaning (i.e., from truth to model). The text perpetuates the illusion that the ancients got it wrong, we know better, and you need only learn what is in the book. But it would be so easy to uncover some of the history and the vital inquiries that emerged from the debate over the postulates. More to the point, students will never understand the postulates until they see them as the sought-for logical underpinnings of theorems we want to prove.

A Lost Opportunity

Compare the preceding textbook omission with a passage from a renowned translator and editor of Euclid's work from the early 20th century. The quote suggests how the textbook authors lost a critical opportunity to help students understand the *system* we call geometry. Edward Heath (1956) constructs an imaginary first-person essay to help us better grasp the subtlety of Euclid's view that postulates only become justified by what they enable us to prove:

> Besides the common notions, there are a few other things which I must assume without proof, but which differ from common notions and are not self-evident. The learner may or may not be disposed to agree to them; but he must accept them at the outset on the superior authority of his teacher, *and must be left to convince himself of their truth in the course of the investigation which follows* (p. 124) (emphasis in original).

It turns out that Euclid and his colleagues had a highly sophisticated view of postulates (and how

a postulate differed from an axiom). Axioms (i.e., common notions) are self-evident logical facts: Equals added to equals yield equals. However, we assume postulates to be true even though *not* self-evident—because the postulate is needed as a logical underpinning for something we *already know we want to prove*. It is vital for understanding to make the student say, "*Now* I see why we assumed those postulates" or "Whoa! When we assumed those to be true they seemed far less of a problem than they do now" (a sign of greater sophistication in mathematics).[2]

The Counterintuitive Role of Postulates

The upshot is that postulates are not developed chronologically in time. They come *last*, as we search for the logical grounds of *understandings we have and proofs we want to make*. To prove that there were 180 degrees in all triangles, Euclid *needed* to postulate (the equivalent of there being) only one possible parallel to a line through a given point not on the line. Given that this counterintuitive idea is rarely explained in math courses, is it any wonder that many students are confused about a basic matter—the difference, if any, between postulates and theorems—as Perkins (1992) reports in *Smart Schools* and as we have seen many times in classrooms? This constant rethinking of basic ideas is central to developing understanding and avoiding misunderstanding. But overreliance on a glib and linear textbook account certainly jeopardizes that rethinking.

The doubting of Euclid's parallel postulate and the trying out of alternatives led to a revolution. It can be said without exaggeration that this event spelled the end of naive faith in reason as the key to understanding the universe, just as the theory of

evolution undermined the static and religiously influenced biology of the day:

> The two concepts which have most profoundly revolutionized our intellectual development since the 19th century are evolution and non-Euclidean geometry. The theory of evolution is generally well recognized as a prime influence, but non-Euclidean geometry, despite its more fundamental and more far-reaching effects, seems to escape attention (Kline, 1985, p. 452).

The Fear of Ridicule

Some of the most highly respected mathematicians in the 19th century who worked in this area *feared publishing their work for the ridicule it would engender*, because it challenged a 200-year-old view that Euclid's geometry described the facts of the world. Do students know—do they imagine—that "pure" mathematics can have such dramas and controversies?

We realize that the example is a bit esoteric. But that is our point, in a way—it *shouldn't* be. Anyone who studies geometry ought to understand the postulates (i.e., their justification and their meaning). Applying the six facets of understanding makes this clear: There is often little meaning to geometry for students, and rarely are they able—notwithstanding the light of history—to radically shift perspective in their study.

Yet few of us know any of this provocative history and analysis of geometry as a system because of the unidirectional and purposeless way we were taught geometry. The postulates, never revisited, are portrayed as unproblematic, and we aren't helped to see the system as a whole and ask, What of it? Students typically conclude their study of geometry with the misconception that postulates are either self-evident or arbitrary statements—neither of which is true.

Even though these kinds of covering up are common and usually unwitting, they have significant pedagogical impact. Shulman (1992), in his discussion of the case method of instruction, cites a recent study whose author argues that many so-called "naive misconceptions" are actually misconceptions generated by teaching:

> Spiro and his colleagues observed that excellent medical students frequently emerged from courses on physiology holding misconceptions with which they had apparently not entered the courses. . . .
>
> The medical students studied by Spiro, however, did not appear to be afflicted with crippling preconceptions. Indeed, their maladies seem pedagogenic; that is, they were created by the instruction rather than antedating it. More specifically, the misconceptions appeared traceable to the power of initial analogies, metaphors, examples, or cases used by teachers to introduce and frame the topics of the course.
>
> Spiro came to realize that the problem lay not in the distortive power of analogies and cases, *but in a pedagogy that permitted single representations to remain unchallenged* (emphasis in original).

In sum, all teaching must simplify, but there is a fundamental difference between developmentally simplified instruction and overly simplistic and inquiry-ending coverage. The latter approach hides the uncertainties, arguments, and subtleties, and it never revisits the simplistic beginnings. Wittingly or unwittingly, such textbooks (and the teaching they foster) imply that thought, qualification, or investigation are no longer needed. The consequence of such a presentation is to close off the student questioning essential to engagement and deeper understanding.

An education for uncoverage, by contrast, involves instruction that regularly requires students to find questions in knowledge, to dig deeper and test, explore, and perhaps rethink what they thought they knew.

Highlighting Big Ideas

The previous discussion is not meant to blame textbooks when students don't think. Didactic instruction of currently accepted knowledge is always prone to making knowledge seem more definite and final, as Kuhn (1970) suggested. Regardless, through assignments and assessments, teacher-designers must help students uncover not just facts or concepts but the big ideas. Our discussion of geometry was meant to suggest by example what we mean by a big idea, but let's consider it in more detail.

We note in Chapter 1 that a big idea can be described two ways: as involving an enduring conception or principle that transcends its origins, subject matter, or place in time; and as a *linchpin* idea— one crucial to a student's ability to understand a subject. All modern subject areas are grounded in nonobvious ideas: The earth does not appear to move; there are no obvious signs of our being descended from primates; *Hamlet* does not appear relevant to 14-year-olds; and derivatives and integrals make no conceptual sense to the novice calculus student (even if the idea of limits does). We struggle to grasp such ideas and see their value, just as great minds before us did.

Surely, then, there are not only performance benchmarks but also conceptual ones. To grasp them is to overcome simplistic and easily misunderstood conceptions. Here are some examples:

■ Impressionism was an attempt to paint scenes in light realistically, not abstractly or by feeling. Impressionism is the *opposite* of what people think, because they don't realize that the painters were using the word in its philosophic sense of "sense impressions."

■ The phases of the moon depend on the relative position of the earth, sun, and moon, so that we see the part of the moon that is not lit by the sun. Ongoing lunar eclipses are not the cause of the phases.

■ Correlation is not causation. Modern science, economics, and medicine deal more with the former as the latter.

■ Fractions when multiplied yield a smaller answer, and when divided, a larger answer. Do we know why?

■ A historian is a storyteller, not a scientist.

■ Two light beams intersecting at crest and trough can cancel each other out and cause darkness—light as waves.

■ Negative and imaginary numbers are no less and no more real than ordinary numbers. They exist to provide the symmetry and continuity needed for essential arithmetic and algebraic laws.

■ The theory of natural selection is what is controversial. Theories of evolution predated Darwin by centuries.

■ The American revolutionaries held that individuals, not governments, had a natural right to property and wages gained through labor. Thus, in one sense, they were "conservatives," not "liberals."

■ Irony is not mere coincidence.

Understanding is under way when curriculum design helps students progress in making sense of these new, more powerful, but not-at-all-obvious ideas. No matter how elegant a student's writing on gravitational force may be, if he persists in discussing gravity as if it were a physical, observable thing, he lacks a sufficient understanding of gravity.

A linchpin idea, once understood, generates powerful ordering and transfer of learning. Bruner's (1960) account of structure in *The Process of Education*, almost 40 years ago, says it best:

> Grasping the structure of a subject is understanding it in a way that permits many other things to be related to it meaningfully. To learn structure, in short, is to learn how things are related. . . . To take an example from mathematics, algebra is a way of arranging knowns and unknowns in equations so that the unknowns are made knowable. The three fundamentals involved . . . are commutation, distribution, and association. Once a student grasps the ideas embodied by these three fundamentals, he is in a position to recognize wherein "new" equations to be solved are not new at all. Whether the student knows the formal names of these operations is less important for transfer than whether he is able to use them.

Because big ideas are essential yet difficult to understand, our instructional designs will work best if they require students to ask and re-ask questions about important ideas. That is why converting objectives into essential, unit, and entry-point questions is so crucial. We signal to the stu-dent what the big ideas are, and her job is to inquire into the meaning, value, and confirmation of important ideas.

Similarly, naive thinking develops into more sophisticated thinking through inquiries and performance tasks. We as educators design those tasks specifically to discover how far a student can go beyond glib generalizations, common misconceptions, and superficial knowledge.

We conclude this overview of uncoverage by offering a rule of thumb for teacher-designers: The big idea at the heart of any unit is not likely to be understood if it is merely taught. To be fully understood, it will have to be explored, questioned, played with, used in realistic contexts, rephrased, and verified as important in some way. In the next chapter, we offer a practical strategy for acting on that idea for each unit and course of study.

Endnotes

1. Rubrics for determining the degree of a student's epistemological naivete are found in material developed by the Harvard Teaching for Understanding project (Wiske, 1997, pp. 184–196). Some of the work derives from groundbreaking work at the college level by William Perry (1970) at Harvard.

2. In this and other examples, readers familiar with educational history will hear an echo of the idea that learning should be designed to "recapitulate" the history of knowledge. Although we do not endorse recapitulation as a sound educational theory, part of what we mean by "uncoverage" is the idea that students should experience authentic inquiry and sometimes re-create or simulate how knowledge was developed. (Chapter 9 offers more on this topic.) For more on recapitulation, see also Egan (1997), Gould (1977), and Wiggins (1987b).

WHAT THE FACETS IMPLY FOR UNIT DESIGN

HAVING LOOKED AT THE KEY CONSIDERATIONS IN THE design of curricular activities, we can now consider the design criteria or filters needed to ensure high-quality curricular units. How can teachers deliberately design activities that will evoke and develop greater student understanding? In this chapter, we examine design guidelines and self-assessment criteria, which we summarize in the acronym WHERE. We also take a closer look at the problems of coverage and consider the seemingly contradictory goals of depth and breadth.

Introducing WHERE

The acronym WHERE stands for *where* are we headed, *hook* the student, *explore* the subject and *equip* the student, *rethink* our work and ideas, and *evaluate* results. Before we engage in a more detailed discussion with examples, here is a thumbnail sketch of how these five elements apply to the classroom experience:

W*here are we headed?* Why are we headed there? What are the student's final performance obligations—the anchoring performance assessments? What are the criteria by which student work will be judged for understanding? Students ask these questions. Help them see the answers up front.

Hook *the student through engaging and provocative entry points:* thought-provoking and focusing experiences, issues, oddities, problems, and challenges that point toward essential and unit questions, core ideas, and final performance tasks.

Explore *and enable/equip.* Engage students in learning experiences that allow them to explore the big ideas and essential questions and cause them to pursue leads or hunches, research and test ideas, and try things out. Equip students for the final performances through guided instruction and coaching on needed skill and knowledge. Have them experience the ideas to make them real.

Reflect *and rethink.* Dig deeper into ideas at issue (through the facets of understanding). Revise, rehearse, and refine as needed. Guide students in self-assessment and self-adjustment, based on feedback from initial inquiry, results, and discussion.

Exhibit *and evaluate.* Reveal what has been understood through final performances and products. Involve students in a final self-assessment to identify remaining questions, set future goals, and point toward new units and lessons.

■ MISCONCEPTION ALERT

We stress here that WHERE, like the facets, serves more as a *criterion* for design than as a *chronology* or step-by-step recipe. Recall that Bloom's *Taxonomy of Educational Objectives* (1956) represents a way of judging assessment items and tasks for cognitive difficulty and is not a rigid prescribed sequence for

teaching. Similarly, WHERE represents a way of testing lessons and units rather than a recipe for building them.

To use an analogy in story telling, a story needs a plot, characters, and setting. Those are story elements, just as WHERE summarizes the design elements. But how should those elements be fashioned into the most engaging and effective whole? There are many possible beginnings, middles, and ends.

Just as a story teller might begin with fragments of dialogue or a character and work toward a plot (or vice versa), design work, too, can emerge over time, following many different paths and sequences. Thus, a teacher might introduce a unit with the final task done in a preliminary form, such as a written draft.

Before discussing the implications of each element of WHERE, we offer a general comment about the importance of design standards. Our work is reaching a crucial stage. We are moving from thinking only about what *we* want to do and need to accomplish as teachers to thinking about what the student—the end user of our design—will need to do to achieve understanding.

If we were software designers, we now would have to ensure that all the code we have written and all the functions we have built into the application are going to become truly user friendly, elegant, and powerful. In a sense, we *are* intellectual software designers: The student is going to use our design to accomplish important learning tasks.

The rest of this chapter explores specific implications of WHERE for creating and implementing a quality curriculum.

Where Are We Headed?

We are headed toward establishing direction, purpose, rationale, performance requirements, and standards, of course. The purpose of this first element in WHERE parallels the first stage of backward design. We begin by thinking purposefully about how to show where teaching is headed (i.e., the specific learning sought).

But the challenge is more than just clarifying or restating our own teaching targets. The first requirement of effective, user-friendly curriculums is that the designer must make the goals clear to *students*. Such work means specifying the desired performances and standards constituting the achievement—not just what we will cover.

Early in a unit, we must orient students to the purposes and obligations that are most relevant to final assessments of their understanding. Through design, we want to maximize the likelihood that students will understand both the work and its purpose.

Performance Obligations

Only rarely do students know where a lesson or unit is headed in terms of their own performance obligations. That a student knows the topic, what chapters will be read, the directions for each activity, or that a test is coming at the end, are not sufficient to focus attention, guide effort, and ensure that goals are understood and met.

As soon as possible in the unit or course of study, students should know not only the overarching questions but also the specifics of final performance (e.g., tasks, tests, assignments, evaluative criteria, and the related performance standards) that must be met by the end.

This requirement is more stringent than it first appears. Students must be able to answer the following questions with specificity and confidence as the work develops:

- What will I have to understand by unit's end, and what does that understanding look like?
- What are my final obligations? What knowledge, skill, tasks, and questions must I master to meet those obligations and demonstrate understanding and proficiency?
- What resources are available to support my learning and performance?
- What is my immediate task? How does it help me meet my overarching obligations?
- How does today's work relate to what we did previously? What is most important about this work?
- How should I allot my time? What aspects of this and future assignments demand the most attention? How should I plan? What should I do next? What has priority in the overall scheme of things?
- How will my final work be judged? Where is my current performance strongest and weakest? What can I do to improve?

Purposeful Work

As the above questions suggest, the work must be purposeful from the *student's* point of view. Regardless of how abstract the key ideas are or the student's degree of naiveté about the subject, we as educators must embody the goals in known, practical tasks and standards that the student can understand from the beginning of the unit. The student must clearly see the purpose of each assignment, in other words, and have an overall sense of the plan and resources available for accomplishing that

purpose. For a student to meet the goal of clarity about direction, he must know the final assessment obligations from the beginning, as well as the focusing or guiding questions that lie behind the design of the work.

Here is an example of how a teacher provides this information for a unit on *The Catcher in the Rye*. Notice how the teacher uses a first-day overview and entry questions (given out in advance) to make clear where the work is headed, how the reading should be approached, and thus how study and note taking might be organized. The teacher says to the class:

> At the end of a close reading of *The Catcher in the Rye*, you will act as part of a peer case-review committee at the hospital from which Holden is telling his story. With access to the transcript of Holden's own words, plus selected related materials, you will write a diagnostic report for the hospital and a prescriptive letter to Holden's parents.
>
> Quizzes and a writing exercise in which you describe Holden from the perspective of another character will act as prompts to your understanding. At the end of the unit, you will also analyze your evolving understanding of the novel, as chronicled in daily journals.
>
> Please respond in the journal at the end of each reading assignment and before the next class to two questions: What is the most important thing you learn about Holden in this section of the novel? What is the most important unanswered question about Holden at this point in the novel? Your responses to these questions will begin and end daily class discussions. In addition, you will address in writing a third question with each assignment, such as: What do you make of the title? What observations do you have about Holden's use of language? What do you make of the line "Allie, don't let me disappear," and what scene early in the book does this line remind you of?

What should we make of Holden's reactions to the obscenities he sees written at Phoebe's school and at the museum?

Final questions for the last days are, What changed in the way you saw Holden as the book went along? and, If, as some people claim, "misunderstanding is inevitable" when you encounter new material, what were your misunderstandings at any point during this unit?

Given your reading, if you were to teach this novel to next year's students, what would you do to ensure they understand the novel as opposed to just knowing some facts about it?

Think how different this approach to literature is from a typical teacher strategy: passing out copies of the book and providing a syllabus of homework assignments showing what pages to be read on which night. Note, too, how the different types of assessment provide a sufficient set of evidence for judging student understanding.

Hook the Student Through Engaging and Provocative Entry Points

The intellectual work leading to sophisticated understanding requires a high degree of self-discipline and delayed gratification. Still, many students come to school somewhat unwilling (and not expecting) to work very hard. Historically, we have assumed that we can solve this problem only through extrinsic means, such as the carrot of praise, awards, prizes, and privileges and the stick of low grades, punishment, and public humiliation.

We take a different view here. We focus on the elements of design that are most likely to engage students, using our knowledge of the student-user and the subject as the basis. Furthermore, we believe schoolwork itself can be designed to be far more interesting without sacrificing rigor. Schoolwork is often needlessly boring, especially when composed of mind-numbing skill worksheets or excessive passive listening—all of it divorced from interesting problems and realistic performance challenges.

Indeed, time-honored and powerful ways of provoking thought, awakening and sustaining interest in ideas, and otherwise making learning exciting do exist. To realize greater student engagement in learning, however, we will have to explicitly design for it.

Organizing work around questions and problems has already been cited as an effective way to entice or provoke students. Other kinds of hooks include immersing students in puzzles, challenging them to solve a real-world problem, and engaging them in role-play. Presenting far-out theories, paradoxes, and incongruities can also stimulate wonder and inquiry.

Educator Frank Lyman (1992), who quips that "education should be an itch, not a scratch," favors the use of "weird facts" to provoke interest in a topic. He suggests beginning a lesson or unit with an anomaly, such as, "Did you know that according to the laws of aerodynamics the bumblebee should not be able to fly [as a picture of a bee in flight is shown]? How can this be(e)?"

Our entry-point questions in Chapter 2 also serve to provoke interest, as do the challenges posed in problem-based learning or through a case study. A mystery is always a good starter. Here is a problem artifact that can be used in a problem-based learning lesson to introduce a unit on westward expansion in the mid-19th century:

You discover a yellowed copy of the following article from the front page of a very old issue of the New York Times *stuck in a library book. Only the first paragraph remains, and there is no date or volume number. It reads:*

Turning Back the Hands

At just 9 o'clock, local time, yesterday morning Mr. James Hamblet, general superintendent of the Times Telegraph Company, and manager of the time service of the Western Union Telegraph Company, stopped the pendulum of his standard clock in Room 48 in the Western Union Telegraph Building. The long glistening rod and its heavy cylindrical pendulum ball were at rest for 3 minutes and 58.38 seconds. The delicate machinery of the clock rested for the first time in many months. The clicking of the electric instrument on a shelf at the side of the clock ceased, and with it ceased the corresponding ticks on similar instruments in many jewelry and watch stores throughout the city. When as nearly as it could be ascertained, the time stated above had lapsed, the heavy pendulum was again set in motion and swung backward and forward in its never-varying trips of one second each from one end of its swing to the other. With the starting of the pendulum, the clicking of the little instruments all over the city was resumed. Mr. Hamblet had changed the time of New York City and State.

Do you know what this article is about? We provide the answer later in the chapter. Once students have solved this particular mystery, they can productively focus on important, big ideas—the causes and effects of the American movement westward—informed by the questions and issues that arise from student inquiry and argument about this introductory puzzle.

An element of mystery is central to provoking thought. Consider how filmmakers raise questions in our mind that remain unanswered as a way of keeping us thinking and wondering. In workshops, we often show the first 10 minutes of Ken Burns's *The Civil War* to show how this technique of questioning works even in a documentary. The opening scenes personalize the devastation wrought by the war. But only tantalizing and limited facts are offered about the people depicted in this dramatic opening, and we are left to wonder with the narrator, How is it that we could kill our brethren in such staggering numbers?

Inviting the Viewer in

Leaving some things unspoken and unanswered invites the viewer in—to help make sense—and sustains interest and thought. Consider, for example, if a narrator were to open a film by stating some personal information about a protagonist in this way:

An archaeologist grew up in the household of a stern ancient history scholar. He was a Boy Scout. He became interested in archaeology when he happened upon some men who were digging up old artifacts. From that encounter he developed a distinctive style of dress as well as a lifelong fear of certain reptiles.

Here is a flat, didactic presentation of facts with little drama, oddities, humor, or mystery. But fans of the Lucas-Spielberg movie trilogy will quickly recognize this character as Indiana Jones. In actuality, however, the first 10 minutes of *Indiana Jones and the Last Crusade* are riveting and funny, filled with mystery and humorously dashed expectations. (The horse moves when Indy tries to jump on it, the bad guys wear white, and the Boy Scout ends up being the thief.)

Contrast those 10 action-filled minutes with a flat textbook biography of the kind we started to sketch out above and you get a sense of what needs to be done to make work more engaging for kids—without sacrificing facts.

For example, one of us, years ago, watched a history course whose entire structure was a sequence of biographies. Each student took turns researching the next character, presenting his research, then joining a press conference, in which four or five other role-players fielded questions from the rest of the class (the press). The biographies were chosen to make the subject (Russian history) interesting and to afford engaging and provocative matches of personality in the press conferences.

Adding to the provocative, sometimes dramatic turns in the course was a devilish trick of the teacher. He set up a reserve library with a few false and disreputable materials about the characters thrown in, so that the students had to cross-check references and be skeptical. Significantly, this teacher never lectured, although he put dozens of his lectures on videotape so they could be checked out of the library.

By framing academic goals through the lens of student issues and interests, teachers frequently see student *engagement* rather than an attitude of minimum compliance—What's the least I have to do to get this done? For example, a middle school language arts teacher used a school board proposal on school uniforms to engage students in understanding the processes of issue analysis, debate, and persuasion in writing and speaking. Members of the class analyzed the proposal, held a simulated school board debate, and wrote letters to the local newspaper editor.

Beyond Entertaining to Essential

The challenge is to point toward what is essential, not merely provide work that is entertaining. The article excerpt, "Turning Back the Hands," is not only engaging but effective in setting up important ideas and issues in U.S. history. Indeed, key questions typically arise from students as the excerpt is deciphered, identified, and discussed. (Have you been wondering what the problem artifact actually is describing? It's the day the United States changed from local time, kept by the rising and setting of the sun, to standard time, which carved the United States into three time zones. The railroads drove this change because of the need for standardized national schedules.)

Many educators who have experienced this problem artifact in workshops propose dozens of plausible but incorrect theories. They therefore have seen firsthand how important questions arise and how those questions can frame both historical and scientific study. Similar models can be modern (e.g., the structure of the World Wide Web) or ancient (e.g., the Gregorian calendar). Either way, the design must blend what is engaging with what is effective.

Another workshop exercise we use involves a series of questions leading to a Venn diagram to address the challenge of engagement and effectiveness. Figure 8.1 shows how we start. We ask, When are students most engaged and committed in their work generally and in their schoolwork in particular? In other words, what kinds of work (putting aside the teacher's influence) engage students and why? Some predictable answers (which are written in the oval) are hands-on tasks, mysteries, a combination of cooperation and competition, real-world challenges, role-play, provocative case studies or

mock trials, audiences for products and performances, choices in process and product, and the ability to personalize the work. But why do these strategies succeed in heightening interest?

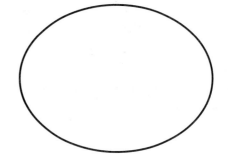

FIGURE 8.1 **BEGINNING OF A VENN DIAGRAM**

When are students most
engaged in their work?

Piquing Interest

The following conditions sum up our knowledge about how to pique intellectual interest:

■ *Instant immersion in questions, problems, challenges, situations, or stories that require the student's wits, not just school knowledge.* This way of thinking is central to problem-based learning and the case method.

■ *Thought provocations.* Anomalies, weird facts, counterintuitive events or ideas, and mysteries appeal to the gut, making the strange familiar and the familiar strange. An example is reading *Flatland* to introduce issues in geometry.

■ *Experiential shocks.* This type of activity is an intellectual Outward Bound where students have to confront feelings, obstacles, and problems personally and as a group to accomplish a task.

■ *Differing points of view or multiple perspectives on an issue.* For example, a U.S. history course might include a reading from another country's textbook to provide a shockingly different point of view on famous events, as we saw in the previous chapter.[1]

Considering Effectiveness

We ask our workshop participants to consider not only engagement but also effectiveness—their own. What is their most effective lesson and why? What determines whether a design is effective, other things being equal? Figure 8.2 shows how we frame the questions in an evolving Venn diagram.

Here, too, the answers are predictable. Work is more effective when

■ It is focused on clear and worthy goals.
■ Models and feedback are provided.

■ Students understand the purpose of, and rationale for, the work.
■ Clear, public criteria and models allow the students to accurately monitor their progress.
■ The ideas are made concrete and real through educative activities linking to students' experiences and the world beyond the classroom.
■ Built-in opportunities to self-assess and self-adjust based on feedback exist.

Finally, workshop participants ponder the center portion of the Venn diagram: What must be true for the work to be both highly engaging *and* effective? The answers become a useful set of criteria for working toward understanding without sacrificing rigor or key content. Figure 8.3 shows the completed framework.

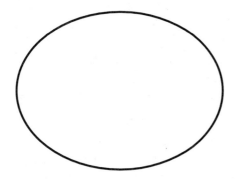

FIGURE 8.2
AN EVOLVING VENN DIAGRAM FOR GOOD DESIGN

When are students most effective
in their work?

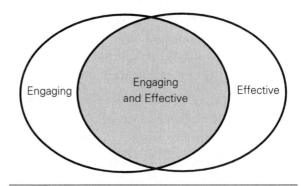

FIGURE 8.3
**DEVELOPING CRITERIA TO MAKE
WORK ENGAGING AND EFFECTIVE**

When are students most engaged
and most effective?

Engaging

Engaging
and Effective

Effective

Explore and Enable/Equip

Here is where uncovering depth and breadth takes center stage in the design work. Uncoverage requires the design of lessons that move the inquiry beyond obvious or flat summary accounts of a textbook. The exploring and equipping must be carefully shaped to evoke and require the relevant facets of understanding, focused on specific final goals:

■ Present and clarify key problems needing solution.

■ Call for students to dig deeper and go broader to make sense of things.

■ Investigate differing points of view that have emerged.

■ Pursue essential questions in depth.

■ Learn needed facts, examine relevant theories, find and explore resources, and develop needed skills.

■ Aim for final performance, study models, and practice or rehearse.

■ Provide as much direct experience as possible to give meaning to key ideas.

Using the Facets as Questions

We can use the six facets of understanding as a set of questions to be asked of key textbook statements to explore key ideas, not just cover them. Our design is then more likely to uncover the inquiries and issues that lead toward a better understanding of a subject. Here are sample questions for screening textbook statements:

■ What is the theory behind this statement of a big idea? How might we test it to verify or justify it? What theory or principle lies behind this idea?

■ What is the story behind this fact? How did this statement come to be argued or believed? Might the statement be interpreted differently? What is important here? Why is this statement significant?

■ What can you do with this knowledge? To what important problems, questions, or puzzles can this knowledge be applied? In what situations do adults or professionals use this knowledge? What tasks require this type of knowledge? What kinds of uses would cause a needed refinement of the idea?

■ Are there other points of view beside the one expressed here? From what perspective is this statement made? How might critics, skeptics, or people different from us view the matter? What is assumed here? What are we being asked to take on faith? Should we?

■ What would it feel like to think that way? What would students need to experience to believe this?

■ What do I know as a student that makes this statement seem true? False? Which of my beliefs and prejudices could be making it hard for me to believe or question this statement?

Questions like these serve as prompts for the teacher-designer, injecting exploration and active inquiry into what otherwise would be passive learning. The teacher then can bring the statements in a textbook to life by designing learning experiences around inquiries, research, discussions, debates, role-play, and shifts of perspective, to name a few.

By using the terms *equip* and *enable*, we underscore the vital role that instructional activities and textbooks should play as a *means* to effective performance. The "equipping" implied also involves what we refer to as highly focused (or enabling) teaching,

derived from an analysis of the performance goals. Teachers in this stage of the design must ask themselves, What kinds of knowledge, skill, habits of mind, and attitudes are prerequisites for successful final performance? What kinds of instructional activities will ensure that students have an equal chance to master the core ideas and performances?

The most overlooked aspect of instructional design is the need to help students self-assess and self-adjust their work as they progress. Our lessons should provide models of exemplary performance, practice in understanding and using the criteria in rubrics, and strategies such as peer review to inform and guide self-adjustment. (For more ideas, see Chapters 2 and 3 of Wiggins, 1998.)

Experiencing Key Ideas

Real or simulated experiences of key ideas are vital in teaching for understanding. The design challenge is to make an abstract idea or remote experience accessible, real, and seemingly important. An example from the teaching of Steven Levy illustrates how experiential activities or simulations can bring the facet of empathy to the fore:

> In September 1992, when Levy's students entered their classroom for the first time, they found to their astonishment that the room was empty—no desks, chairs, computers, or bookshelves. Like the Pilgrims, whom they would be studying all year, the students would be shaping their new environment to their needs. Throughout the year, they were given opportunities to experience the concepts specified in the 4th grade curriculum: They built their own desks and chairs; formed a cooperative, acquired shareholders, and gave out dividends to finance their activities; grew and harvested wheat for baking bread; and dyed and spun wool for weaving mats (Regional

Laboratory for Educational Improvement of the Northeast & Islands, undated, p. 1).

Accessible Introductions to Complex Ideas

We have used non-Euclidean geometry as an example of a complex, important, but poorly understood topic that ought to be more prominent if we want the entire system of geometry understood. Consider the following methods to introduce students to the topic in an interesting and accessible way:

- Ask students to bring in the rules of their favorite games and sports. Discuss whether the rules can change and the game still be the same. Can they name major rule changes in sports they all know? Why were the rules changed, and with what effect on the game? (And how does this history inform our insight into a big idea we discussed in Chapter 1— the letter versus the spirit of the law?)

- Have students develop a crude geometry of the physical plant of their school. In other words, what are the postulates needed to describe the "space" of the building and human movement through it? (Clearly, in many cases, a straight line is not the shortest practical distance between two points.)

- Using a globe, explore the problem of setting airline routes and minimizing fuel costs. Show how Euclidean geometry is not the right system for determining the shortest distances.

Recasting Each Facet

Again, teacher-designers can profit from recasting the six facets as design questions—questions about how students might better use experiences and be better equipped and enabled to achieve understanding in performance:

Facet 1: Explanation. What kind of data, problems, and experiences must students encounter if they are to grasp that which is not obvious, meet new ideas and theories, test and verify them, and build their own (or fully internalize someone else's) theory or explanation?

Facet 2: Interpretation. How will the work require *students* to make interpretations, derive meaning, explore the importance, or find the significance in material or knowledge? What texts, events, or people will be provided as grist for student interpretation?

Facet 3: Application. How will the work require and enable students to use and test their understandings in apt and varying contexts, where authentic situations, purposes, and audiences require it? How can the work encourage students to propose or even invent new applications?

Facet 4: Perspective. How will the materials, assignments, experiences, and discussions be delivered so that students can not only generate multiple points of view but also critically evaluate them?

Facet 5: Empathy. What kinds of direct or simulated experiences in class might cause students to viscerally connect with the experiences of others? How might the work help students get beyond empty words and abstractions to find worth or possible value in the ideas and experiences of people that might initially strike them as dumb, unappealing, or alien?

Facet 6: Self-Knowledge. What kinds of experiences will help students self-assess and reflect on what they do or do not know and understand? How will the lessons evoke the habits of mind and biases students bring to the work?

Reflect and Rethink

The likelihood of a more sophisticated understanding depends on enticing and requiring the student to constantly use and rethink her concepts, points of view, and theories, as we have repeatedly suggested.

When overarching and recurring tasks and questions anchor the curriculum, it stands to reason that important ideas can and must be revisited. In designing for understanding, we are deliberately uncovering ideas, counter to the linear scope-and-sequence view of curriculum that fosters coverage.

For example, an elementary class explores the idea of friendship by reading various stories featuring friends and acts of friendship. Students derive a theory of friendship and create a concept web for the topic. The teacher then presents them with a proverb from the Middle East, "The enemy of my enemy is my friend," and asks them to reexamine their theory based on this idea.

Here is an example of a middle school unit on ancient civilization. The unit is designed around increasingly demanding induction, and it requires rethinking both the process and the product. Simulated and genuine artifacts are used. As students learn about Mesopotamia and read *The Epic of Gilgamesh*, they learn to think like archaeologists:

1. Introduce the unit using the essential questions, What is civilization? How do we know what we know? Have students write a brief definition of civilization. For an additional activity, students can bring in an object they believe symbolizes civilization.

2. In class, students examine the U.S. penny. They make observations and a list of observable facts that will be called *near facts*. They share facts

and near facts to accumulate as many as possible. Magnifying glasses and microscopes can be used to inspect the penny. After each student selects facts and near facts, they all copy each one onto a small card. Facts are pink and near facts are blue.

3. Students arrange the layers of facts and near facts at the bottom of a pyramidal tower. By arranging and rearranging the cards, they combine facts and near facts to make knowledge claims. The knowledge claims go on yellow cards.

4. After sharing knowledge claims with each other, each student makes a final interpretation of the penny and writes it on a green card. They do this work at home. Some students will make one interpretation for each side of the artifact. They next make a final interpretation on another card of a different color and write a journal entry on the strengths and weaknesses of the interpretation.

5. Students share their interpretations.

6. In partnerships, students accumulate facts and near facts based on a close observation of the "Standard of Ur," an artifact discovered earlier this century. The name of the artifact is not shared with the students because it may influence their interpretation. The same color coding is used.

7. At home, each student makes knowledge claims and a final interpretation of the artifact. To keep material organized, students should arrange all the facts, near facts, and knowledge claims based on each side of the artifact in separate sections of the tower.

8. Students present their finished inductive towers to the class. Classmates are encouraged to question the validity of the interpretation.

9. The published interpretation of *The Standard of Ur* by Sir Leonard Woolley is read. At home, students compare and contrast his interpretation and their own.

10. Students write another definition of civilization with the intention of making a more sophisticated definition based on what they learned in the inductive process.

11. Students write a journal entry on the strengths and weaknesses of the inductive method based on their experiences with the penny, the Standard of Ur and Woolley's interpretation. A discussion titled "How Do We Know What We Know?" ends the unit.

Rethinking as a design element causes students, after developing their initial idea, explanation, concept, or theory, to encounter and make sense of

- Related but dissimilar experiences.
- Shifts in perspective (different people's views, books, theories, and events).
- Weird facts, anomalies, or surprises.

Exhibit and Evaluate

Exhibit and evaluate understandings, findings, and solutions through authentic products and performances that involve a meaningful context, clear purpose, and audience (real or simulated). Evaluate in terms of quality and effectiveness.

As we have argued throughout the book, the final assessment serves to reinforce what understanding actually means and thus teaches students what we are after. Teachers sometimes do not see that their *talk*—their verbalized aims ("I really want you to think critically about what we read") is not always reflected in their *walk*—their final test ("Choose the best answer to each of the 20 questions after reading the short story").

Again, by thinking up front about the most appropriate assessments of understanding—performance tasks and projects—we are likely to realize greater congruence between means and ends. By teaching toward known purposes embodied in worthy performance tasks and projects, we signal to students what we consider to be most important in the unit or course. *What* and *how* we assess signals what we value.

Moreover, if we establish the evaluative criteria and performance standards at the outset, we are working with clear and explicit priorities that can inform student learning and self-adjustment. This specificity provides students with a clear and public answer to their constant questions: What do you expect? How good is good enough? What is excellent work?

Another typical question, What do we have to do to get a top grade? can be turned around: Do you, the student, know what evidence of understanding looks like? Have you shown evidence of understanding? In other words, self-assessment (and perhaps built-in self-adjustment) must be central to any formative and summative assessment if the teacher is to fully assess for student understanding.

The six facets again supply key design criteria. The designer must ensure that the final tasks (as well as the enabling work) require the performances at the heart of each facet, and that the exploring and refining stages of the work require the student to develop and perhaps rethink theories, interpret events, and encounter multiple perspectives. No single lesson or unit is likely to reflect all six facets, but an entire course of study no doubt will cycle through the facets many times.

Here is an example of a middle school unit in mathematics that addresses many facets of understanding as well as the WHERE sequence. This award-winning unit by David Foster involves a study of systems:[2]

Preface. Students read "The Road Not Taken" by Robert Frost and analyze the meaning of the poem. The initial journal entry will be revisited in the final assessment.

Preview Problem: Rush hour. Given a map and a problem situation, students determine the best route to travel and time to travel to ensure on-time arrival.

Lesson 1: Daily walk. Students are introduced to examples of networks. They examine paths walked each day and draw at least two different representations of their networks.

Lesson 2: Intersections and roads. Each student pair plays a series of games involving graphs. Students work to devise winning strategies. They use their experience to make conjectures about pathways, then construct their own graphs and analyze possible pathways.

Lesson 3: The shortest route. A map and questions are given to groups. Students examine the map, finding the shortest paths from house to school, shortest route in minutes, and paths that avoid signals and stop signs.

Lesson 4: Count the ways. Students use the computer program Logo to identify the number of possible pathways through a city, then write reports on their findings.

Lesson 5: Pick-up sticks. Students engage in a series of games involving sticks along a path.

Lesson 6: Bay Area tour. Students act as tour directors for a Bay Area travel agency. Their task is to design a couple of tours to visit various sights, crossing the five major bridges that span the bay. Groups design tour routes using city maps that satisfy agency objectives.

Lesson 7: Public works. Students explain a menu of four situations involving tours with best possible routes.

Lesson 8: The commute. Three commuting alternatives are presented in narrative form. Students examine cost, time, and environmental issues.

Lesson 9: Bus stop. For each student in the class, groups investigate the best possible bus routes to school, optimum number of buses, and costs incurred.

Lesson 10: Rapid transit. Students choose one of three tasks: design a rapid transit system for the Los Angeles basin; design a rapid transit system for any community; or design a complex network in another setting (e.g., airplane hub-and-spoke system or Federal Express distribution center). This lesson requires research, cost/benefit analysis, and written and oral presentations.

Final reflection: Again, read the Frost poem from the first day and write a journal entry.

Two brief unit outlines based on the WHERE framework are shown in Figure 8.4. They expand on two examples used earlier—the time-zone artifact problem and the geometry inquiries.

A Return to the Nutrition Unit

Setting: Teacher Bob James was beginning to design his unit on nutrition in Chapter 2. He now considers how he might add to or modify his design in light of the criteria and guidelines provided by WHERE.

Just when I think I've got it nailed, I'm finding that my thinking about the nutrition unit is being stretched by WHERE. Here are my current ideas:

W – The backward design process has really helped me clarify where *I'm* going with the unit. Now I need to think about how I can help the students know where *they* are headed, and why. I think that the essential and entry-point questions will help give direction, especially since I plan to post these questions on the classroom bulletin board. But I probably can make the goals even clearer by introducing the assessment tasks, project, and my evaluation criteria and rubrics early in the unit.

With these performance targets in mind, I'm hoping that the kids will more clearly see the purpose for the particulars they'll be learning— the food groups, the food pyramid, how to read nutrition information on food labels, things like that.

H – I like the suggestion of starting with a hook, something to capture students' interest in the topic. Our social studies textbook has a section on the explorers that will work well, I think. The kids love mysteries and this is one—the story of the 16th and 17th century ocean-going sailors. They developed a mysterious disease, called scurvy, during their long months aboard ship, but their condition improved dramatically once they were back on land.

Once the kids learn that the disease resulted from a lack of vitamin C, and that consuming fresh fruits and vegetables was the "medicine," we will be poised to examine the role of nutrition in health.

E – I think that my new lessons will go far to equip my students for the performance tasks and project. And I believe that my teaching will be much more focused now that I've thought through my desired understandings and the assessment evidence I need to collect.

R – The rethinking portion of unit design is probably the greatest stretch for me. Other than when we use revision as a part of the writing process, I have rarely asked my students to

FIGURE 8.4 **APPLYING WHERE**

WHERE Sequence	Application in Geometry	Application in History/Government
Where are we headed?	Was geometry discovered or invented? Task: Write an essay and do research.	Antitrust and government regulation of business: Necessary or intrusive?
Hooks (Work is designed to engage and build interest in the key learnings.)	PBL exercise on mysterious letters back and forth over fear of publishing controversial math work (on non-Euclidian geometry). George Brett pine-tar bat incident. Can you change the rules of a game and have it be the same game?	Modern link: Microsoft-DOS browser war; government regulation of Internet development in Malaysia and Scandinavia. PBL mysterious artifact and event— article from the *New York Times* on the changing of clocks all over New York. Why? When?
Explore and equip (Work is designed to induce learning, sharpen thinking, and establish agenda and purpose.)	Some work in proving theorems in alternative geometries; issues and research needs emerge from solving puzzle of letters on geometry (written by Bolyai and Gauss).	Who invented the time zones? Why? How did they come about? What was the effect? Power of the railroads. Role of media. Westward expansion.
Tasks and assignments that build knowledge and capacity.	Key postulates and theorems. History and import of the parallel postulate. Kline reading on Euclidean and non-Euclidean geometry, *Mathematics in Western Culture.*	Readings on the period of 1820–1880 Study of the Industrial Revolution and westward expansion. Having solved the problem, the class explores the entire era in text-driven ways.
Refine and rethink	The postulates and the point of geometry.	The pros and cons of business power and antitrust laws.
Exhibit and evaluate	Was geometry discovered or invented? Why has the answer changed over time? What difference does the answer make? Write a paper that includes your research into at least one other geometry.	Write an editorial, a letter to the editor, or an article on how differently the time change affected four to five people in the United States, or a news article marking the 25th or 100th anniversary of the time change. List the pros and cons of government versus commercial control of common resources.

formally rethink the ideas we discuss. Yet I'm beginning to realize how important it can be.

Two very interesting questions came up over lunch with the other teachers. One or both should be good midway into the unit to challenge the students to refine their thinking about nutritious eating. If allowed to eat anything they wanted, would children eat a balanced diet? Do animals eat foods that provide for their nutritional needs?

These questions point to another essential question: Does Mother Nature lead living creatures in the direction of nutritious eating? These provocations should stimulate discussion, and rethinking, and lead to interesting questions for further research.

E – The performance tasks and culminating camp menu project will give them several opportunities to show me they understand healthy eating—the major goal of the unit. Before evaluating, I'll involve the class in a peer review of the camp menus in cooperative learning groups so that the students will receive feedback. And I'll allow them time for menu revisions before their final menus are due.

Finally, I'll ask each student to complete two self-assessments—one for their camp menu using the rubric, and the second a reflection on if (and how) their personal eating habits have changed because of what they've learned during the unit. These activities should bring the unit to an effective closure.

I think that the nutrition unit has definitely been enhanced by WHERE and I intend to use it when planning other units. I'm anxious to see what the results will be with my students.

Altering the Textbook's Role

Obviously, we are altering the textbook's role—from a sacred text to an outline of possibilities and a resource and reference book of summary ideas. In its changed role, the textbook now supports purposeful, educative work through its focus on overarching questions and performance tasks, not coverage. Now it is a means for students to address explicit ends, framed as questions and tasks, and for teachers to check understanding as it emerges from inquiry.

One of the chief recommendations of the Carnegie report on Secondary Education in 1983 was to demand more primary-source material and more direct experience of how knowledge becomes knowledge. The report discusses the shortcomings of textbooks:

> Most textbooks present students with a highly simplified view of reality and practically no insight into the methods by which the information has been gathered and the facts distilled. Moreover, textbooks seldom communicate to students the richness and excitement of original works (Boyer, 1983, p. 143).

Figure 8.5 offers a brief guide of indicators for thinking through using a textbook when the goal is understanding through uncoverage as opposed to coverage.

FIGURE 8.5 **A COMPARISON OF TEXTBOOK UNCOVERAGE AND COVERAGE**

Uncoverage	Coverage
The text serves as a resource and reference book for core inquiries and performances.	The text is the syllabus.
The main ideas suggest the kinds of performances for which the text can serve as one resource.	Assessment is viewed as a test based solely on what is stated in the textbook, often involving exclusive use of publisher-supplied tests and quizzes.
The text is construed as offering a helpful summary of "answers" to essential and unit questions, but where other answers will likely arise and be explored.	The students' job is to know the text; there are no overarching questions.
Sections of the text are read to support overall objectives, and not necessarily in the order of textbook pagination.	The text is read more or less with the intent of moving from cover to cover, with no clear overarching purpose.
The textbook is seen as one resource, supplemented as needed with primary-source materials.	Primary-source materials are not used.
The textbook provides a summary of desired learnings, for which active lessons, inquiries, and problems need to be found to lead to those summaries, in addition to lectures provided.	The textbook is viewed as lecture notes in a course dominated by lectures.

■ MISCONCEPTION ALERT

"I would *like* to go into greater depth, but I *have* to cover the content. This all takes so much time!" We believe this statement is plausible, but incorrect, and based on a misunderstanding about the relationship between results and teaching.

The root of the misunderstanding is the very real problem of having to make difficult choices and priorities in instruction. All teaching involves deciding in part what *not* to teach or emphasize. All teaching involves the feeling that we are making great sacrifices in likely and desirable understanding. No good teacher has ever complained of having too much time.

The "coverer" acts under an illusion, we believe: Textbook and test-driven instruction operate under an *untested* assumption that coverage maximizes test scores. But there is little evidence to support that view. In fact, the recent Third International Mathematical and Science Study (TIMSS) reveals that the opposite is true. So much is simply passed over without inquiry. Weaker students get confused and lost. Memory is overtaxed in the absence of central questions and ideas upon which organized inquiries and answers can be placed. Ultimately, coverage is based on an egocentric fallacy: If I talked about it and we read about it, they got it. (Or as a high school teacher we know once termed it, "teaching by mentioning it.")

Coverage involves a sad irony. In the absence of guiding questions, ideas, and methods that are meant to recur and inform all learning, students are left to guess about what is most important and what is going to be tested. Test results reflect this lack, even when the teaching is otherwise good.

The time-honored justification for this type of content coverage is that the syllabus and upcoming tests somehow demand it. Yet, teachers who make this claim rarely subject it to critical scrutiny. Should we think that teaching *worse* causes higher test scores? That's what is implied by their rationale. But let's stop and rethink this understanding:

■ *What methods of teaching ensure the greatest retention and recall of facts?* Surely, not one that is essentially composed of unconnected lectures and reading, with no prioritized knowledge containing overarching ideas or performance goals to guide note taking and studying. Recall depends on meaningful, prioritized ideas and uses to organize what is to be remembered.

■ *When we compare classrooms with the highest test scores and those with the lowest test scores, do we see more or less uncoverage and performance-based*

work in the former or the latter classrooms? In our experience, the best test scores correlate with more diverse, active, and intellectually provocative forms of instruction. The worst scores come from classrooms that rely on simplistic worksheets, homework problems having no larger purpose, and "copy down my notes from the blackboard" kinds of work. Recent research by Newmann (1997) and his colleagues supports the idea that more authentic work leads to better overall student performance.

■ *Has the teacher who covers only content conducted action research to justify that the coverage approach yields equally optimal results—to determine what forms and diversity of teaching maximize test scores?* Few teachers have ever done systematic research into their own practice. Rather, they grow comfortable with their habits, which invariably are developed with limited exposure to other ways of teaching. They fear that new approaches to instruction will jeopardize results. That is a *reasonable* fear, we allow, but not quite the same thing as their having evidence that their coverage approach is demonstrably the most effective.

Coverage thus works under a false logic, one that betrays a misconception about cause and effect in test validity. We can easily confuse *correlation* with *causality*: Short-answer test results correlate with important performance; teaching to items in a coverage way doesn't *cause* important performance.

For example, it would be ludicrous to practice the doctor's physical exam as a way of becoming fit and well. The reality is the opposite: If we are physically fit and do healthy things, we will pass the physical. The separate items on the physical are not meant to be taught and crammed for; rather, they serve as indirect measures of our normal healthful living. Multiple-choice answers *correlate* with more genuine abilities and performance; yet mastery of those test items does not *cause* achievement.

Lastly, standardized tests were not invented to be directly "taught to." Indeed, we corrupt their meaning if we teach to them. Rather, they were meant to be the easiest ways possible of testing classroom-developed knowledge and skills indirectly and inexpensively. (This point is discussed at greater length in Wiggins, 1998, Chapters 10 and 11.)

Although we have provided a set of criteria and guidelines for the elements of good design, we still need to explore curriculum design as a whole, whether the "whole" is a unit, course, or program. In particular, we must consider the organization and flow of curriculum relative to the need for uncoverage, iteration, and coherence from the learner's point of view. To do all this will require rethinking of what we mean by the "logic" of a course of study. To that challenge we now turn.

Endnotes

1. A unit built upon such a provocation is provided in the next chapter. In the *Teaching for Understanding* framework developed by the Harvard researchers at Project Zero, this idea is summed up as part of what they call "generative topics." Two of the four criteria are interesting and accessible to students, and interesting to the teacher (Wiske, 1997, pp. 63–64).

2. This unit won the 1993 Geraldine R. Dodge Curriculum Design Award in mathematics, sponsored by the Center on Learning, Assessment, and School Structure. It is used with the permission of CLASS.

9

IMPLICATIONS FOR ORGANIZING CURRICULUM

*Much
assistance in the selection of
appropriate material may be derived by
considering the eagerness and closeness of observation
that attend the following of a story or drama. Alertness of
observation is at its height whenever there is plot interest. Why? The
balanced combination of the old and new, of the familiar and the unexpected
. . . alternatives are suggested, but are left ambiguous, so that our whole being
questions: What happened next? Which way did things turn out?
When an individual is engaged in doing or making something, there is an analogous
situation. Something is going to come of what is present, but just what is doubtful. The
plot is unfolding toward success or failure, but just when or how is uncertain. Hence the keen
and tense observation that attends construction. [Even] when the subject matter is of
a more impersonal sort, the same principle of movement toward a dénouement may apply.
Mere change [in the experiences and situations] is not enough. The changes must
(like the incidents of a well-arranged story or plot) take place in a certain cumulative order.*
—DEWEY, 1933, P. 253

The Problem of Sequence

When important problems and questions anchor the curriculum, a clear overarching purpose for student learning and performance is established. Student engagement and rethinking takes priority when our curricular designs are guided by the criteria in WHERE, as illustrated in Chapter 8.

Designers, however, still need guidance on how to plan the sequence of individual units to lead to greater student understanding. So now we confront the question of sequence in the design of curriculum.

Our ongoing discussion of the need for constant rethinking suggests the challenge, as well as possible solutions. The typical organization of curriculum—the scope and sequence—provides a linear march through content topics; it is the logic of detailed and patient explanation (Facet 1). But our theory of understanding suggests that there are at least two other kinds of logic, reiterative in nature, that may more appropriately organize learning: the logic of narrative (Facet 2) and the logic of application/ task analysis (Facet 3).

Both alternative methods are time-honored ways we conceive of teaching. But they unfold in a different, nonlinear order. An explanation of supply and demand has a step-by-step sequence, very different from a case study about supply and demand; a lecture on the stock market has a different logic from the task of learning to invest funds. Even when content knowledge is the same, the order in which it is taught and learned will vary. The newspaper account and the movie portrayal of a crime are different.

The point we wish to make is that although a clear explanation is sometimes just what we need, the logics of narrative and of learning to perform may better suit coming to understand. We are not likely to thoroughly understand any subject that is new to us, based on one-shot explanations, no matter how clear and thorough. As the facets imply, when we understand, we go from surface to deep grasps of the same idea over time; we need to try to use the idea; we need to shift point of view, and so on. Indeed, the whole discussion of the facets should alert us to the constant need for any student, of any age and experience, to continually revisit and rethink key ideas.

Much student misunderstanding derives from a one-way, one-stop march through knowledge in textbooks, where teachers assume that because the explanation is clear—to them—it must be understandable to their students. The logic of understanding is thus more like intelligent trial and error than follow the leader. Though efficient, the logic of explanation can be ineffective. To teach the textbook only, instead of using it as a resource, may further exacerbate the natural problem of misunderstanding.

Form Follows Function

In light of how understanding unfolds, curricular design may be best construed through the phrase often heard in recent decades, but rarely honored: *the spiral curriculum*. The idea of the curriculum as a spiral is that big ideas, important tasks, and ever-deepening inquiry must *recur*, in ever-increasing complexity and through engaging problems and sophisticated applications if students are to understand them. Units and courses of study that are primarily fact or discrete-skill based can still be woven into such a framework, but their organization and sequencing needs to allow for constant rethinking of ideas and refining of performance.

To use an old architecture adage that applies to all design, including curricular design, "form follows function." If the goal (function) of curriculum is increased understanding, then a more spiral-like logic (form), may be necessary.

Two examples of this spiral at the unit level can be found in the unfolding of the archaeology and mathematics units discussed in Chapter 8. The same ideas and materials are revisited in more and more complex ways to arrive at sophisticated judgments and products. Similarly, to confront students with the poetry of e. e. cummings and the stories of James Joyce on the heels of more familiar forms is to cause a deeper understanding of earlier lessons in form, mechanics, and impact on the reader.

As mentioned in Chapter 4, Joseph Schwab (1978), a professor at the University of Chicago in the mid-20th century, proposed such a design approach for college courses. He called the approach the art of "eclectic," which he built around the goal of rethinking the same ideas. Students would consider psychological and social problems through the lens of different and competing theories (e.g., Freud, Skinner, and Adler), in which each theory took a turn seeming like the best one.

Or, consider a more spiral-like structure for an entire program. At the beginning of a series of photography courses one of us took, the instructor described the goals of the first course: learning the principles of composition in photography. For

example, to place the prominent feature in a picture, the students learned the "rule of thirds." In the advanced course, however, the instructor began with examples of pictures where these rules were broken to achieve dramatic effects. The unfolding of the courses illustrates a similar deliberate rethinking of the convention found in the poetry course.

Another function of curriculum is to be maximally engaging, and such rethinkings naturally enhance it. The problem of engaging students is not just a problem about content and teaching strategy, but also about structure and sequence. The predictable yet directionless form of typical scope and sequence, of clear and patient explanation, is less likely to suit the function of the student's needs for engagement than work focused on goals, as Dewey's opening chapter quote suggests.

Toward a More Natural Unfolding of Lessons

A curricular logic based on topical analysis and explanations in analytical order is so natural and familiar that we have a difficult time seeing its weaknesses. How can it be otherwise, we wonder? Start with the basics or elements—definitions, axioms, parts of speech—and build up the knowledge in a sequence of clear explanations. It seems so obviously the best way to manage learning.

And yet, that approach is not how we learned to raise children, tell jokes, understand our finances, learn violin using the Suzuki method, or gain proficiency in software. Nor is it the logic of how our favorite books unfold their story and the facts that make them up. In personal, civic, and professional adult life, we typically learn just enough things to accomplish something specific. For example, when learning a new software pro-

gram, most adults do not read the entire manual first. We begin at a simplistic level and develop increasing skill with repeated use as we tackle more sophisticated applications.

Understanding a subject is like such real-world proficiency. It is more like learning skills than facts, more like solving a complex crossword puzzle than memorizing vocabulary lists. We try out new ideas, try on new skills, rethink prior learnings, and thus constantly reassemble old ideas into new ones as we come to an understanding. Being taught the puzzle answers, like memorizing the vocabulary, in fact undercuts the understanding and transfer needed to master later linguistic challenges. In contrast, learning by using the logic of explanation best suits step-by-step tasks or analysis to help us clarify what we have already considered or experienced.

Circling back to previous ideas is not a waste of time. On the contrary, this work is how learners come to understand. Learning becomes more coherent as topics arise and re-arise naturally in response to questions, problems, results, inquiries, and reactions. The spirit is one of, "We began with a black-and-white statement and now must see the shades of gray." The sequence of work must cause this realization in students and not come from teacher pronouncements or from the textbook. In other words, the need and opportunity to rethink must arise out of the curricular structure, not the teacher's style or the learner's persistence in interrupting an otherwise unbroken march through content.

It is an all too common teacher misunderstanding to think that coverage is effective—that just because the subject is clear to the teacher, it will be clear to the students if laid out in efficient, logically ordered explanations. If misunderstandings are likely, if understanding requires shifts of perspective and rethinking, if understanding is revealed through student application and interpretation, then we should be wary of believing that teaching predominantly through explanation and its logic can yield understanding.

A Different Logic to Stories and Applications

To more easily rethink curricular unfolding, consider first the organization of a narrative. Stories rarely lay out all facts and ideas in a step-by-step fashion. A story is constructed using the logic of drama—suspenseful buildups, surprising twists and turns, and multiperspective accounts are routine, yet memorable to the reader. Stories are idiosyncratic, not generic, and any truth contained within them is implicit, not explicit. Though illogical and incomplete from an explanatory-analytic point of view, narratives are often more likely to engage the reader and far easier to recall than textbook accounts:

> We do not easily remember what other people have said if they do not tell it in the form of a story. . . . We hear, in the stories of others, what we personally can relate to by virtue of having in some way heard or experienced that story before (Schank, 1990, p. 83).

Problem-based learning (PBL), for example, is a narrative-based logic. To achieve more effective and engaged learning, PBL reverses the typical logic of instruction, which is explanation based. In PBL, students are thrust into problem situations immediately, just as readers are thrust into the middle of a story, from which they must learn their way out:

> Problem-based learning turns instruction topsy-turvy. Students meet an "ill-structured problem" before they receive any instruction (Stepien & Gallagher, 1993, p. 26).

So, too, with the case method in law and business schools. In all effective stories, there is a reversal of explanation logic:

> Narrative, whatever its medium—words, film, strip-cartoon—holds the interest of an audience by raising questions in their minds, and delaying the answers (Lodge, 1992, p. 14).

The logic of learning how to do things is also different from the logic of an explanation. Attempts to perform begin with a specific goal in mind, an end that shapes how the content is introduced and unfolds. People don't need the whole subject laid out to master a challenge; rather, they need specific knowledge tools to accomplish a specific task. The requirements of the task, not an outline of topics, supply the logic of instructional design.

Thus, a one-shot, step-by-step series of lessons explaining each piece of the automobile and its function prior to ever touching a car engine will not be the best way to make us fully understand the car, how it works, and how to fix it. Through coaching, trial, error, adjustment based on a constant focus on the narrower performance goal—a smooth-running engine—we gradually increase our abilities in auto maintenance and our understanding of cars. Application requires an iterative curriculum: We keep returning to the problems of fixing the engine in increasingly sophisticated ways. And much important teaching often occurs *after,* not before, student attempts to perform—when students are ready to hear and grasp its value.

A simple thought experiment in the teaching of history points out how structure might be rethought, *without* changing content, to tell a more insightful and coherent story from the student's point of view. By beginning history courses in a remote and distant past, unmoored from interests, overarching questions, and specific tasks, students are far more likely to be passive and in the dark. In reality, there is no story in the typical history textbook. There is just information laid out using narrative language on discrete topics.

If our goal is to have students understand historically, we might well begin and end in the *present* to better view the past in light of a more familiar present. We must at least ensure that we start with specific questions about the present to pursue in the past: Who are we? How did we get here? And we must make sure that in addition to reading stories, students construct them and perform other specific tasks that inform the unfolding—that they *do* history, not just read it contained in texts.

Suppose that a history course began with a two-week summary of the whole period of history to be covered. It was then followed by an uncovering of that summary during the rest of the year—in separate strands, moving from the present to the past and back again. It culminated in performance tasks based on questions from the teacher and student questions that arise from the summary and their experience in the present:

■ Where are we now? How did we get here? Who is the "we"? E pluribus unum?

■ Is history a history of progress? Are we better off?

■ Are we free? Are we freer? Again, who is the "we"?

■ How does your story illuminate the United States' story?

■ Whose story is the United States'? Whose story isn't getting told, and why? Has the story changed over time, and if so, why?

■ Can things be changed? Can you make a difference? Does history make a difference? Is history bunk? Or are those who ignore history condemned to repeat it?

The textbook, along with other primary and secondary material, would serve as a key resource—it is not to be confused with being the syllabus or the sole resource. The core content is thus resource material for addressing specific unit questions and essential questions. The particular strands and content chosen could vary from year to year and would be based on student interest and contemporary events. The movement would be logical though not necessarily chronological. (How sad to observe that many teachers don't take advantage of relevant current events in a history course because they don't fit the pages the class is on in the textbook!)

The following history unit and its culminating performance further the idea that the logic of coming to understand history can and should deviate from the logic of the textbook. The student must enter a provocative set of narratives, construct a narrative, and perform an authentic historical task, going backwards in time from the present. Here is the unit:

A Backward History Design Project
Essential Question: Whose story is it?
Unit Question: Is it true that "one man's revolutionary is another person's terrorist is a third person's criminal"?

1. Start with the Oklahoma City and World Trade Center bombings:

■ Look at a set of newspaper clippings chronologically.

■ What turned out to be true? Not true?

■ What do we know? What do we still not know?

2. Work on jigsaw projects to research other notable U.S. bombings and terrorist acts:

■ What have been the most notable or important acts or events? Is terrorism new? Worse? The same? Are students aware of the long history of U.S. terrorists' acts related to Puerto Rico, including an assault on the U.S. Congress?

■ What generalizations, if any, can be made about the rationale or motives of terrorists?

■ Leaving aside morality, is terrorism effective? What are the evidence and arguments pro and con?

■ What counterterrorism steps have been taken historically? Have they been effective?

■ What is the difference between terrorism and other criminal activity? Consider gangs or crimes like blackmail and rape. Is assassination terrorism?

■ Are economic embargoes a form of terrorism?

3. Compare terrorism to revolutionary behavior. Are these terms only a question of semantics and relative perspective? Consider these people and events:

■ The Boston Tea Party—the founding of the United States and the founding of other countries like Israel and France.

■ The Weathermen during the '60s and '70s.

■ Hamas, Sinn Fein, and Muslim militants in Turkey, Egypt, and Algeria.

■ The anarchists in our midst today: the Texas militia, the Posse Comitatus, and the unabomber.

4. Read John Locke's "Second Treatise on Government," which discusses the nature of rebellion and natural rights. How does Locke justify the legitimate overthrow of an unjust government?

5. Read Thoreau's "Essay on Civil Disobedience" and King's "Letter from Birmingham Jail." Then read Orwell's provocative essay on Gandhi.

Culminating Performance: Write a magazine article on the history of terrorism, back to the time of the founding of the United States, focusing on the unit question.

The Logic of Narrative: The Story Structure as a Curricular Design

> Narrative, whatever its medium, holds the interest of an audience by raising questions in their minds, and delaying the answers. . . . The questions are broadly of two kinds, having to do with causality (e.g., whodunit?) and temporality (what will happen next?).
>
> —Lodge, 1992, p. 14

Facet 2, interpretation, as well as common sense, suggests that a curriculum grounded in the structure, logic, and drama of stories offers the potential for more engagement, more deliberate rethinking (hence deeper understanding), and more

coherence in the overall design than does sole use of the logic of explanation.

The Presence of a Mystery or Dilemma

The most basic feature of all compelling stories is the presence of some mystery or dilemma; we are plopped into a specific world that has to be figured out. Instead of presenting a straightforward sequence of events, the story teller deliberately raises questions and delays answering them, while still teaching us about people, situations, and ideas along the way. This structure is also, not coincidentally, that of every successful computer simulation game. Think of a course designed to provide drama, to offer surprises, twists, and turns. Think of how your syllabus might be designed by Stephen King or Steven Spielberg to move back and forth between provoking thought and resolving questions. Any course can be designed to honor this logic if we work at it. For example, we know of a chemistry course taught entirely as forensics. Students must take the usual chemistry in the curriculum and use it to solve crimes. The teacher stages clues, and the students solve the cases.

User Friendly

Stories have to be not only engaging but also user friendly if they are to work for the audience. Stories need a coherent flow, or they end up confusing and disengaging. The "logic" is then conceived in terms of the *recipient's* need to be engaged, leading to the more deliberate construction of meaning. By thinking of our design as a story, we are more likely to avoid the boredom of schooling, the haphazardness of coverage, and the "I taught it but they didn't get it" syndrome. Stories also make learning easier because

memory works better when structured into narrative (see, for example, Schank, 1990; Bruner, 1990).

In a good story, events lead naturally to events, and questions lead naturally to answers and new questions, consistent with an overall plot provided by the designer-author. But stories derive their teaching value, in part, from another feature—drama or tension:

> A "story" (fictional or actual) involves an Agent who Acts to achieve a Goal in a recognizable Setting by the use of certain Means. What drives the story, what makes it worth telling, is Trouble: some misfit between Agent, Acts, Goals, Settings, and Means (Bruner, 1996, p. 94).

Thinking of curriculum as narrative helps us see why problem-based learning (PBL) works as an engaging and effective design, even in such abstract disciplines as chemistry and calculus—and why textbooks are so often dull. To understand, we need to want to understand, and a good story or task makes understanding more likely. Immersion in real problems involves the unfolding of a story. The work of involved students brings the story to fruition or dénouement; the students, in effect, become part of the story. PBL works well as a vehicle for developing uncoverage and understanding because its form suits its object. We often understand complex matters through stories, and we often reveal that we understand by our ability to tell meaningful but accessible stories.

A problem-based learning unit developed at the College of William and Mary, Center for Gifted Education (1997), provides a wonderful example of the drama and twists of fate that can be made part of a unit in science on ecosystems. Here is the first problem given to students early in the unit:

Julie and Josh Miller's grandfather has come back to Virginia for one of his periodic visits. When the family goes to Sam's Restaurant in the Phoebus section of Hampton, Grandfather Miller becomes very upset to find that sea trout is no longer on the menu.

"I came here to eat sea trout because Sam is the only one who can prepare it the way it should be cooked. Let me talk to Sam about this!" exclaims Grandfather Miller. . . .

Julie and Josh are understandably upset by these events. Wondering why sea trout is not available for their grandfather, they decide to investigate.

You are Julie's and Josh's science teacher, and they are your favorite students. They've come to ask for your help in the investigation. How can you help Julie and Josh?

After much inquiry, using the PBL questions—What do we know? What do we need to know? How can we find out?—students begin to explore and understand the problems of pollution in the Chesapeake Bay. Using firsthand and secondhand research, hearing from real experts in class, and performing experiments about salinity and algae, students see the story unfold—from different perspectives and with some twists and turns—and causing the key learnings in the middle school science curriculum to unfold. But the story has a nice dramatic twist: It turns out that Josh and Julie's father is a farmer, and there may be a correlation between fertilizer runoff from the farm and the problem in the bay that killed off the fish! Thus, the unit graphically underscores, in a way all students can appreciate, why we call it an *ecosystem*.

Again, we point out that the structure of the story, not only its content or the pedagogy involved, is different from the sequence of a unit developed through explanatory logic. In a more conventional treatment of the science material, few if any surprises would be involved in the textbook. Yet, we see how treating the student as a virtual participant in an unfolding story may well lead to more focused and engaged learning.

Even mathematics can be taught using narrative if we work at it. *Flatland* (Abbott, 1884/1963) remains a treasured story 100 years after it was written because it takes the subject of spatial dimensions and casts it as a dramatic and provocative story about a two-dimensional person's discovery of, and difficulty in believing in, a three-dimensional world.[1]

The history of non-Euclidean geometry, alluded to in earlier chapters, shows the tale to be more than fanciful. Correspondence reveals that one of the discoverers of non-Euclidean geometry was afraid to publish his findings for fear of being ridiculed (see, for example, Greenberg, 1972). Yet, few people are aware of this history. Imagine a unit on the problem of the parallel postulate and other geometries, beginning with excerpts from these letters set up as a PBL exercise: Who wrote them and what are they writing about? The answers to that mystery open up bigger mysteries about a key idea: Can there be other "spaces," and how do we know which one is ours? If students were introduced to mathematics using narrative more often—through cases and intellectual problems—more students would become interested in math, a vital aim. A recent television program and books on the discovery of a proof for Fermat's 200-year-old theorem shows how dramatic mathematical discovery, like any discovery, can be.[2]

There is, of course, an irony in calling for curriculum to be structured more like a story. As teach-

ers, we are trained to believe our job is to remove doubts and explain things. Teaching is meant to take away the deadends, false starts, and surprises of inefficient inquiry. But teaching engagingly and effectively for understanding often requires that we persist in asking questions, delaying or avoiding giving answers, confronting students with problems, and putting mysteries and the need to re-think things constantly before them. (A folksy indicator that we value such indirect and inefficient learning is that people who give away the ending to movies and stories are sometimes annoying. Well-intentioned teachers and textbook writers are often guilty of this without realizing it.)

Narrative and Questions

How might we tell more engaging, coherent, yet enabling stories from the learner's point of view, given a pre-existing set of content standards and textbook? What can we learn from the best storytellers about how to make curriculums more effective and engaging? Stories raise questions and delay answers. A practical way to cast the idea of curriculum as narrative, then, is to ensure that curriculums are built upon the logic of essential and unit *questions*, not the logic of published *results*.

The challenge is to map out the most natural and engaging flow of such questions and (delayed) answers, as we saw in the Chesapeake Bay problem. The science content provides the material for the story, not the structure. The content is uncovered by design in response to a provocative sequence of questions—questions and tasks framed to be mindful of the answers that need to emerge and tend to emerge when such challenges are posed.

The phrase, "one question naturally leads to another," catches the spirit of the proposed solutions and serves as the criterion and guideline for sequencing topics. Do the guiding questions for all units seem to suggest a natural flow of inquiry? Does it seem to the students that the next unit follows from the issues raised or knowledge gaps of the current unit? Then the logic of inquiry is guiding the design.[3]

An example in meteorology illustrates the endlessly diverse possibilities that the natural sequences of questions can provide. Instead of starting with definitions, laws, and an array of facts, we use questions designed to suggest inquiries that require key content. Why does the bathroom mirror fog when you shower? What prevents it from fogging and why? Is bathroom fog like real fog? Is a fog the same as a cloud or different? What causes each? As Dewey noted in the opening chapter quote, such problem-solving tasks create their own narrative tension.

Tension

Greater drama is made possible by considering the structure of the best stories. A story falls flat without some form of tension—Trouble with a capital T—as Bruner termed it. Kieran Egan has written extensively on curriculum as storytelling (Egan, 1986; Egan, 1997). He initially proposed that we think of teaching as more like storytelling than training, precisely because of its dramatic nature:

> A model for teaching that draws on the power of the story, then, will ensure that we set up a conflict or sense of dramatic tension at the beginning of our lessons and units. Thus, we create some expectation that we will satisfy at the end. It is this rhythm of expectation and satisfaction that will give us a principle for precisely selecting content. . . . We need, then, to be more conscious of the importance of beginning with a conflict or problem whose resolution at the end can set such a rhythm in motion (Egan, 1986, pp. 25–26).

The psychological movement, the heightening of engagement, is especially enabled by the key tension inherent in all children's stories. Such tension is the struggle between opposing forces, such as good and evil or old and young, that Egan terms "binary opposites." To maximize interest, the narrative we construct as teachers of *any* topic should focus on the inherent opposites—the plausible multiple perspectives of Facet 4—findable in all subjects. These opposites serve as "criteria for the selection and organization of content" (Egan, 1986, pp. 26–27).

Not only does the logic of a story better suit the needs of students for coherence and meaning, but that logic also calls into question a time-honored habit of organizing teaching as a movement from the simple to the complex:

> Ironically in the face of the presently dominant [views of teaching], it is the most important aspects of a topic that need to be brought to the fore if children are to understand it (Egan, 1986, p. 45).

Centering on a Big Idea

A good story centers on what is essential—a big idea, made concrete and virtually real. And it always attends to our need for affective involvement, a useful reminder about needlessly boring curriculums that ignore the connection of ideas to emotions.

The overall structure and direction for design that Egan (1986) initially proposed had five components:

1. Identifying importance
- What is most important about this topic?
- Why should it matter to children?
- What is affectively engaging about it?

2. Finding binary opposites
- What powerful binary opposites best catch the importance of the topic?

3. Organizing content into story form
- What content most dramatically embodies the binary opposites, in order to provide access to the topic?
- What content best articulates the topic into a developing story form?

4. Conclusion
- What is the best way of resolving the dramatic conflict inherent in the binary opposites?
- What degrees of mediation of those opposites is it appropriate to seek?

5. Evaluation
- How can one know whether the topic has been understood, its importance grasped, and the content learned (p. 41)?

Egan cautions us that casting issues, ideas, and controversies as binary opposites runs the risk of either-or thinking and other forms of simplistic presentation (such as we find in glib media accounts of national and international problems). But he argues that such a schema suits the mental needs of children, and in his later work, he stresses that stereotypes are avoidable through the critical discussion that occurs when the stereotypes are made explicit in the story (Egan, 1997, pp. 184–185).

To show the value in this way of thinking for all subjects, especially in the sciences where one might not expect to find it useful, Egan (1986) applies it to the teaching of arithmetic:

1. Identifying importance

What is important is that children understand the ingenuity of our decimal system. We will want to convey this as something wonderful, almost magic. . . .

2. Finding binary opposites

As our concern is to convey the ingenuity and wonder of the decimal system, we might choose the binary opposites of ingenuity and cluelessness.

3. Organizing content into story form

Our number sense is intuitive, but counting is learned. . . . [Egan goes on to use various stories and experiments to help students realize the abstraction of numbers and to show that without counting, our intuition would not take us far. The upshot is to show how only a few repeating counters can be used to count reliably large numbers of things and how place value helps us. Students would then apply the idea using a system of marbles or other objects to count phenomena.]

4. Conclusion

The conclusion should stress the basic ingenuity of our number system. The task for the teacher is in large part to make wonderful what has become routine. Or rather to uncover what wonder lies behind the routine.

5. Evaluation

There is a range of standard tests which can show whether the basic concept of placement in the decimal system has been mastered. What is more difficult to evaluate is whether or to what degree the magic of numbers has been felt by individual children. [Egan notes the importance of observing and recording evidence in support of that wonder] (pp. 76ff.).

Though Egan provides only sketches of what is possible, two important consequences of this approach stand out, reinforcing themes we have addressed throughout the book. First, skill is taught but in a wider intellectual context. Second, the goal is to tell a story that is likely to engage at many different levels, both cognitively and affectively. All designers of curriculums and units should try to be better storytellers in this sense.

The Logic of Application: Curriculum as Task Analysis

This discussion rejects the doctrine that students should first learn passively, and then, having learned, should apply knowledge. It is a psychological error. In the process of learning, there should be present, in some sense or other, a subordinate activity of application. In fact, the applications are part of the knowledge. For the very meaning of things known is wrapped up in their relationships beyond themselves. Thus, unapplied knowledge is knowledge shorn of its meaning.

—Whitehead, 1947, pp. 218–219

The logic of application derives its sequence from specific performance goals. In coaching, we organize a sequence backward from specific tasks and standards: Lessons are derived from desired results. Here Whitehead's maxim of "get your knowledge and use it quickly" always applies: We head right to the desired performance, even if it has to be in simplified or scaffolded form (e.g., T-ball for six-year-olds); we build up performance progressively; and we revisit the fundamentals as we do so.

Though the idea "get your knowledge and use it quickly" makes clear sense, many educators, habituated to textbook-driven learning, resist it. Many argue that "students need to learn all the basics before they perform" or that "inexperienced students aren't ready to do complex tasks." But consider how *unlikely* mastery of any performance would be if the performance were organized as mostly front-loaded knowledge taught in a linear scope and sequence. Imagine, for example, if the syllabus for a mock trial involved a linear march of didactic teaching through all relevant laws as codified in legislative archives, followed by a sequence of drills that went from the opening to the closing—without ever once involving students in complete preparation and execution of a trial plan until the end of instruction.

In short, educators wisely do not front-load all knowledge and discrete skills in performance-based instruction. Ski classes no longer require the learner to learn snowplows, stem christies, and other overly analytical approaches to build up performance; instead, the learner starts to parallel ski using short skis. Similarly, software manufacturers now provide tutorials and usage ideas in brief manuals, separate from the complete reference manual organized into topics analytically. We often ignore in practice the truism in the Chinese proverb: I hear, I forget; I see, I remember; I do, I understand.

The flip side of this iterative logic is also true. Coaches invariably revisit the basics with each new group, no matter how expert a student is—how to hold the instrument, how to pass and shoot, and how to sing from the diaphragm and not the throat. They do not think of this as time lost or coverage sacrificed because they know they will gain better results by embedding a review of the basics in the context of meaningful performance. It is understood that two kinds of learning by doing must keep occurring: Students must practice the new ideas in simplified drill or exercise form, and they must then practice using those discrete skills or moves in a more complex and fluid performance. Didactic teaching occurs *while* they play and *after* they play as a way of making the learning by doing more self-conscious and informed.

What is wanted, said Dewey (1933), is a logic like that in art:

> Practice, exercise, are involved in the acquisition of power, but they do not take the form of meaningless drill, but of practicing the *art*. They occur as part of the operation of attaining a desired end. . . . All genuine education terminates in discipline, but it proceeds by engaging the mind in activities worthwhile for their own sake (pp. 86–87) (emphasis in original).

This movement back and forth, from discrete learning to whole performance, from part to whole to part and back to whole again, is a familiar one to all performers in writing, the performing arts, and athletics. In acting, we rehearse a few lines of dialogue, then put them back into act 2, scene 4, and rehearse again, as needed. In writing, we fine-tune our story introductions, read the whole story to see if it works, then have the work peer edited. Alas, the introduction confuses the reader, so we work on it again. Similarly, in basketball, we practice shooting and dribbling in isolation, work on drills that combine the two, then have a controlled scrimmage to see if we can put everything together in context. On the basis of the feedback from results in the whole performance, we go back to drillwork to overcome misunderstandings, bad habits, or forgotten lessons. Work on specific elements, chunks of performance, and performance as a whole constantly recycles. The work is structured as many sequences of model, practice, feedback, practice, perform, and feedback, followed by more such loops as the complexity of each exercise increases toward the complexity of the whole performance.

The Logic of Backward Design

The logic of application is another way of describing backward design discussed at length in Chapter 2 and throughout the book. The designer begins with the end in mind and maps back from the desired result to the present to determine the best way to reach the goal. Sequence for the student is established by asking, What is the most logical (i.e., effective and efficient) way to reach the performance goal?

This approach to curricular design also calls for ongoing task analysis. We design toward standards, fleshing out assessment and lessons as we go. The performance targets then serve to guide both teaching and learning. Without such clear performance goals, neither the teacher-designer nor performer-student can work on task analysis. In such a situation, teachers will resort to the sequence provided by the textbook, and students will be basically directionless and purposeless by not being able to answer, Where am I headed? What is most important for me to learn, and why?

An example of such task analysis is planning a big meal, such as Thanksgiving dinner. One starts with the time the turkey dinner must be ready, say 5 p.m. Then, one plans backward to the starting time and the order of events—in short, the most efficient way to have the stuffed bird, gravy, creamed onions, sweet potatoes, beans, cranberry relish, and cornbread all ready at the same time. What is a good recipe, in fact, if not an already worked out backward design of a meal?

There is a mature stage beyond using recipes, of course. From recipes, we graduate to an understanding of how recipes work—how to create recipes. We move from apprenticeship to creative application on the basis of understanding food, chemistry, and how ingredients work together. In the curriculum, it is vital to clarify that such performance is the goal. We need to beware of overreliance on recipes, whether in writing, mathematics, or cooking:

> Recipes, which began as such useful things, have become tyrants, leaving even the most well-meaning cook unsure of his own instincts. A slavish devotion to recipes robs people of the kind of experiential knowledge that seeps into the brain. . . . Most chefs are not fettered by formula; they've cooked enough to trust their taste. Today that is the most valuable lesson a chef can teach a cook (O'Neill, 1996, p. 52).

Here again, such sophisticated learning is nonlinear. An accomplished cook has developed such instincts through intelligent trial and error, not a unidirectional march through recipes. Recipe-driven instruction, if carried too far, would inhibit a more sophisticated and fluent understanding.

But a handed-down task analysis recipe is still superior to the purposeless structure of many academic courses. The goal of a good recipe writer, after all, is to enable others to perform. By contrast, most academic courses, organized around the content to be covered, are equivalent to giving cooks mere descriptions of finished meals. Such information, while complete in terms of the content, offers no explicit help in using the knowledge to accomplish cooking goals.

This approach may help explain why some teachers struggle to find authentic performance tasks for their content and to make their instruction more inquiry- and performance-based. The context-less and goal-less content in textbooks makes imagining or designing tasks difficult, by virtue of both form and content. The books are not written to support specific performance goals; they often end up serving *teacher* explanation, not student inquiry and performance. Such a lack is another reason that effective teaching for understanding requires that we first identify target performances before we specify how and what we will teach. In the absence of such target performances, teachers will be unclear about how to treat the textbook as a resource for performance and easily succumb to turning the textbook into the syllabus.

Building upon the logic of reiteration for performance is relatively new in academic content areas. One hundred years ago, writing was still taught primarily through learning grammar, syntax, parsing, and reading good writing. One supposedly learned to write by first learning its elements intellectually. The modern writing process is more faithful to the act of mature writing because it gets students going right from the start, even if they haven't yet mastered all the mechanics. We now understand that the act of writing provides the context for helping students develop and revise their ideas, as well as for teaching them the necessary conventions.

Through the writing process and using the teacher as coach in the skill areas, we are well on our way to coaching for skilled performance. But with the goal of understanding big ideas, we are back in the premodern era: talking and reading, leading somehow to a step-by-step assembly of abstract ideas in the student's mind. Ideas, like skills, require practice in use to be understood, yet we still organize the teaching of understanding as if the learnings were merely facts to be stored away for recall—as if reading an encyclopedia from cover to cover were sufficient to understand all subjects.

An example of deriving a logic of inquiry from essential questions and culminating tasks, whereby a student recapitulates the tasks of the historian, can be seen in the following culminating performance task. The task is for our course and is organized around questions and backward design:

Performance Task: Design a History Text
Part I: Assigning the Performance Task
You and your student colleagues (groups of six to eight) have been asked, along with other groups, to write a U.S. history textbook for middle school students. The publishers demand two things above all else: that the book hit the most important facts and ideas, and that it seem relevant to middle school students.

Because of your expertise in 18th century U.S. history, you will propose a chapter on the 18th century. The publishers want to be sure that you have covered all the most important elements, so they have asked you and your colleagues to fill in an "importance" chart for each of the three sources of history: events, people, and ideas (see Figure 9.1 on p. 148). By filling in the charts, your group will be responsible for deciding three different kinds of importance:

■ Which events, persons, or ideas are most important?
■ Which of the three *sources* of history—events, people, and ideas—is most important?
■ Which of the six history *categories*—arts, economics, military, politics, social, and science and technology—is most important?

FIGURE 9.1 **"IMPORTANCE" CHARTS FOR A HISTORY UNIT**

SOURCE: EVENTS

DEGREE OF IMPORTANCE	LIST OF EVENTS BY CATEGORY					
	Arts	Economics	Military	Politics	Social	Science and Technology
#1 in Importance						
#2 in Importance						
#3 in Importance						

SOURCE: PEOPLE

DEGREE OF IMPORTANCE	LIST OF PEOPLE BY CATEGORY					
	Arts	Economics	Military	Politics	Social	Science and Technology
#1 in Importance						
#2 in Importance						
#3 in Importance						

SOURCE: IDEAS

DEGREE OF IMPORTANCE	LIST OF IDEAS BY CATEGORY					
	Arts	Economics	Military	Politics	Social	Science and Technology
#1 in Importance						
#2 in Importance						
#3 in Importance						

You will also be expected to make some judgments about your current textbook. Therefore, you must be prepared to justify your choices of importance in a letter to the editors. How will you do it? What patterns might all the charts provide as an answer? How does your textbook emphasize what is important? Are the authors' decisions justified? What about other textbooks?

By the due date, you should have completed the following activities:

■ Divided up the responsibilities in your group so that the three sources of history charts can be efficiently filled in.

■ Coded each of the three charts and answered questions (see Part II below).

■ Filled in a group chart based on a group consensus (see Figure 9.2 on p. 150).

■ Agreed on your book title and subtitles for the 18th century chapter and its different sections; designed a book cover.

■ Picked two or three reporters to give a brief summary of your work and judgments about importance for the publisher (i.e., teacher and class) to hear.

Part II: Coding Your Charts to Determine "What *Is* History?"

After you have decided on the most important stories for 18th century U.S. history, consider the following questions:

■ *Is history predictable and linear?* Or chaotic and discontinuous? Do people determine history— or does history happen in spite of the best-laid plans? Do ideas determine actions or vice versa? Is history evolutionary or revolutionary? Code your three source charts as follows:

❑ Put an **A** by those *events* that were accidents, and a **D** by those that were deliberately caused by a person or group.

❑ Put a **B** by those *people* who were before their time, and an **O** by those who were of their time.

❑ Put an **E** by those *ideas* that were evolutionary and an **R** by those that were revolutionary.

■ *What is the relevance of your choices?* Why should a middle schooler care about your choices today? In general, are the same sources and categories from the 18th century charts the most important in 1993? Explain. If not, why not? Are there completely new sources and categories for understanding modern history than had existed or had influenced the 18th century? Include your answers in your group report.

■ *Whose story is it?* From what historical point of view is your own textbook written? Find at least two events, people, or ideas of importance that the authors either left out, overemphasized, or underemphasized. In general, does the book emphasize more the role of ideas, people, or events? Which category do they most emphasize? Give evidence.

The Logic of Process Versus Products

Whether we think more like storytellers or coaches, the problem of sequence is worsened by the common tendency to teach the textbook. A textbook is like an encyclopedia or almanac, an analytically organized account of adult knowledge in a field of study. But although the textbook seems exhaustive, it only

FIGURE 9.2 **GROUP "IMPORTANCE" CHART**

Area	Item or Person of Most Importance
Event	
Person	
Idea	
Category	
Source	

provides a series of distilled content. It is a catalog of summary information—a reference book.

As with an encyclopedia or almanac, therefore, it doesn't follow that we should teach the textbook from page to page. Learning from only the summaries of what is known in a field is like learning baseball from newspaper box scores, law from only the final written legislation, or meteorology from old weather reports. Worse, the sequence of such products is ill-suited for developing understanding. The logic derives from a catalog of the completed content instead of from the needs of learners to ponder, question, explore, and apply the knowledge.

A Need for the Story Behind the Results

To understand any set of results, we need the story behind it. How did the baseball game unfold? How did the law come into being? Why is it foggy? Is such fog predictable? How does it happen? What were the decisive moments, by what process did the results happen, and how should they be interpreted? *These* are our unanswered questions of results. A

curriculum should be organized to pursue our questions, not simply catalog what is known. That process requires not just different content but a different structure to curriculum—more akin to narrative than to an almanac. Teaching the textbook by itself, in the order of its pages, can as little cause understanding as teaching the dictionary can cause understanding of language and use.

John Dewey, more than any other writer in the history of education, grasped the unwitting harm in teaching the residue of other people's learnings in a sequence logical to the writer and explainer only. The adult educator, Dewey (1916) argued, is constantly prone to a misunderstanding that the content and organization suitable for experts are best for novices:

There is a strong temptation to assume that presenting subject matter in its perfected form provides a royal road to learning. What more natural than to suppose that the immature can be saved time and energy, and be protected from needless error by commencing where competent inquirers have left off? The outcome is written large in the history of education. Pupils begin their study . . . with texts in which the subject is organized into topics according to the order of the specialist. Technical concepts and their definitions are introduced at the outset. Laws are introduced at an early stage, with at best a few indications of the way in which they were arrived at. . . . The pupil learns symbols without the key to their meaning. He acquires a technical body of information without ability to trace its connections [to what] is familiar—often he acquires simply a vocabulary (p. 220).

In other words, from the learner's point of view, the linearity and vocabulary-laden quality of finished explanation are illogical for learning what is new, problematic, and opaque:

Every subject in the curriculum has passed through—or remains in—what may be called the phase of "anatomical" method: the stage in which understanding the subject is thought to consist of multiplying distinctions . . . and attaching some name to each distinguished element. In normal growth, specific properties are emphasized and so individualized only when they serve to clear up a present difficulty (Dewey, 1933, p. 127).

Both the complexity and sequence of knowledge are parceled out more carefully, in other words, when teachers provide students with performance goals and questions that move the purpose beyond coverage and recall. The finished results must be uncovered in yet another sense: made less finished, more crude, more informal—in the same way the cookbook analyzes the finished meal into its ingredients—so that students can more easily understand what the final knowledge helps accomplish and how it came to be.

Overarching demands of performance and inquiry alter the sequence, precision, and pace of

knowledge introduction. Think of the difference in software between the user manual and a comprehensive reference book on all topics related to the software, often put into separate books for users. Would-be performers need a logic that postpones a thorough march through all features, facts, and formal vocabulary in favor of a sequence derived from new user needs. The same is true in narrative: The author does not first lay out every detail about characters, scene, and plot in analytic order as a precondition of our following the story. Facts and generalizations are introduced as appropriate to the story's direction and drama. As we noted in the previous chapter, this approach is what the case and PBL methods do: postpone a great deal of teaching and formal summaries of knowledge until learning and attempts to perform have occurred.

Dewey's genius grasped the educational principle underlying such sequences. Coming to understand an established idea in school must be made more like discovering a *new* idea than like hearing adult knowledge explained point by point. We learn complex and abstract ideas through a zigzag sequence of trial, error, reflection, and adjustment. As the facets tell us, the student needs to interpret, apply, see from different points of view, and so forth—all of which imply different sequences than those found in a catalog of existing knowledge.[4] We cannot fully understand an idea until we retrace, relive, or recapitulate some of its history—how it came to be understood in the first place. The young learner should be treated as a discoverer, even if the path seems inefficient. That's why Piaget (1973) argued that "to understand is to invent."

Efficient summary explanations are only effective when we already know a great deal or have a

specific need. Those situations are when the organization and approach of the encyclopedia are most useful. Then the logic of explanation helps us find what we need. But when we do not yet know much about the subject, when we lack an interest in the subject, or when the encyclopedia summary is easily misunderstood and abstract because of the absence of prior experience or future performance aims, the alphabetic and analytic structure of the encyclopedia makes it seem without direction and meaning.

Geometry, like all mathematics subjects, has been traditionally taught using a logic based on the logic dictated by a sequence of proofs: One begins with postulates and definitions, working through the most basic to the most complex theorems. This sequence seems so obvious that an alternative approach to organizing teaching is difficult to imagine.

Yet, René Descartes, the father of modern analytic geometry as well as modern philosophy, thought the normal explanatory logic approach to teaching and sequencing geometry as a catalog of results to be downright sneaky and misleading. Studying finished theorems in deductive order hides the fact that *the results were derived by completely different methods—methods far simpler to use than is suggested by studying the final products.* This recognition led Descartes (1628/1961) to a cynical conclusion:

> Indeed, I could readily believe that this mathematics was suppressed by [the Greek mathematicians] with a certain pernicious craftiness, just as we know many inventors have suppressed their discoveries, being very much afraid that to publish their method, since it is quite easy and simple, would make it seem worthless. And I believe they

preferred to show us in its place, as the product of their art, certain barren truths which they cleverly demonstrate deductively so that we should admire them [Note: Descartes was guilty of the same crime in his analytic geometry, as history and his own writing reveal.] (p. 160).

Indeed, a highly successful software program and a discovery-method textbook use this approach to teach geometry (see, for example, Serra, 1989). Though inductive or discovery-based instruction has sometimes been overdone or mishandled, its reasonableness is clear: Students will better understand results if they learn how the results were derived and why they were sought.

Rethinking as Rediscovery

The discovery method has its roots in a fascinating theory of curriculum that has waxed and waned in importance, called "recapitulation."[5] As the term suggests, the theory argued that to best understand a subject, the student should recapitulate the original discovery and development of the knowledge we want them to learn. In other words, rather than using a logic of results to guide scope and sequence, we should use more of a logic of efficient (re-)discovery.

In light of the discussion in this chapter, the theory has an obvious plausibility. If the aim of curriculum is to make adult knowledge accessible to the student, the challenge is not merely to provide a simple summary of what we know. The student must come to see the value and verify the correctness of the knowledge—a scaffolded version of what the original knowledge creators did. Thinking of curriculum as a sequence of stories to enter or tasks to master can make that more likely.

Unfortunately, the theory of recapitulation, which seemed so promising as a way to honor developmentalism and the student's need to be more active, yielded a rigid and eccentric system at the turn of the last century (Gould, 1977). Yet, modern developmental psychology sprang from the idea, and constructivism represents one of its most important modern guises. A new form of recapitulation, grounded in the development of linguistic and philosophic tools, has been proposed by Egan (1997).

The Spiral Curriculum

As we noted at the chapter's start, this way of thinking can be understood as embodiments of the spiral curriculum. The idea was championed by Bruner; first articulated by Dewey; and rooted in a long philosophical and pedagogical tradition running back through Piaget, G. Stanley Hall, and the recapitulationists, and further back to Hegel and Rousseau. But few curriculums have been built to embody it. The scope-and-sequence approach is still typically done as a linear parceling out of topics.

Bruner (1960) popularized the ideal of the spiral curriculum with his stark postulate that "any subject can be taught effectively in some intellectually honest form to any child at any stage of development" (p. 33). It is, as he said, a "bold" hypothesis, but central to a coherent education for rethinking and eventual understanding:

> The foundations of any subject may be taught to anybody of any age in some form. Though the proposition may be startling at first, its intent is to underscore an essential point often overlooked in the planning of curricula. It is that the basic ideas

at the heart of all science and mathematics and the basic themes that give form to life and literature are as simple as they are powerful. To be in command of these basic ideas, to use them effectively requires a continual deepening of one's understanding of them that comes from learning to use them in progressively more complex forms. *It is only when such basic ideas are put in formalized terms as equations or elaborated verbal concepts that they are out of reach of the young child, if he has first not understood them intuitively and had a chance to try them out* (pp. 12–13) (emphasis in original).

The spiral image guides the teacher in making the student's experience continually developmental while also enabling the student *from the outset* to encounter what is essential. An explanatory logic is deductive; a spiral logic is inductive, as the Bruner quote suggests. The issue is one of timing, not exclusion: Formal explanations come *after* inquiry, not before (or in place of) inquiry.

Dewey (1938) first used the analogy of the spiral to describe how subject matter should be organized to move from problem to problem, while causing knowledge to increase in depth and breadth. In this way, coursework could develop student thinking and interest, but do so purposefully and systematically, pointing toward the full fruits of each discipline.

The task was to move back and forth between the known and the problematic; otherwise, "no problems arise, while problems are the stimulus to thinking" (p. 79). The teacher's task was to construct a genuinely "educative experience" out of authentic contexts—the result of which was that learning should end in, as it does for the scholar, "the production of new ideas." The new facts and ideas "become the ground for further experiences in

which new problems are presented. *The process is a continual spiral*" (p. 79) (emphasis in original).

Ralph Tyler, Dewey's student and the dean of modern student assessment, underscored in his seminal brief book on design, *Basic Principles of Curriculum and Instruction* (Tyler, 1949), the need to think about curricular matters from the perspective of desired outcomes and the learner's needs. Indeed, more than anyone, Tyler laid out the basic principles of backward design. He proposed three criteria for effective organization—*continuity, sequence,* and *integration*—to show how the logic of curriculum should suit the learner's, not the experts', sense of order:

> In identifying important organizing principles, it is necessary to note that the criteria, continuity, sequence, and integration apply to the experiences of the learner and not to the way in which these matters may be viewed by someone already in command of the elements to be learned. Thus, continuity involves the recurring emphasis in the learner's experience upon these particular elements; sequence refers to the increasing breadth and depth of the learner's development; and integration refers to the learner's increased unity of behavior in relating to the elements involved (p. 96).

Tyler warns that such common organizing approaches as marching through chronology in history do *not* pass the test of being most helpful to the novice learner. A logical-to-the-learner ordering of schooling must make possible increasing breadth of application, increasing range of activities, description followed by analysis, specific instances followed by broader and broader principles, and the building of a unified worldview out of discrete parts. Moving toward a curriculum design approach that attempts to build in a logic of inquiry, rethinking, and application can better honor that idea.

The Spiral Through the Facets of Understanding

> Children rarely [are provided work in] redefining what has been encountered, reshaping it, reordering it. The cultivation of reflectiveness is one of the great problems one faces in devising curricula: how to lead children to discover the powers and pleasures that await the exercise of retrospection.
> —Bruner, 1973a, p. 449

The six facets of understanding can help us imagine a practical structure for incorporating such structured rethinking and spiraling. One way to realize the idea is to routinely build in reflection on prior learning by moving across the six facets within and across units. An effective way to raise important questions, keep them in view, and cause rethinking by design is to build units and groups of units out of loops back and forth across the various facets. Examples in this section suggest some possibilities. The numbers in parentheses refer to the six facets: 1 = explanation, 2 = interpretation, 3 = application, 4 = perspective, 5 = empathy, 6 = self-knowledge.

Interpretation-Application-Explanation (2-3-1)

Students confront data or experiences needing interpretation. By applying their ideas in diverse contexts, they develop a refined and thorough explanation of what they have learned and link it to core content knowledge. Here are some beginning ideas:

■ Test a theory of friendship against different "Dear Abby" scenarios.

■ Apply the theory of physics to the practice of physics. Build a balsa bridge or M&M's container to specifications in which the situational demands require adjustments to the mathematically predicted answers.

■ Consider this statement from a sign on a water tower: "Yarmouth Public Works: One Million Gallons of Fresh Water for Our Town." Is this statement plausible? How can we prove that the tower holds that much water?

Interpretation-Self-Knowledge-Perspective-Interpretation (2-6-4-2)

Students move back and forth between having to interpret events or ideas and arguing for their importance—why, how, and what of it? They also consider the historical origins, contexts of the theories in question, different perspectives, and their own biases—culminating in full-blown analysis. Here are examples of where to start:

■ The facts and causes of the '60s versus the meaning of the '60s (oral history).

■ Evolution versus creationism, and the extent to which it is a debate about science and meaning.

■ The role of key analogies and metaphors in science, and the power and limits of such metaphors.

Application-Perspective-Explanation (3-4-1)

The student develops a working hypothesis, based on the evidence and argument to date and on prior beliefs. Through materials, class discussion, and role-play, the design of the work injects numerous new and different plausible perspectives into the conversation. Students must now fully develop, test, and modify their theory, as appropriate, in light of the new points of view. Here are some ideas:

■ Study the American Revolution, using British and French texts.

■ Read *Flatland*; do "taxicab" or "walkway" geometry (the geometry of city streets or of inside buildings); review the criticisms of Euclid's postulates; and consider alternate theories of space.

■ Read short stories such as "The Lottery" and "The Stranger," which provoke rethinking of social norms, customs, and habits.

Interpretation-Empathy-Interpretation-Perspective-Interpretation (2-5-2-4-2)

Students read as well as construct narratives of real or fictional events and test the interpretation against the diverse experiences, values, points of view, and narratives of others. Here are examples:

■ Compare *The Three Little Pigs* with *The Real Story of the Three Little Pigs* by A. Wolf.

■ As part of a foreign policy simulation, translate a passage containing numerous colloquialisms and distinctively Spanish experiences from Spanish to English.

■ Beginning with the textbook account of World War II, interview veterans, including Japanese-Americans and Germans, then propose revisions to the textbook.

Interpretation-Explanation-Empathy-Explanation (2-1-5-1)

Students study data and develop theories on the causes of poverty, then take oral histories of poor people and engage in a simulation game about poverty and wealth. Their original thesis is rethought as needed.

Criteria for Designing a Sequence for Learning

Regardless of how literally or figuratively we take the idea of narrative, application, and spiral, any organization and sequence of work must ultimately meet different criteria. The organization must have

■ *An engaging and coherent unfolding of topics that seems logical and sensitive to learners.* Resist the urge to front-load too much information. Rather, immerse the student in stories or performance needs that give rise to the need for focused and enabling teaching and coaching along the way. As in problem-based learning curriculums, try to imagine cases, vignettes, and inquiries that might serve as the focal point for each unit.

■ *Reiterations and rethinkings of key ideas and skills.* Organize around tasks that constantly call for and require core knowledge, like a coach does.

■ *A curriculum construed as a narrative, with each unit being a chapter.* What might the titles be? How might you develop a storyline and fashion titles to maximize interest and natural-to-the-learner unfolding of the story?

■ *Some "hook" to maximize student interest and persistence.* Build in drama in the unfolding of lessons and ensure that interesting and thought-provoking surprises are included in how ideas are presented and how needed rethinking is made obvious.

■ *Flexibility with clear goals.* Build in room to change course resulting from unanticipated difficulties, emerging questions, and student performance results, without losing sight of core objectives. Use unit questions to build the outline and stay focused, regardless of interesting diversions based on student interests and responses.

We have considered the design elements of an instructional unit (using WHERE), and we have considered the overall coherence and flow of the design. What, then, should we consider as users of the design? What kinds of considerations go into teaching for understanding that deserve attention up front—issues that may well affect our design as we consider the needs of the design users (teachers and learners). To those pedagogical considerations we now turn.

Endnotes

1. The story builds upon all six facets of understanding. Beyond explaining the geometry involved and the application of it to the demands of the story, we are made to empathize with Mr. A Square, we must shift perspective twice—as he confronts a world of one and three dimensions—and we must confront our own prejudices in a variety of ways. Instead of a dry, linear treatment of dimensionality, we get a morality play: The now-wiser lineperson cannot convince his two-dimensional friends that he is anything but crazy or dangerous. We are likewise made to wonder if our own failure to see in more than three dimensions may be equally narrow minded.

2. The NOVA episode is called "The Proof," and a recent book is titled *Fermat's Enigma* (Singh, 1997).

3. For background reading on a logic of inquiry, see Collingwood (1939), Gadamer (1994), and Bateman (1990).

4. Compare to Popper's (1968) discussion on all scientific and philosophic inquiry as intelligent trial and error.

5. For a history of the idea, see Gould (1977) and Wiggins (1987b).

IMPLICATIONS FOR TEACHING

> *Americans
> hold the notion that good teaching
> comes through artful and spontaneous
> interactions with students during lessons. . . . Such views
> minimize the importance of planning increasingly effective
> lessons and lend credence to the folk belief that good teachers are born,
> not made. . . . Our biggest long-term problem is not how we teach now but
> that we have no way of getting better.*
> —STIGLER & HIEBERT, 1997, P. 20

THE BACKWARD APPROACH TO DESIGN SUSPENDS instructional planning—the development of specific lessons and selection of teaching strategies—until the last phase of the process. Though such an approach runs counter to the habits of many educators, the delay should make sense to the reader in light of what we have said thus far. For until we have specified the targeted understanding, the assessment tasks implied, and the enabling knowledge and skill necessary to master such tasks and display understandings, a discussion of learning activities and teaching strategy is premature. Teaching "moves" must be made in light of our goals and what they require.

Historically, U.S. education has minimized the role of planning and design in teaching. The frenetic pace of daily school schedules, the demands of nonteaching duties, and the general lack of time reserved for planning (within and beyond the teaching day), make it difficult for educators to engage in substantive curricular planning and design work, especially with colleagues. These realities are in contrast to the practices in some other countries:

During their careers, Japanese teachers engage in a relentless, continuous process of improving their lessons. . . . A key part of this process is their participation in "lesson study groups." Small groups of teachers meet regularly, once a week for about an hour, to plan, implement, evaluate, and revise lessons collaboratively. Many groups focus on only a few lessons over the course of the year with the aim of perfecting these (Stigler & Hiebert, 1997, p. 20).[1]

Good teaching is dependent upon good design, in other words. Until we are more comfortable with designing complex learning for uncoverage, and thus familiar with the kinds of instruction needed to develop deeper understandings, our teaching strategies are likely to remain rooted in traditional coverage, activity-based instruction, or the coaching of skill.

But good design and good teaching are dependent upon clear purposes. Teaching for understanding is not the same thing as teaching for skill or recall of facts. Clarity about different teaching purposes and the designs that best support those purposes can also better inform teaching. We have found it helpful to list the key instructional moves under the three broad categories of teaching types derived from Adler (1982) in *The Paideia Proposal:* didactic (or direct) instruction, coaching of skills, and facilitation (maieutics, as he terms it). Figure 10.1 shows the "three columns" in Adler's original proposal; Figure 10.2 (see p. 160) shows how we relate them to student and teacher actions. Note that the three columns in the Paideia proposal explicitly link educational aims and teaching means.[2] And understanding as a goal is explicitly distinguished from knowledge and skill.

Understanding is developed through discussion, not instruction. Socratic seminar, using primary texts or experiences, is how learning for understanding must be explicitly designed, according to the Paideia group.

To talk at great length about teaching for understanding would take us too far afield in a book about design. Nor are we advocating that all schools should construe all teaching for understanding as requiring Socratic seminar. There are other appropriate methods and dozens of wonderful books and programs on effective teaching, including new books on teaching for understanding, that readers should consult (see, for example, Wiske, 1997; White & Gunstone, 1992; Saphier & Gower, 1997; Marzano & Pickering, 1997). But the need to challenge unthinking teaching habits is central to our message because many common teaching moves

FIGURE 10.1 **THE THREE COLUMNS OF THE PAIDEIA PROPOSAL**

Acquisition of Organized Knowledge	**Development of Intellectual Skills**	**Enlarged Understanding of Ideas and Values**
by means of	*by means of*	*by means of*
Didactic Instruction	Coaching, Exercises, and Supervised Practice	Maieutic or Socratic Questioning and Active Participation

Source: Adler (1982), p. 23.

FIGURE 10.2 **TEACHING TYPES**

What the Teacher Uses	What Students Need to Do
Didactic/Direct Instruction -	*Receive, take in, respond:*
Demonstration/modeling	Observe, attempt, practice, refine
Lecture	Listen, watch, take notes, question
Questions/convergent	Answer, give responses
Coaching -	*Refine skills, deepen understanding:*
Feedback/conferencing	Listen, consider, practice, retry, refine
Guided practice	Revise, reflect, refine, recycle through
Facilitative/Constructivist/Reflective - - - - - - - - - - - - -	*Construct, examine, extend meaning:*
Concept attainment	Compare, induce, define, generalize
Cooperative learning	Collaborate, support others, teach
Discussion	Listen, question, consider, explain
Experimental inquiry	Hypothesize, gather data, analyze
Graphic representation	Visualize, connect, map relationships
Guided inquiry	Question, research, conclude, support
Problem-based learning	Pose/define problems, solve, evaluate
Questions (open ended)	Answer and explain, reflect, rethink
Reciprocal teaching	Clarify, question, predict, teach
Simulation (e.g., mock trial)	Examine, consider, challenge, debate
Socratic seminar	Consider, explain, challenge, justify
Writing process	Brainstorm, organize, draft, revise

support goals other than understanding, and excessive didacticism—documented in every major critique of secondary schooling in the past 20 years—undercuts the questioning, research, discussion, and performance needed to develop understanding.

The aim of this chapter is to offer some general instructional guidelines relating to what we have said about backward design for understanding. We will examine

■ The need to think of teaching for understanding as involving less teaching and more questioning.

■ The importance of frequent checks for understanding, in light of the problems of misconception, predictable misunderstanding, and apparent understanding.

■ Application of the six facets to understanding *people* (in the context of teaching) as well as ideas.

■ Ways to develop and reinforce those habits of mind that are key to the development of understanding.

We conclude the chapter by turning the light from students to ourselves as educators. What habits of mind do we need in teaching for understanding, and what blind spots do we need to overcome?

Toward More Learning Through Less Teaching

> Teachers . . . are particularly beset by the temptation to tell what they know. . . . Yet no amount of information, whether of theory or fact, in itself improves insight and judgment or increases ability to act wisely.
>
> —Gragg, 1940

This quotation comes from a Harvard Business School publication, in which the rationale for the case method in business school is offered. Its title says it all: "Because Wisdom Can't Be Told."

At its most basic, teaching for understanding means, ironically, less teaching. As Sizer (1984) put it:

> Understanding . . . [is] the development of powers of discrimination and judgment. . . . Understanding is more stimulated than learned. It grows from questioning oneself and being questioned by others (pp. 116–117).

Much of understanding is about thoughtfulness, and thoughtfulness is awakened more than trained—developed by design, not exhortation. In teaching for understanding, students must come to

see that understanding means that *they* must figure things out, not simply wait for and write down teacher explanations. That effort requires teachers to alter not only the curriculum (as discussed in previous chapters) but also their teaching style. Constructivist approaches become more vital: The learner must make meaning of ideas, not just receive explanations from teachers, if complex ideas are to be understood (Brooks & Brooks, 1993).

The idea is as old as Plato. In his famous dialogue entitled *Meno*, Socrates demonstrates how learning to understand is more akin to clarifying one's ideas than to being taught facts—that there is no "teaching" for understanding, strictly speaking, only learning. When Meno is incredulous, Socrates "proves" it through his dialogue with an uneducated slave boy. Through questioning only and the boy's critical ability to follow the logic and admit ignorance when his hunches don't work out, Socrates is able to show that an uneducated boy can understand a geometrical fact—in this case, how to double the area of a given square. In being taught such a fact and in the absence of such questioning, the boy (like any other student) would have only a "true opinion" without understanding—an easily forgotten thing, as Socrates later notes:

> For the true opinions, as long as they stay, are splendid. . . . but they do not stay long. Off and away they run out of the soul, so they are not worth much unless we fasten them up with reasoning (Warmington & Rouse, 1956, p. 65).

This old idea was once again recently proven correct in the Third International Mathematics and Science Study (TIMSS). A key finding explained the United States' poor showing on the international tests in the cross-cultural 8th grade mathematics

teaching study: U.S. teachers were found to merely *present* key ideas, whereas teachers from the better-performing nations tend to *develop* key ideas through examples, inquiries, and discussions (see Figure 10.3).

The data were even more striking when the more sophisticated performance areas—"applying concepts" and "inventing new applications and procedures"—were examined (see Figure 10.4).

Figures 10.3 and 10.4 reinforce the importance of clear and appropriate achievement targets and the logic of backward design. We will fall back on textbook coverage if our goals do not clarify what students must be able to do themselves at the end of instruction. Student autonomy requires carefully designed units that point all work toward complex and self-directed intellectual performance.

Adapting Teaching to Purposes

Given the complexity of all instructional methods, there is no one best or preferred approach to teaching for understanding. No single method of teaching will work all the time. Particular instructional methods and techniques follow from the specific types of learning needed to achieve the desired results (evidence of understanding) in the unit or course. Let's consider Bob James's 5th grade nutrition unit from the vantage point of the three types of teaching:

■ *Didactic.* Direct instruction is certainly needed. Explicit teaching and student reading, followed by checks for understanding, are best to teach knowledge about fats, protein, carbohydrates, and

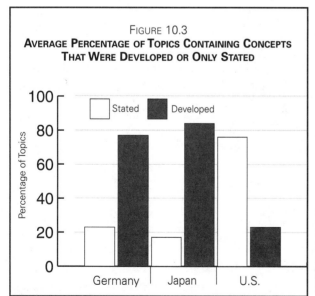

Source: U.S. Department of Education, NCES (1998a).

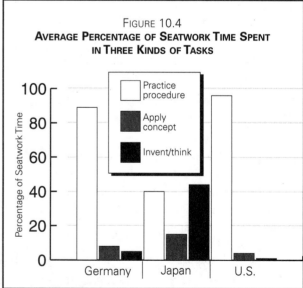

Source: U.S. Department of Education, NCES (1998b).

cholesterol; the food pyramid; and the relationship among food consumption, caloric intake, and energy expenditure.

■ *Coaching.* Coaching comes into play when the teacher provides feedback and guidance to students as they work.

■ *Constructivist.* The unit has numerous opportunities for guided inquiry and discussions around the essential, unit, and entry-point questions (e.g., What do we mean by "healthy eating"?). In addition, students will need to do individual and group research for the performance tasks and the camp menu project.

To teach for understanding requires teachers to routinely use all three types of teaching. Far from being a second-class form of teaching, direct instruction is vital for developing enabling skill and knowledge. An education devoted *exclusively* to guided discovery is inefficient and may be ineffective.

As an example, if you become lost while driving and stop to ask for directions, you don't want Joe Socrates, the gas station attendant, asking: "And why are you trying to get there as opposed to some other place? What does it mean that you are driving? How do you think you became lost? Have you considered that maybe you are not lost and have found something important?" You want directions. In the same vein, if you are learning entry-level computer skills, procedures for library research, or a foreign language, you will probably do best with step-by-step instructional coverage and highly directed skill-building exercises. But to overemphasize didactic teaching is to bypass the constructive work students must do to understand what they learn.

Rather than succumb to either-or thinking about direct or indirect teaching approaches, we need to carefully consider the issues of strategy and choice. When should we teach what we know, and when should we structure experiences that cause inquiry and constructive understanding? When should we cover and when should we uncover? These are the key questions for teachers of understanding.

As we have said throughout the book, as teachers, we should use direct instruction and focused coaching for discrete, unproblematic, and enabling knowledge and skill. We should reserve uncoverage—and the kinds of facilitative or indirect teaching it implies—for those ideas that are subtle; most prone to misunderstanding; and in need of personal inquiry, testing, and verification. Figure 10.5 offers insights into how to choose from various teaching approaches. When the educational aims in a given lesson involve the items in the first column, direct instruction will tend to be more effective—that is, understanding will be furthered by learning the knowledge that teachers and textbooks have to teach. The items in the first column can be grasped through straightforward apprehension. When the aims involve the items in the second column, direct instruction is less likely to be effective. Some form of inquiry or "meaning construction" by the student will be necessary for understanding.

But we can also look at the chart from another perspective: as elements on a continuum of conceptual complexity from the *learner's* perspective. For the novice student, understanding of any kind requires first paying attention to the elemental, the discrete, the unproblematic, and the unambiguous. However, the expert student will likely find that what was once opaque, counterintuitive, or complicated has now become obvious, straightforward, and clear.

FIGURE 10.5 **CHOOSING A TEACHING APPROACH**

Didactic	Constructivist
Facts	Concepts and principles
Discrete knowledge	Systemic connections
Definitions	Connotations
Obvious	Subtle
Literal	Symbolic
Concrete	Abstract
Self-evident	Counterintuitive
Predictable result	Anomaly
Discrete skills and techniques	Strategy (using repertoire and judgment)
Recipe	Invention
Algorithms	Heuristics

We might also view Figure 10.5 as the beginning of a spiral of instruction (explained in Chapter 9). Regardless of our current level of understanding, we possess a mixture of understanding, ignorance, and confusion; we constantly need to move back and forth between the known and unknown, the familiar and the strange if we are to further our understanding.

Here are some principles and guidelines for teaching that support student inquiry for greater understanding and autonomous learning:

■ Engage students in inquiry and inventive work as soon as possible when no problem or performance challenge exists to guide and focus the learning. Otherwise, teaching becomes excessively didactic. Resist front-loading all the needed information. Save lectures for "half-time" and "post-game analysis," when they are more likely to be understood and appreciated.

■ Use the textbook as a reference book, not a syllabus.

■ Teach by raising more questions and answering fewer questions. Ask and re-ask big questions and answer little ones.

■ Make clear by deed and word that there is no such thing as a stupid question.

■ Reverse roles: Ask naive questions and make students come up with answers that are explanations and interpretations.

■ Raise questions with many plausible answers as a way to push students to consider multiple perspectives and give empathetic responses. Follow up with assignments that make students investigate and support diverse points of view.

■ Coach students to conduct effective final performances (e.g., oral presentations or graphic displays).

■ Strive to develop greater autonomy in students so that they can find knowledge on their own and accurately self-assess and self-regulate. The ultimate aim is to make ourselves unneeded as teachers who tell students only what and how to understand.

■ Assess for understanding periodically, not just at the end of a lesson, unit, or course. Never assume that covering a topic once will result in student understanding.

The last two points in particular relate to the development of student understanding. Students must develop greater autonomy—self-regulation—if we expect them to understand on their own. And "thinking like an assessor" while teaching will prove vital to detect the kinds of misunderstandings this book describes.

The link to our design work should be clear. In the absence of a design grounded in essential and unit questions, and tasks that embody the questions, teachers will be reduced to didactic instruction and leading questions only.

Assessing Along the Way

Thinking like an assessor means effectively assessing how our design is working while we teach: Are the students beginning to understand the big ideas we're focusing on? That understanding is more likely if we are doing constant assessments (both formal and informal), rather than assessing only through end-of-teaching performance tasks, culminating projects, and final exams.

The purpose of assessment-in-progress is to ferret out apparent from genuine understandings. Teachers need to be vigilant about this work because of their propensity to construe correct answers as understanding and the students' desire to appear that they understand (whether they do or not). Over the years, teachers have developed a variety of techniques to make sure students understand *while* they are learning. Figure 10.6 (see p. 166) offers eight of these techniques.

These suggestions underscore perhaps the most common teacher misconception about teaching: "If I said it clearly and they answer correctly, then they must have understood it." The bottom line is that there is no such thing as teaching for understanding by recipe and recitation. Naturally, we play to our strengths and predilections as teachers; however, teaching for understanding may require us to develop new teaching strategies, create opportunities for meaning making, and do more assessing of student responses.

It is ironic but true that less teaching can yield better learning if we use good judgment in designing our assignments and assessments—that is, if we evoke and require understanding rather than merely trying to hand it over.

William James (1899/1958) argued that *tact*—sensitivity in context, based on the demands of a particular situation—was central to good teaching. Tact helps us understand the interplay between the known and the knower—what is to be understood as well as the students who are trying to understand.

Using the Six Facets for Understanding Students

All design is ultimately for the client and must satisfy the client's needs. Thus, the design that pleases the teacher may not work with students. This is the tension inherent in design work throughout the

FIGURE 10.6 **TECHNIQUES TO CHECK FOR UNDERSTANDING**

1. Index Card Summaries and Questions

Periodically, distribute index cards and ask students to write on both sides, with these instructions:

> (Side 1)
> Based on our study of (*unit topic*), list a big idea that you understand and word it as a summary statement.

> (Side 2)
> Identify something about (*unit topic*) that you do not yet fully understand and word it as a statement or question.

2. Hand Signals

Ask students to display a designated hand signal to indicate their understanding of a specific concept, principle, or process:

- I understand _____ and can explain it (*e.g., thumbs up*).
- I do not yet understand _____ (*e.g., thumbs down*).
- I'm not completely sure about _____ (*e.g., wave hand*).

3. Question Box or Board

Establish a location (e.g., question box, bulletin board, or e-mail address) where students may leave or post questions about concepts, principles, or processes that they do not understand. This technique may benefit students who are uncomfortable saying aloud that they do not understand.

4. Analogy Prompt

Periodically, present students with an analogy prompt:
(*A designated concept, principle, or process*) is like _____
because _____.

5. Visual Representation (Web or Concept Map)

Ask students to create a visual representation (e.g., web, concept map, flow chart, or time line) to show the elements or components of a topic or process. This technique effectively reveals whether students understand the relationships among the elements.

FIGURE 10.6   (CONTINUED)

6. Oral Questioning

Use the following questions and follow-up probes regularly to check for understanding:

- How is _____ similar to/different from _____?
- What are the characteristics/parts of _____?
- In what other ways might we show/illustrate _____?
- What is the big idea, key concept, moral in _____?
- How does _____ relate to _____?
- What ideas/details can you add to _____?
- Give an example of _____?.
- What is wrong with _____?
- What might you infer from _____?
- What conclusions might be drawn from _____?
- What question are we trying to answer? What problem are we trying to solve?
- What are you assuming about _____?
- What might happen if _____?
- What criteria would you use to judge/evaluate _____?
- What evidence supports _____?
- How might we prove/confirm _____?
- How might this be viewed from the perspective of _____?
- What alternatives should be considered _____?
- What approach/strategy could you use to _____?

7. Follow-Up Probes

- Why?
- How do you know?
- Do you agree?
- Explain.
- Give your reasons.
- But what about _____?

- What do you mean by _____?
- Could you give an example?
- Tell me more.
- Can you find that in the text?
- What data support your position?

8. Misconception Check

Present students with common or predictable misconceptions about a designated concept, principle, or process. Ask them whether they agree or disagree and explain why. The misconception check can also be presented in the form of a multiple-choice or true-false quiz.

professions. The craft of teaching is the art and science of blending adult objectives with student needs and interests (notwithstanding the realities of school resources).

These considerations recall the double meaning of the word *understand* alluded to in Chapter 2: We seek to understand *people* as well as *ideas*. Those two kinds of understanding are intimately related in teaching. Unless we understand students, we will not get them to understand ideas.

To teach for understanding, then, what must we understand about students and our relationship to them? How can we better understand the relationship between complex ideas and naive minds? We teach a variety of students and therefore must teach to a variety of learning styles. Figure 10.7 shows how the six facets affect both the understanding of important ideas and people.

Diversity in Learning Styles

The facets alert us to diversity in learning styles, natural intelligences, and styles of understanding, as shown in everyday classroom experiences. Rarely do we find students who are fluent and flexible with all facets. A student can

- Provide a brilliant interpretation of a text but lack empathy for the characters and hence be poor at explaining their individual psychology.
- Display psychological insight into the characters of a play but completely misunderstand the themes and significance of the writing.
- Solve complex math problems but be unable to explain how.
- Have a fascinating scientific hunch but little or no convincing evidence to support it.

Moreover, each student can think that other students who fit a different profile "just don't get it." A goal of teaching for understanding, then, should be to help students develop all the facets and to realize the facets' importance.

Facets and Habits of Understanding

Because we settle into habits of understanding, we are predisposed to favor the facet in which we are strongest. Conversely, we may devalue those facets in which we are weak or fail to appreciate students who understand differently from us. The question, "How can you see it that way?" may have more to do with our way of understanding than the particular idea expressed.

Deficiencies in one or more facets are a problem; excessive dominance of a particular facet may be more serious because it may foreclose future understanding in even a bright and able student. Consider the dangers in each facet if it is overdeveloped at the expense of the others.

Facet 1. Explanation. *Rational or rationalization?*

Ideological rigidity results from having developed one's theoretical understanding at the expense of the other facets. Explanation or theorizing is rendered more appropriately open, cautious, fluid, and improvable when we can openly and honestly consider other explanations, theories, and points of view as well as unfamiliar ways of living or perceiving. This flexibility becomes progressively harder as we age and become more sure of our knowledge.

The best theorists are open to being wrong and eager to have their ideas tested. But many highly theoretical people can be just the opposite: closed-minded and confirmed in their prejudices. A highly developed sense of explanation, without a similar sophistication of critical and empathic ability, can lead to dogma and rationalization.

In schoolwork, simply teaching and testing constantly for right answers can foster an orthodoxy of opinion and performance. For their part, students who view their primary role as receivers and repeaters of truth can develop a kind of ideological rigidity or unwarranted faith in the pronouncements of texts and teachers, such that they have difficulty in understanding.

FIGURE 10.7 **THE SIX FACETS OF UNDERSTANDING, ENHANCED**

Facet	Realm of Ideas and Knowledge	Realm of People and Emotions
1: Explanation	Deep and broad knowledge. Sophisticated theory, evidence, and argument.	Sophisticated grasp of human psychology (child development, research on learning, and misconceptions).
2: Interpretation	Subtle and thorough grasp of meaning of texts, events, and data. Ability to assess importance.	Ability to grasp the meaning of classroom behavior and performance in terms of individual student lives and understandings.
3: Application	Authentic use of ideas and processes. Technical skill in context.	Effective use of *Understanding by Design* ideas and tools.
4: Perspective	Critical analysis. Awareness of diverse yet plausible points of view.	Sophisticated classroom management. Ability to see the plausibility as well as the weakness in diverse student ideas and responses.
5: Empathy	Sensitivity.	Sympathy for the insecurity of novice learners. Tactful in response to naive questions or novel ideas.
6: Self-Knowledge	Awareness of one's ignorance —the limits of one's knowledge. Sensitivity to the interference of one's beliefs and habits.	Awareness of one's prejudice, biases, and projected feelings toward different students and ways of learning.

Source: Based on a five-trait rubric for assessing understanding found in Wiggins (1998), p. 95.

Facet 2: Interpretation. *Insightful or a closed loop, impervious to feedback?*

Conspiracy theorists, numerologists, dooms-dayers, and utopians exemplify those people who have overly developed Facet 2. They see signs everywhere (signs overlooked by ordinary mortals) of a deeper, fundamental meaning. Entire lifestyles, myths, and cults are created from a few small events or findings. They "explain" things, but not using the analytical and well-supported theory implied in Facet 1. Fanciful storytelling is involved.

We are, of course, meaning-making animals. The point is not to criticize this capacity for finding and creating significance. But we need not go far afield to see evidence of such excess. In schools, we often hear a student state an opinion defiantly as if a strong belief is the same as truth. Or, a student frequently offers interesting anecdotes or stories that cannot be substantiated or are irrelevant to the task or lesson.

Facet 3: Application. *Effective repertoire or thoughtless plugging in?*

The danger here is overreliance on skill and cleverness, leading to an anti-intellectual and unprincipled smugness that values practical results above all else. A person strongest in this facet can grow disdainful of all intellectual work and efforts to understand, or become the kind of person who solves problems and cuts deals with no moral or intellectual integrity.

Facet 4: Perspective. *Critical insight or alienated detachment?*

The dangers of too much critical distance (e.g., an armchair perspective) are cynicism, relativism, disengagement, inaction, and alienation—in other words, too much criticism or doubting and not enough believing and acting. As Elbow notes, many highly trained academics have overdeveloped their critical faculties at the expense of others.[3] Here again, we see the educational importance of balancing the facets in tension to ensure mature development in students.

Facet 5: Empathy. *Disciplined openness or soft-headedness?*

The danger here is the loss of perspective—thinking that simply because one feels it or relates with it, it must be true or important. Shattuck (1996) says that when we understand empathically, we easily veer into relativism because

> We tend to interpret that person's behavior as caused by some form of fate. . . . That form of understanding denies responsibility for one's actions and heads easily to moral laxness where *all* is forgiven (pp. 153–154) (emphasis in original).

In everyday classroom experience, we may encounter a student who has a strong emotional response or conviction about a lesson, text, or experience but who cannot apply critical judgment.

Facet 6: Self-Knowledge. *Wisdom or self-centered inaction?*

Too much self-knowledge? Sounds like a contradiction in terms. But excessive student self-doubt and fatalism can arise from unending self-criticism, undue attention to one's own learning style, or too much emphasis on every thought and feeling.

The independence of each facet and the tensions between them suggest that assessment must also be used to examine the student's ability to balance and draw on all the facets. Soccer and basketball coaches attempt this balance in drills designed to discourage players from favoring the foot or hand that seems most natural for shooting and passing.

Natural favoritism should never serve as an excuse for playing to the student's dominant facet at the expense of understanding. It is the job of teaching, reinforced by assessment, to help the student not only to develop a more fluent and powerful repertoire but also to see the value in other (perhaps unnatural or difficult) forms of knowing, inquiry, and performing.

The Disposition to Understand

> Because of the importance of attitudes, ability to train thought is not achieved merely by knowledge of the best forms of thought. Moreover, there are no set exercises in correct thinking whose repeated performance will cause one to be a good thinker. . . . Knowledge of the methods alone will not suffice; there must be the desire, the will to employ them. This desire is an affair of personal disposition.
>
> —Dewey, 1933, pp. 29–30

Using all six facets does not come easily or naturally. How then do we develop all the facets, given the propensity of students (and teachers) to favor some over others? We believe that one key to successful teaching for understanding is to grasp the role of attitudes and habits of mind.

Rethinking and Our Habits

The reality is that we will only rethink our preferred understandings if we are accustomed to doing it. The development of understanding greatly depends on such attitudes and habits of mind as open-mindedness, self-discipline (autonomy), tolerance for ambiguity, and reflectiveness. Mature self-discipline is critical; tolerance of ambiguity makes possible seeing the world through multiple lenses, as the facets theory requires.

We cannot "teach" a habit per se, and knowledge alone will not lead to or change a habit. A new habit of mind, like any habit, has to be cultivated over time—evoked, reinforced, required by the performance challenges, and supported by teacher modeling, exhortation, coaching, and feedback.

Dewey (1933) succinctly enumerated the habits needing development for understanding:

> Alertness, flexibility, curiosity are the essentials; dogmatism, rigidity, prejudice, caprice arising from routine, passion, and flippance are fatal (p. 214).

Dewey also stressed that training in "thinking skills" is *insufficient* to develop thoughtful, mature thinkers (p. 283). Rather, he believed, as we do, that the problems and performances encountered—the design—should make the habits necessary.

The Dimensions of Learning program, developed by Marzano and Pickering (1997), highlights three categories of habits of mind that influence learning, and offers practical suggestions to introduce, label, and reinforce them (see Figure 10.8 on p. 172). Marzano and his colleagues note that Dimension 5 (habits of mind) is "probably the most important dimension because it permeates all the others."

Thoughtful Judgment

The Bradley Commission on the Teaching of History (Gagnon, 1989) developed a list of habits of mind best suited to study in that field, though they apply generally to most subjects:

FIGURE 10.8. **SUGGESTIONS FOR DEVELOPING HABITS OF MIND**

Self-Regulation	Critical Thinking	Creative Thinking
Monitor your own thinking. Plan appropriately. Identify and use the necessary resources. Respond appropriately to feedback. Evaluate the effectiveness of your actions.	Be accurate and seek accuracy. Be clear and seek clarity. Maintain an open mind. Restrain impulsiveness. Take a position when the situation warrants it. Respond appropriately to others' feelings and level of knowledge.	Persevere. Push the limits of your knowledge and abilities. Generate, trust, and maintain your own standards of evaluation. Generate new ways of viewing a situation outside the boundaries of standard conventions.

Adapted from Marzano & Pickering (1997), p. 262.

The perspectives and modes of thoughtful judgment derived from the study of history are many, and they ought to be its principal aim. Courses in history, geography, and government should be designed to take students well beyond formal skills of critical thinking, to help them through their own active learning to

■ Understand the significance of the past to their own lives, both private and public, and to their society.

■ Distinguish between the important and the inconsequential, to develop the "discriminatory memory" needed for a discerning judgment in public and personal life.

■ Perceive past events and issues as they were experienced by people at the time, to develop historical empathy as opposed to present-mindedness.

■ Comprehend the interplay of change and continuity, and avoid assuming that either is somehow more natural, or more to be expected, than the other.

■ Prepare to live with uncertainties and exasperating, even perilous, unfinished business, realizing that not all problems have solutions.

■ Grasp the complexity of historical causation, respect particularity, and avoid excessively abstract generalizations.

■ Appreciate the often tentative nature of judgments about the past, and thereby avoid the temptation to seize upon particular "lessons" of history as cures for present ills.

■ Appreciate the force of the nonrational, the irrational, [and] the accidental in history and human affairs.

■ Read widely and critically in order to recognize the difference between fact and conjecture, between evidence and assertion, and thereby to frame useful questions.

Students must learn what is taught, but teaching for understanding also involves cultivating and reinforcing mature intellectual habits. As teachers, our tasks are to model, evoke, and reinforce the formation of habits of mind, and to make clear in assignments and assessments that we value habits of mind.

Big Ideas and Reflection

Big ideas are often obscure or counterintuitive, as we have seen. To grasp them requires reflection and persistence. Consider some once-controversial ideas: The earth, not the sun, moves; life evolves through adaptation and selection; there can be many different valid systems for describing space; motion on earth can best be described through a theory of a frictionless world and force acting at a distance; and freedom of speech helps rather than hurts the social order. Even well-educated people of the times resisted these ideas. Habits of mind such as a tolerance for ambiguity and suspension of disbelief—habits key to the discovery of big ideas—must be seen as valued and useful in accomplishing learning goals.

We can summarize the habits of mind that relate to the development of understanding as the propensity to "thoughtfulness." Dewey (1933) noted,

> When we say someone is *thoughtful* we mean someone who is not only "logical" but who has the right habits of mind: They are heedful, not rash; they look about, are circumspect. . . . [they do not] take observations at face value but probe them to see whether they are what they seem to be (emphasis in original).

Dewey also described the thoughtful person as "taking delight in the problematic."

Both Dewey's remarks remind us that all the brain power in the world is for naught if one fears uncertainty and cares more about being right than understanding. Our understandings improve, paradoxically, if teaching requires students both to learn new ideas and to challenge familiar ones. Students of philosophy will recall that Descartes, the so-called father of modern philosophy, used the method of doubting everything to attain greater knowledge.

A Delicate Balance

We must therefore strike a delicate balance as teachers between respecting our students and challenging their thinking and beliefs. We must provide them with useful knowledge but also alert them to problems in their thinking about the knowledge. Thus, teaching for understanding means more than designing opportunities to learn: It also means teaching in ways that challenge *resistance* to new ideas.

We occasionally must cause doubt in students to counter the propensity we all have to believe we understand. Winnie the Pooh and Piglet "prove" with ever-growing fear that the number of Woozles they are following is growing: They see increasing numbers of what are in fact their own footprints.[4]

Yet scientists and philosophers, despite their intelligence and training, often cannot grasp their own prejudices of thought (as the philosopher Kant noted 200 years ago, and as Thomas Kuhn [1970] underscored in his famous book on the history of science and its paradigm shifts).[5]

Of course, we want students to be thoughtful. But having students rethink—what a difficult thing to do! Really thinking things through is daunting and perilous, as Socrates found. It unravels fixed and sometimes hallowed ideas. Consider a 6th grader rethinking neighborhood norms after studying civil rights, or physics researchers publicly challenging their mentors. No one relishes the idea that years of living and thinking a certain way

might have been based on falsehoods. Yet, thoughtlessness is even more dangerous as a habit because of its potentially lethal consequences, as the Holocaust has shown.

Confronting Our Rationalizations and Resistance

To challenge any habit takes more than intelligence and knowledge. We can resist and explain away the problem if we are so inclined—and we often are. We call such post-hoc ideas *rationalizations*. There is no foolproof way to increase a student's understanding without her permission or to ensure that she avoids rationalizations.

The implications for teaching are significant. Deep understanding takes courage and mutual respect. Learning requires trust in the teacher because new understandings are threatening—sometimes at the personal, sometimes at the cultural level. Good ideas may be rejected in favor of older ideas. Great minds—not just naive and ignorant ones—are subject to intellectual inertia, blind spots, and resistance.

Two thousand years ago, Plato stated the problem in his allegory of the cave. We are asked to imagine being in chains, alone, in a cave. We can only look in one direction, at shadows cast by moving objects—objects illuminated by a fire that we cannot see. The release from our misunderstanding is painful, not welcome. We are not initially "enlightened" but "blinded by the light"; we must be "dragged" and "compelled" to understand the cause of the shadows:

Now consider what their release and healing from bonds and folly might be like. . . . Take a man who is released and suddenly compelled to stand up, to turn his neck round and look toward the light . . . who, moreover, in doing all this is in pain, and because he is dazzled, is unable to make out the shadows he knew before. . . . And if he were compelled to look at the light itself, would his eyes hurt and he would flee. . . . And if someone dragged him by force along the rough ascent, wouldn't he be distressed and annoyed? (Warmington & Rouse, 1956, p. 516a).

Even when the student grasps that the light of the sun causes shadows to fall on objects and thus causes him to realize that the cave offers merely shadows of real things, the return to the cave robs him of the ability to see anything clearly. The one with understanding—now the *teacher*!—will have little luck in helping others understand; they will resist even more:

Then again, just consider; if such a one should go down again and sit on his old seat, would he not get his eyes full of darkness coming in so suddenly out of the sun? And if he should have to compete with those who had been always prisoners, by laying down the law about those shadows while he was blinking before his eyes settled down . . . wouldn't they all laugh at him and say he had spoiled his eyesight by going up there, and it was not worthwhile so much as to try to go up? (Warmington & Rouse, 1956, p. 516d).

Socrates calls this a parable of our education and ignorance, and he draws this conclusion:

The nature of education is thus not what some professors say it is; as you know, they say that there is not understanding in the mind, but they put it in, as if they were putting sight into blind eyes. . . . But our reasoning indicates that this power is already in the soul of each one (Warmington & Rouse, 1956).

As teachers, our best hope is not in teaching what we know. It is in designing learning that confronts students with the limits of their ideas and the promise of new ones. It is the constructed understandings that compel us to leave the cave, not the teachings. *We* must will ourselves to overcome our constraining habits and resistance as students, hard though it is; the newly enlightened figure in the allegory of the cave first imagines that he is worse off than before.

Those are sobering thoughts for a teacher. Even clear, thorough teaching doesn't cause understanding. Understanding is caused by the learner who willingly overcomes old ideas and habits—and even otherwise successful students may not yet have that ability. Teachers can only design possibilities and build trust.

Teacher Habits and the Understanding of Learning

Everything we have said about habits of mind, resistance, and courage applies not only to students but also to teachers. We resist change in our teaching style, and we must model overcoming resistance for our students. We use our preferred facets of understanding, but we must work on all of them for the benefit of our subject and our students. Otherwise, *we* are in danger of misunderstanding what students need to understand. Teaching, like learning, demands that we keep working to develop all our facets of understanding.

Emphasizing Our Design Skills

Ultimately, our success in teaching for understanding depends on our design skills: our ability to design activities and assessments that *naturally* raise questions and new ideas instead of telling students what we know, and assuming that they understand. But our teaching, too, must become more responsive. If students are not understanding, we may need to alter the design (e.g., change the lesson or revise the curriculum).

It is a humbling but true fact that the best curriculum design may fail with a particular group of students. More often, though, when we have designed well, we are free to appreciate how students are learning instead of thinking about our own next move as a teacher.

This is the great irony of teaching. At times, being observant and silent is the best way to teach, because it allows us to listen for weak insights or misconceptions that may inhibit student understanding. To teach for understanding, then, we as educators also must be aware of how our teaching habits can undercut learning.

Being Diligent and Open

The happier news is that if we are diligent and open to the evidence, we will be the first to find the shortcomings in our ongoing assessment of student performance and our design work. When we say *assessment*, we mean more than tests and direct questions to students. We mean attending to feedback about whether they understand. Unless we succeed regularly in inviting students to reveal their misunderstandings and confusion, we are likely to overlook their lapses in understanding. Feedback from students is crucial to improving their learning, our designs, and our teaching.[6]

In addition to the strategies mentioned earlier in the chapter for soliciting feedback, we offer this one: Each week, hand out index cards to students. On one side ask them to list or identify "What worked for you this week?" and on the other "What didn't work for you this week?" (and *why* in each case). Note that the focus is on the design of learning experiences and instruction, not on the student or the teacher. We strongly encourage teachers to solicit such feedback, either directly from students or observations from colleagues, or indirectly through peer reviews of their designs.

These reflections on teaching for understanding only hint at a lifetime's undertaking. We trust, though, that we have proposed some essential questions and fruitful directions for research into—and reflection about—one's practice.

Endnotes

1. We realize that many readers may not (yet) work in schools where such time is routinely available. It is our hope, however, that the design process described in this book will stimulate conversations about the need for new schedules and different uses of existing time to facilitate the collaborative design, review, and revision of curriculum and assessment. Something other than one day of in-service training is required if quality curriculum is to result, given the iterative nature of the work. Specific ideas for incremental changes to the schedule and calendar can be found in Wiggins (1998), Chapter 12.

2. For further insight into the rationale for the three columns and how to decide what kind of teaching best suits what kind of objective, refer to Adler (1984) and follow-up volumes.

3. Compare Elbow (1973), pp. 162, 173, to Elbow (1986), p. 257.

4. The problem is solvable only by a shift in perspective: Christopher Robin sits in the tree above and sees the scene unfold (Milne, 1926).

5. "One thinker may be more interested in manifoldness, another in unity. Each believes that his judgment has been arrived at through insight into the object, whereas it really rests entirely on the greater or lesser attachment to one of two principles. . . . So long as these maxims are taken as yielding objective insight . . . they will not only give rise to disputes, but will be a positive hindrance and cause long delays in finding truth" (Kant, 1787/1929, pp. B695–696).

6. These points are developed at length in Wiggins (1998), Chapters 2 and 9.

PUTTING IT ALL TOGETHER: A DESIGN TEMPLATE

HAVING DESCRIBED THE BACKWARD DESIGN PROCESS, the facets of understanding, and the facets' implications for curricular organization, assessment, and teaching, we now strive to "put it all together" in this final chapter. We present a design template and a set of corresponding "intelligent" tools for teachers to use in the design of units of study that focus on understanding. Examples of the tools and template are provided for the nutrition unit. We also examine design standards for each phase of the backward design process and discuss their use for self-assessment, peer review, and quality control.

Form and Function

The Understanding by Design template provides a format in which all the design elements come together to enable the designer and others to take stock. Each page of the three-page template contains key questions to help the user focus on one of the three stages of backward design:

- Identify desired results.
- Determine acceptable evidence.
- Plan learning experiences and instruction.

The page then presents a graphic organizer that

contains several frames for summarizing design ideas. Figures 11.1 to 11.3 (see pp. 181–183) present a blank version of the template.

The first page (Figure 11.1) asks designers to consider what they want students to understand and then to frame those understandings in terms of questions. In completing the top two sections of the template page, users are prompted to identify overarching understandings and essential questions to establish a larger context into which a particular unit is nested. For example, Bob James identified the essential questions, "What does it mean to live a healthy life?" and, "What is 'wellness'?" as the conceptual umbrella for the specific unit on nutrition. The bottom part of the page is used to specify the particular understandings and questions that will guide the unit of study.

Page 2 (Figure 11.2) prompts the designer to consider a variety of assessment methods for gathering evidence of the desired understandings. The four-box graphic organizer then provides spaces for specifying the particular assessments to be used during the unit. Designers need to think in terms of collected evidence, not a single test or performance task.

Page 3 (Figure 11.3) contains two sections related to the planning of learning experiences and instruction. The top section asks the designer to specify what students will need to *know* (facts, concepts, principles, and generalizations) and *be able to do* (skills, processes, and strategies) to demonstrate their understanding through performance. In addition to such prerequisites for understanding, the designer notes here other unit goals of desired knowledge and skill, unrelated to the targeted understandings. The section helps establish teaching priorities. Rather than covering everything equally, we are reminded to identify the knowledge and skills that are most relevant and necessary to equip students for the performances required to demonstrate their understanding and to achieve all other unit goals.

The bottom section calls for a listing of the major learning activities and lessons. When it is filled in, the designer should be able to discern the major organizational patterns of the unit—explanation, narrative, and application—as well as the elements of WHERE. A completed template for the nutrition unit is shown in Figures 11.4, 11.5, and 11.6 (see pp. 184–186).

The *form* of the template offers a means to succinctly present the design unit; its *function* is to guide the design process. When completed, the template can be used for self-assessment, peer review, and sharing of the completed unit design with others.

Design Standards

Accompanying the design template is a set of design standards corresponding to each stage of backward design. The standards offer criteria to use during development, as well as quality control of completed unit designs (see Figure 11.7 on p. 187).

Framed as questions, the criteria are categorized according to the three stages of backward design. The first set evaluates the targeted understandings and the extent to which they represent big ideas, are specific enough to guide teaching and assessing, and are framed in terms of provocative questions. The second set of criteria examines the assessment evidence in terms of validity, reliability, sufficiency, and feasibility. The third set focuses on the elements of WHERE.

The design standards serve curriculum designers in the same way that a scoring rubric serves students. When presented to students *before* they begin their work, the rubric provides them with a performance target by identifying the important qualities toward which they should strive. Similarly, the design standards specify the qualities of effective units according to the Understanding by Design framework.

The standards contribute to design work in three ways:

■ *As a reference point during design.* Teachers can periodically check to see, for example, if the identified understandings are truly big and enduring, or if the assessment evidence is sufficient. Like a rubric, the questions serve as reminders of important design elements to include, such as a focus on essential questions.

■ *For use in self-assessment and peer reviews of draft designs.* Teachers and peers can use the criteria to examine their draft units to identify needed refinements, such as using the facets to dig deeper into an abstract idea.

■ *For quality control of completed designs.* The standards can then be applied following classroom trials by independent reviewers (e.g., curriculum committees) to validate the designs prior to their distribution to other teachers.

Our profession rarely subjects teacher-designed units and assessments to this level of critical review. Nonetheless, we have found structured peer reviews, guided by design standards, to be enormously beneficial—both to teachers and their designs (Wiggins, 1996–1997). Participants in peer review sessions regularly comment on the value of the opportunity to share and discuss curriculum and assessment designs with colleagues. We believe that such sessions are a powerful approach to professional development, because the conversations focus on the heart of teaching and learning:

■ What is worthy of understanding in this unit?

■ What counts as evidence that students *really* understand and can use what we're teaching?

■ What knowledge and skills must we teach to enable them to apply their knowledge in meaningful ways?

In addition to the value of the process, the quality of the product is enhanced when teachers are able to refine their unit designs based on feedback and guidance about the strengths of their designs, along with suggestions for improvement. Lastly, the peer review provides an opportunity to see alternate design models, to say, "Gee, I never thought about beginning this unit with a problem. I think I'll try that the next time I teach this unit."

Design Tools

In addition to the design standards, a set of design tools is available to support teachers and curriculum developers as they work. Each design tool contains a focusing question, prompts and idea starters, and one or more graphic frames for recording design ideas. This chapter presents three design tools for the backward design process: generating guiding questions, six facets of understanding, and WHERE. Examples from the nutrition unit show how the tools can be used.

The design tool, generating guiding questions (see Figure 11.8 on p. 188), offers several prompts to stimulate thinking about fruitful questions to focus the unit. Curriculum designers often find it useful to brainstorm possible guiding questions and then select the most promising to frame the desired understandings and engage students. Examples of potential questions for nutrition are provided, including the unit question eventually chosen: "What is healthy eating?"

The facets sheet (see Figure 11.9 on p. 189) asks designers to consider which of the facets of understanding are appropriate to the unit being constructed. A review of the facets often sparks new ideas to stretch students' thinking, as well as suggesting ways of framing the targeted understandings and constructing assessment prompts and tasks.

The WHERE design tool (see Figure 11.10 on p. 190) poses a set of key questions to remind designers of effective instructional practices, such as providing provocative entry points to hook students and offering opportunities for them to rethink and revise.

Intelligent Tools

We think that a good template or design frame serves as an "intelligent" tool. It provides more than a place to write in our ideas. It focuses and guides our thinking throughout the design process to make high-quality work a more likely result.

In this book, we have deliberately "uncovered" the elements and complexity of design piece by piece and iteratively. In practice, however, curriculum designers would work from a blank copy of the template, supported by specific design tools and numer-ous filled-in examples of good unit designs. In this way, we practice what we preach with students: There are models and design standards provided up front to focus designer "performance" from the start.

But why do we refer to the template, design standards, and corresponding design tools as "intelligent"? Just as a physical tool (e.g., telescope, automobile, or hearing aid) extends human capabilities, an intelligent tool enhances performance on cognitive tasks, such as the design of learning units. For example, an effective graphic organizer, such as a story map, helps students internalize the elements of a story in ways that enhance their reading and writing of stories. Likewise, by routinely using the template and design tools, it is likely that users will develop a *mental* template of the key ideas presented in this book: the logic of backward design, thinking like an assessor, the facets of understanding, WHERE, and design standards.

By embodying the Understanding by Design elements in tangible forms (i.e., the template and design tools), we seek to support educators in learning and applying these ideas. Thus, the design tools may be thought of as training wheels, providing a steadying influence during those periods of disequilibrium brought on by new ideas that may challenge established and comfortable habits. Once the key ideas of Understanding by Design are internalized, however, and regularly applied, the explicit use of the tools becomes unnecessary, just as the young bicycle rider sheds the training wheels once she achieves balance and confidence.[1]

Endnote
1. For additional information and examples of cognitive tools, see McTighe & Lyman (1988).

Figure 11.1 **Results**

IDENTIFY DESIRED RESULTS

**What overarching understandings
are desired?**

_____
_____
_____
_____

**What are the overarching
"essential" questions?**

_____
_____
_____
_____

**What will students understand
as a result of _this_ unit?**

_____
_____
_____
_____
_____
_____
_____
_____
_____
_____

**What "essential" and "unit"
questions will focus this unit?**

_____
_____
_____
_____
_____
_____
_____
_____
_____
_____

FIGURE 11.2 **EVIDENCE**

DETERMINE ACCEPTABLE EVIDENCE

What evidence will show that students understand _____ ?

Performance Tasks, Projects

Quizzes, Tests, Academic Prompts

Other Evidence *(e.g., observations, work samples, dialogues)*

Student Self-Assessment

FIGURE 11.3 **LEARNING EXPERIENCES AND INSTRUCTION**

PLAN LEARNING EXPERIENCES AND INSTRUCTION

Given the targeted understandings, other unit goals, and the assessment evidence identified, what knowledge and skill are needed?

Students will need to know . . .	Students will need to be able to . . .
_____	_____
_____	_____
_____	_____
_____	_____
_____	_____
_____	_____
_____	_____

What teaching and learning experiences will equip students to demonstrate the targeted understandings?

_____

_____

_____

_____

_____

_____

_____

_____

_____

_____

_____

_____

✦ *Use additional sheets as needed.* ✦

FIGURE 11.4 **RESULTS (NUTRITION UNIT)**

IDENTIFY DESIRED RESULTS

What overarching understandings are desired?

Elements of "wellness"

- Healthy habits
- Nutrition/diet
- Exercise
- Mental health

What are the overarching "essential" questions?

- What does it mean to lead a healthy life?
- What is "wellness"?

What will students understand as a result of *this* unit?

- Students will understand that a balanced diet (as described by the USDA food pyramid) contributes to optimal health and "healthy" living.
- Students will understand elements of good nutrition (human nutritional needs, nutritional values of various foods, USDA food pyramid recommendations) by analyzing the nutritional value of menus and planning a balanced diet for themselves and others.

What "essential" and "unit" questions will focus this unit?

- What is healthy eating?
- What is a "balanced" diet?

FIGURE 11.5 **EVIDENCE (NUTRITION UNIT)**

DETERMINE ACCEPTABLE EVIDENCE

What evidence will show that students understand *elements of good nutrition* **?**

Performance Tasks, Projects

- *Family Meals.* Students analyze a hypothetical family's diet for one week and make recommendations for improving its nutritional value.
- *You Are What You Eat.* Students create an illustrated brochure to teach younger children about healthy eating.
- *Chow Down.* Students develop a three-day menu for meals and snacks for an upcoming Outdoor Education camp experience. Their menu must be tasty while meeting the USDA food pyramid recommendations.

Quizzes, Tests, Academic Prompts

Quiz 1: The food groups	**Prompt:** Describe two health problems
Quiz 2: The USDA food pyramid	that could arise as a result of poor
	nutrition and explain how these could
	be avoided.

Other Evidence *(e.g., observations, work samples, dialogues)*

Informal observations/discussions
during work on the performance
tasks and the camp menu project.

Student Self-Assessment

1. Self-assess your brochure.
2. Self-assess the camp menu.
3. Self-assess the extent to which you "eat healthy" two times: at the start and at the end of the unit.

FIGURE 11.6 LEARNING EXPERIENCES AND INSTRUCTION (NUTRITION UNIT)

PLAN LEARNING EXPERIENCES AND INSTRUCTION

Given the targeted understandings, other unit goals, and the assessment evidence identified, what knowledge and skill are needed?

Students will need to know . . .	Students will need to be able to . . .
■ Key terms: for example, proteins, fat, calorie, carbohydrate, cholesterol ■ The food groups ■ Types of food in each group ■ USDA food pyramid guidelines ■ Health problems caused by poor nutrition	■ Read and analyze nutrition information on food labels ■ Scale up food recipes

What teaching and learning experiences will equip students to demonstrate the targeted understandings?

1. Present the story of the sailors' "mystery" disease (scurvy).
2. Introduce essential and unit questions and key vocabulary terms.
3. Present concept attainment lesson on food groups, then categorize foods.
4. Have students read and discuss the nutrition brochure from the USDA.
5. Present lesson on the food pyramid and identify foods in each group.
6. Present and discuss the video Nutrition and You.
7. Have students design an illustrated nutrition brochure for younger children.
8. Assess and give feedback on the brochures; allow students to self-assess and assess their peers.
9. Working in cooperative groups, have students analyze a hypothetical family's diet.
10. Give feedback regarding the diet analysis.
11. Have students conduct research on health problems resulting from poor eating.
12. Have students work independently to develop the three-day camp menu.
13. Evaluate and give feedback on camp project; have students self-assess and assess their peers.
14. Conclude the unit with student self-evaluation of their personal habits. . . .

✦ *Use additional sheets as needed.* ✦

FIGURE 11.7 **DESIGN STANDARDS**

How will we judge our unit designs?

	extensively	somewhat	minimally

IDENTIFY DESIRED RESULTS

To what extent are the targeted understandings

	extensively	somewhat	minimally
■ Big ideas (as opposed to basic facts and skills) in need of *uncoverage*?	☐	☐	☐
■ Specific enough to guide teaching and assessing?	☐	☐	☐
■ Framed by provocative *essential* and *unit* questions?	☐	☐	☐

DETERMINE ACCEPTABLE EVIDENCE

To what extent does the assessment evidence provide

	extensively	somewhat	minimally
■ A valid and reliable measure of the targeted understandings?	☐	☐	☐
■ Sufficient information to support inferences about *each* student's understanding?	☐	☐	☐
■ Opportunities for students to exhibit their understandings through authentic performance tasks?	☐	☐	☐

PLAN LEARNING EXPERIENCES AND INSTRUCTION

To what extent will

	extensively	somewhat	minimally
■ Students know *where* they're going and *why* (in terms of unit goals, performance requirements, and evaluative criteria)?	☐	☐	☐
■ Students be *engaged* in digging into the big ideas of the unit (through inquiry, research, problem solving, and experimentation)?	☐	☐	☐
■ Students receive explicit instruction on the knowledge and skills needed to *equip* them for the required performances?	☐	☐	☐
■ Students have opportunities to *rehearse, revise*, and *refine* their work based on feedback?	☐	☐	☐
■ Students *self-assess* and set goals prior to the conclusion of the unit?	☐	☐	☐

FIGURE 11.8 **GENERATING GUIDING QUESTIONS (NUTRITION UNIT)**

A unit can often be more focused and engaging for students if it is framed by guiding questions. Use the design sheet below to help you generate possible questions to guide your unit.

The understandings to be developed in this unit

> elements of good nutrition

To generate guiding questions for the unit consider the following:

1. If the textbook offers key "answers" (content knowledge), then what were the key questions that led to that knowledge?

2. Given what you wish students to understand, what questions are key to the understanding of this knowledge?

3. What interesting questions have arisen when you have taught (or studied) this content?

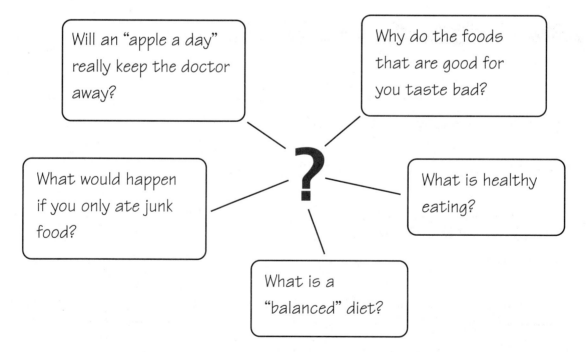

FIGURE 11.9 **SIX FACETS OF UNDERSTANDING (NUTRITION UNIT)**

Through which facets will students develop and reveal their understandings?

- *Explanation.* Students develop an illustrated brochure to explain the principles and practices of healthy eating to younger students.

- *Interpretation*

- *Application.* 1. Students analyze a hypothetical family's diet for nutritional balance. 2. Students develop a menu for meals and snacks for an upcoming three-day trip to the outdoor education camp.

- *Perspective.* Students investigate healthy eating from the perspective of different regions and cultures.

- *Empathy.* Students modify their eating habits for two days to have a "taste" of the experience of people who must restrict their diets because of specific conditions (e.g., diabetes, lactose intolerance, and food allergies).

- *Self-Knowledge.* Students reflect on their own eating habits and evaluate the extent to which they are "eating healthy."

FIGURE 11.10
UNIT DESIGN CONSIDERATIONS (NUTRITION UNIT)

Questions for the Teacher	**Responses from the Teacher**
How will you help students know *where* they are headed and *why* (e.g., major assignments, performance tasks, and the criteria by which the work will be judged)?	▪ Post essential questions on bulletin board. ▪ Present description of the performance tasks early in the unit, along with scoring rubrics.
How will you *hook* the student through engaging and thought-provoking experiences (issues, oddities, problems, and challenges) that point toward essential and unit questions, core ideas, and performance tasks?	▪ Begin unit with a "mystery"—for example, the seafarers' disease (scurvy) that cleared up once fresh fruits and vegetables were consumed. This mystery serves as a doorway into exploration of the unit question.
What learning experiences will *engage* students in exploring the big ideas and essential and unit questions? What instruction is needed to *equip* students for the final performances?	▪ The performance tasks are relevant, real-world applications of nutrition knowledge. ▪ The planned learning activities and lessons (e.g., guest speaker) will support work on tasks.
How will you cause students to *reflect* and rethink to dig deeper into the core ideas? How will you guide students in *revising* and *refining* their work based on feedback and self-assessment?	▪ Students evaluate hypothetical family diets for nutritional balance, then reflect on their own eating habits. ▪ Students will have an opportunity to revise their health brochures based on peer review.
How will students *exhibit* their understanding through final performances and products? How will you guide them in *self-evaluation* to identify the strengths and weaknesses in their work and set future goals?	▪ The tasks (illustrated brochure and camp menu) will provide evidence of understanding. ▪ Students self-evaluate their task and project using the rubrics. ▪ Unit concludes with student self-assessment on their own healthy eating.

AFTERWORD

Of course, a completed template is only the creative phase of curricular design. Although we might have confidence in our plan as an actual tool for teaching real students in real schools, testing and adjustment lie ahead. Having the design reviewed by others, piloting it, and revising it based on feedback in use are the only ways to ensure that the design accomplishes its purpose.

Bringing Design to Fruition

Thus, the process-to-product chart we have considered throughout the book actually has more columns than the four we last saw in Figure 7.1. An expanded version of the chart (see Figure A.1 on p. 193) clarifies what will bring the design to fruition. We have tested our design against design standards (see Figure A.1, Column 4). The final stage involves the movement from blueprint to use.

Note that the language and focus in the last column look outward to other would-be users of the design. A challenge is to make our design so explicit and complete that other teachers could successfully use it. Think about the template elements described in the previous chapter and throughout the book as potential fields in an electronic database. Instead of working in isolation and from scratch each time we design, we can learn and borrow from what others already have done.

Consider, for example, a new teacher's struggle to design good lessons—and how such a cumulative database over many years would help. This database would provide a means of "working smarter, not harder" by incorporating Understanding by Design units and assessments into a searchable database—one sharable across schools, districts, and states.

The expanded chart also evidences a concept we discussed in Chapter 11: Any good piece of design becomes better with feedback. No one can anticipate every possible use or bug in a design. In fact, recent studies have shown that in the field of high technology, users are responsible for more than half of the important innovations (von Hippel, 1988).

Teachers should, therefore, *routinely* take a worthwhile action that is currently atypical: Seek feedback about the design not only from other teachers but also from the end user—the student.

The Students Know

The students know whether or not the design helped them understand, regardless of their youth or inexperience in a subject. (For a refresher on some techniques, see Figure 10.5 and also the suggestion about index cards at the end of Chapter 10.) Even though educators are only beginning to overcome their reluctance about actively seeking reactions from the student-client, feedback solicitation is business as usual in hotels, restaurants, airlines, and hospitals.

All these lessons about debugging based on feedback apply to the authors' work here. This book

has gone through extensive overhaul and editing based on peer review. To the extent that the book is clear, useful, and thought provoking, our peer reviewers played an essential role. To the extent that the book is unclear and not useful, we seek your feedback and guidance, either to us directly via e-mail or through ASCD.

A book about design in discursive form can only do so much. That is why we are working with ASCD to prepare a companion design manual that will be available from ASCD in the future. The manual will provide templates, resource tools, worksheets, and examples to guide you through the complete process of design spelled out in this book. The templates in Chapter 11 here provide a few examples of what the manual will contain. In addition, the References list other books and articles that offer more in-depth guidance and examples about design and design issues.

Please consider sharing your designs—and your design problems—with us. Look at the CLASS web site (www.classnj.org) for bulletin boards, databases, and troubleshooting advice on the Understanding by Design process. An ASCD Web site is forthcoming.

Finally, we have not overlooked the restructuring considerations of this work. A comprehensive Understanding by Design toolkit from ASCD, filled with tools, strategies, handouts, self-assessment rubrics, and approaches to teacher supervision, will also be developed. It should help local change agents redesign the structures of schooling to better support Understanding by Design.

Happy designing!

FIGURE A.1 THE BACKWARD DESIGN PROCESS, ENHANCED

Key Design Question	Design Considerations	Filters (Design Criteria)	What the Final Design Accomplishes	Design Tested Against Design Standards	Peer Review and Pilot Questions	Complete Design	Sharable Design
Stage 1. What is worthy and requiring of understanding?	National standards. State standards. District standards. Regional topic opportunities. Teacher expertise and interest.	Enduring ideas. Opportunities for authentic, discipline-based work. Uncoverage. Engaging.	Unit framed around enduring understandings and essential questions.	What students will understand by design.	Is the focus apt and rigorous?	Feasible and appropriate allocation of time, given overall priorities.	What users will need to know to judge the unit's value and usefulness to them.
Stage 2. What is evidence of understanding?	6 facets of understanding. Continuum of assessment types.	Valid. Reliable. Sufficient. Authentic work. Feasible. Student friendly.	Unit anchored in credible and educationally vital evidence of the desired understandings.	Evidence of the desired understandings.	Is the proposed assessment plan sound?	Rubrics and models developed or made available.	What users will need and need to know for assessment.
Stage 3. What learning experiences and teaching promote understanding, interest, and excellence?	Research-based repertoire of learning and teaching strategies. Essential and enabling knowledge and skill.	WHERE Where is it going? Hook the students. Explore and equip. Rethink and revise. Exhibit and evaluate.	Coherent learning experiences and teaching that will evoke and develop the desired understandings, promote interest, and make excellent performance more likely.	Learning and teaching to evoke the desired understandings.	Is the overall design clear, coherent, and engaging? Will the work likely cause understanding?	Handouts and materials for students prepared.	What users will need and need to know to teach and modify the unit.

BIBLIOGRAPHY

Abbott, E. (1884/1963). *Flatland: A romance of many dimensions.* New York: Barnes and Noble Books. (Original work published 1884)

Adler, M. (1982). *The Paideia proposal: An educational manifesto.* New York: Macmillan.

Adler, M. (1984). *The Paideia program: An educational syllabus.* New York: Macmillan.

American Association for the Advancement of Science. (1993). *Benchmarks for science literacy.* New York: Oxford University Press.

American Association for the Advancement of Science. (1995). *Assessment of authentic performance in school mathematics.* Washington, DC: Author.

Arendt, H. (1963). *Eichmann in Jerusalem: A report on the banality of evil.* New York: Viking Press.

Arendt, H. (1977). *The life of the mind.* New York: Harcourt, Brace, Jovanovich.

Association for Supervision and Curriculum Development. (1997). *Planning integrated units: A concept-based approach* [video]. Alexandria, VA: Producer.

Bacon, F. (1620/1960). In F. Anderson (Ed.), *The new organon* (Book I). New York: Bobbs-Merrill. (Original work published 1620)

Barell, J. (1995). *Teaching for thoughtfulness.* White Plains, NY: Longman.

Barnes, L., Christensen, C. R., & Hansen, A. (1977). *Teaching and the case method.* Cambridge, MA: Harvard Business School Press.

Baron, J. (1993, November). *Assessments as an opportunity to learn: The Connecticut Common Core of Learning alternative assessments of secondary school science and mathematics.* (Report No. SPA-8954692). Hartford:

Connecticut Department of Education, Division of Teaching and Learning.

Baron, J., & Sternberg, R. (1987). *Teaching thinking skills: Theory and practice.* New York: W. W. Freeman and Co.

Barrows, H., & Tamblyn, R. (1980). *Problem-based learning: An approach to medical education.* New York: Springer.

Bateman, W. (1990). *Open to question: The art of teaching and learning by inquiry.* San Francisco: Jossey-Bass.

Beane, J. (Ed.). (1995). *Toward a coherent curriculum: The 1995 ASCD yearbook.* Alexandria, VA: Association for Supervision and Curriculum Development.

Bernstein, R. (1983). *Beyond objectivism and relativism: Science, hermeneutics, and praxis.* Philadelphia: University of Pennsylvania Press.

Bloom, B. S. (Ed.) (1956). *Taxonomy of educational objectives: Classification of educational goals. Handbook 1: Cognitive domain.* New York: Longman, Green & Co.

Bloom, B., Madaus, G., & Hastings, J. T. (1981). *Evaluation to improve learning.* New York: McGraw-Hill.

Blythe, T., & Associates. (1998). *The teaching for understanding guide.* San Francisco: Jossey-Bass.

Boyer, E. (1983). *High school: A report on secondary education in America by the Carnegie Foundation for the Advancement of Teaching.* New York: Harper & Row.

Brooks, J., & Brooks, M. (1993). *In search of understanding: The case for constructivist classrooms.* Alexandria, VA: Association for Supervision and Curriculum Development.

Bruner, J. (1960). *The process of education.* Cambridge, MA: Harvard University Press.

Bruner, J. (1965). Growth of mind. *American Psychologist, 20*(17), 1007–1017.

Bruner, J. (1966). *Toward a theory of instruction.* Cambridge, MA: Harvard University Press.

Bruner, J. (1973a). In J. Anglin (Ed.), *Beyond the information given: Studies in the psychology of knowing.* New York: W. W. Norton.

Bruner, J. (1973b). *The relevance of education.* Cambridge, MA: Harvard University Press.

Bruner, J. (1990). *Acts of meaning.* Cambridge, MA: Harvard University Press.

Bruner, J. (1996). *The culture of education.* Cambridge, MA: Harvard University Press.

Burns, J. M., & Morris, R. (1986). The Constitution: Thirteen crucial questions. In Morris & Sgroi (Eds.), *This Constitution.* New York: Franklin Watts.

Carroll, J. M. (1989). *The Copernican plan: Restructuring the American high school.* Andover, MA: The Regional Laboratory for Educational Improvement of the Northeast Islands.

Cayton, A., Perry, E., & Winkler, A. (1998). *America: Pathways to the present.* Needham, MA: Prentice-Hall.

College of William and Mary, Center for Gifted Education. (1997). *The Chesapeake Bay: A problem-based unit.* Dubuque, IA: Kendall Hunt.

Collingwood, R. G. (1939). *An autobiography.* Oxford, UK: Oxford-Clarendon Press.

Costa, A. (Ed.). (1991). *Developing minds: A resource book for teaching thinking. Volume 1* (Rev. ed.). Alexandria, VA: Association for Supervision and Curriculum Development.

Coxford, A., Usiskin, Z., & Hirschhorn, D. (1993). *Geometry: The University of Chicago School mathematics project.* Glenview, IL: Scott Foresman.

Darling-Hammond, L., et al. (1993). *Authentic assessment in practice: A collection of portfolios, performance tasks, exhibitions, and documentation.* New York: National Center for Restructuring Education, Schools and Teaching (NCREST), Teachers College, Columbia University.

Darwin, C. (1958). *The autobiography of Charles Darwin.* New York: W. W. Norton.

Delisle, R. (1997). *How to use problem-based learning in the classroom.* Alexandria, VA: Association for Supervision and Curriculum Development.

Descartes, R. (1628/1961). Rules for the direction of the mind. In L. LaFleur (Ed. and Trans.), *Philosophical essays.* Indianapolis, IN: Bobbs-Merrill. (Originally published 1628)

Dewey, J. (1916). *Democracy and education: An introduction to the philosophy of education.* New York: Macmillan.

Dewey, J. (1933). *How we think: A restatement of the relation of reflective thinking to the educative process.* Boston: Henry Holt.

Dewey, J. (1938). *Experience and education.* New York: Macmillan/Collier.

Dillon, J. T. (1990). *The practice of questioning.* New York: Routledge.

Drucker, P. F. (1985). *Innovation and entrepreneurship.* New York: Harper & Row.

Duckworth, E. (1987). *"The having of wonderful ideas" and other essays on teaching and learning.* New York: Teachers College Press.

Educational Testing Service/College Board. (1992). *1991 Advanced placement United States history free-response scoring guide and sample student answers.* Princeton, NJ: Author.

Educators in Connecticut's Pomperaug Regional School District 15. (1996). *A teacher's guide to performance-based learning and assessment.* Alexandria, VA: Association for Supervision and Curriculum Development.

Egan, K. (1986). *Teaching as story-telling: An alternative approach to teaching and curriculum in the elementary school.* Chicago: University of Chicago Press.

Egan, K. (1997). *The educated mind: How cognitive tools shape our understanding.* Chicago: University of Chicago Press.

Elbow, P. (1973). *Writing without teachers.* New York: Oxford University Press.

Elbow, P. (1986). *Embracing contraries: Explorations in learning and teaching.* New York: Oxford University Press.

Erickson, L. (1995). *Stirring the head, heart, and soul: Redefining curriculum and instruction.* Thousand Oaks, CA: Corwin Press.

Erickson, L. (1998). *Concept-based curriculum and instruction: Teaching beyond the facts.* Thousand Oaks, CA: Corwin Press.

Freedman, R. L. H. (1994). *Open-ended questioning: A handbook for educators.* Menlo Park, CA: Addison-Wesley.

Gadamer, H. (1994). *Truth and method.* New York: Continuum.

Gagnon, P. (Ed.). (1989). *Historical literacy: The case for history in American education.* Boston: Houghton-Mifflin.

Gardner, H. (1991). *The unschooled mind: How children think and how schools should teach.* New York: Basic Books.

Gould, S. J. (1977). *Ontogeny and phylogeny.* Cambridge, MA: Harvard University Press.

Gould, S. J. (1980). Wide hats and narrow minds. In S. J. Gould (Ed.), *The panda's thumb.* New York: W. W. Norton.

Gragg, C. (1940, October 19). Because wisdom can't be told. *Harvard Alumni Bulletin.*

Grant, G., et al. (1979). *On competence: A critical analysis of competence-based reforms in higher education.* San Francisco: Jossey-Bass.

Greenberg, M. J. (1972). *Euclidean and non-Euclidean geometries: Development and history.* San Francisco: W. H. Freeman Co.

Griffin, P., Smith, P., & Burrill, L. (1995). *The American literacy profile scales: A framework for authentic assessment.* Portsmouth, NH: Heinemann Press.

Gruber, H., & Voneche, J. (1977). *The essential Piaget: An interpretive reference and guide.* New York: Basic Books.

Hagerott, S. (1997). Physics for first graders. *Phi Delta Kappan, 78*(9), 717–719.

Hakim, J. (1993). *A history of us: From colonies to country.* New York: Oxford University Press.

Hammerman, E., & Musial, D. (1995). *Classroom 2061: Activity-based assessments in science, integrated with mathematics and language arts.* Palatine, IL: IRI/Skylight.

Haroutunian-Gordon, S. (1991). *Turning the soul: Teaching through conversation in the high school.* Chicago: University of Chicago Press.

Heath, E. (1956). *The thirteen books of Euclid's elements* (Vols. 1–3). New York: Dover.

Heath, T. (1963). *Greek mathematics.* New York: Dover.

Hegel, G. W. F. (1977). *Phenomenology of spirit* (A. V. Miller, Trans.). London: Oxford University Press.

Heidegger, M. (1968). *What is called thinking?* (J. Gray, Trans.). New York: Harper.

Hirsch, E. D., Jr. (1967). *Validity in interpretation*. New Haven, CT: Yale University Press.

Hirsch, E. D., Jr. (1988). *Cultural literacy: What every American needs to know*. New York: Vintage Books.

Hunter, M. (1982). *Mastery teaching*. Thousand Oaks, CA: Corwin Press.

Jacobs, H. H. (Ed.). (1989). *Interdisciplinary curriculum: Design and implementation*. Alexandria, VA: Association for Supervision and Curriculum Development.

Jacobs, H. H. (1997). *Mapping the big picture: Integrating curriculum and assessment K–12*. Alexandria, VA: Association for Supervision and Curriculum Development.

James, W. (1899/1958). *Talks to teachers on psychology and to students on some of life's ideals*. New York: W. W. Norton. (Original work published 1899)

Johnson, A. H. (Ed.). (1949). *The wit and wisdom of John Dewey*. Boston: Beacon Press.

Kant, I. (1787/1929). *The critique of pure reason* (N. Kemp Smith, Trans.). New York: Macmillan. (Original work published 1787)

Kierkegaard, S. (1959). *Journals*. (A. Dru, Trans.) New York: Harper.

Kline, M. (1953). *Mathematics in western culture*. Oxford, UK: University Press.

Kline, M. (1970, March). Logic vs. pedagogy. *American Mathematical Monthly, 77*(3), 264–282.

Kline, M. (1972). *Mathematical thought from ancient to modern times*. New York: Oxford University Press.

Kline, M. (1973). *Why Johnny can't add: The failure of the new math*. New York: Vintage Press.

Kline, M. (1980). *Mathematics: The loss of certainty*. Oxford, UK: Oxford University Press.

Kline, M. (1985). *Mathematics and the search for knowledge*. New York: Oxford University Press.

Kobrin, D. (1996). *Beyond the textbook: Teaching history using documents and primary sources*. Portsmouth, NH: Heinemann.

Koestler, A. (1964). *The act of creation: A study of the conscious and unconscious in science and art*. New York: Macmillan.

Krause, E. (1975). *Taxicab geometry: An adventure in non-Euclidean geometry*. New York: Dover Publications.

Kuhn, T. (1970). *The structure of scientific revolutions* (2nd ed.). Chicago: University of Chicago Press.

Lewis, N. (1981). *Hans Christian Andersen's fairy tales*. Middlesex, UK: Puffin Books.

Light, R. (1990). *The Harvard assessment seminar: Explorations with students and faculty about teaching, learning, and student life* (Vol. 1). Cambridge, MA: Harvard University Press.

Lodge, D. (1992). *The art of fiction*. New York: Viking.

Lyman, F. (1992). Think-pair-share, thinktrix, and weird facts. In N. Davidson & T. Worsham (Eds.), *Enhancing thinking through cooperative learning*. New York: Teachers College Press.

Mansilla, V. B., & Gardner, H. (1997). Of kinds of disciplines and kinds of understanding. *Phi Delta Kappan, 78*(5), 381–386.

Marzano, R., & Kendall, J. (1996). *A comprehensive guide to designing standards-based districts, schools, and classrooms*. Alexandria, VA: Association for Supervision and Curriculum Development.

Marzano, R., & Pickering, D. (1997). *Dimensions of learning teacher's manual* (2nd ed.). Alexandria, VA: Association for Supervision and Curriculum Development.

Marzano, R., Pickering, D., & McTighe, J. (1993). *Assessing student outcomes: Performance assessment using the dimensions of learning model*. Alexandria, VA: Association for Supervision and Curriculum Development.

Massachusetts Department of Education. (1997a). *English language arts curriculum framework*. Boston: Author.

Massachusetts Department of Education. (1997b). *History curriculum framework*. Boston: Author.

McCarthy, B. (1981). *The 4-Mat system*. Barrington, IL: Excel.

McCloskey, M., Carramaza, A., & Green, B. (1981). Naive beliefs in "sophisticated" subjects: Misconceptions about trajectories of objects. *Cognition, 9*(1), 117–123.

McGuire, J. M. (1997, March). Taking a storypath into history. *Educational Leadership, 54*(6), 70–72.

McTighe, J. (1996, December–1997, January). What happens between assessments? *Educational Leadership 54*(4), 6–12.

McTighe, J., & Lyman, F. (1988). Cueing thinking in the classroom: The promise of theory-embedded tools. *Educational Leadership, 45*(7), 18–24.

Milgram, S. (1974). *Obedience to authority.* New York: Harper.

Milne, A. A. (1926). *Winnie the Pooh.* New York: E. P. Dutton.

National Assessment of Educational Progress. (1988). *The mathematics report card, are we measuring up? Trends and achievement based on the 1986 national assessment.* Washington, DC: U.S. Department of Education.

National Center for History in the Schools, University of California. (1994). *History for grades K–4: Expanding children's world in time and space.* Los Angeles: Author.

National Center for History in the Schools, University of California. (1996). *National standards for United States history: Exploring the American experience, Grades 5–12* (Expanded Version). Los Angeles: Author.

National Center on Education and the Economy. (1997). *Performance standards: English language arts, mathematics, science, applied learning.* Pittsburgh, PA: University of Pittsburgh.

Newmann, F. N., & Associates. (1997). *Authentic achievement: Restructuring schools for intellectual quality.* San Francisco: Jossey-Bass.

Newmann, F. N., Secada, W., & Wehlage, G. (1995). *A guide to authentic instruction and assessment: Vision, standards and scoring.* Madison: Wisconsin Center for Education Research.

New York State Department of Education. (1996). *Learning standards for the arts.* Albany, NY: Author.

New York Times. (1996a, September 27). p. A1, Col. 3.

New York Times. (1996b, September 27). p. A14, Col. 5.

New York Times. (1997, May 4). p. 19.

New York Times Sunday Magazine. (1997, January 5). The soulman of suburbia, Sec. 6, p. 22.

Nickerson, R. (1985, February). Understanding understanding. *American Journal of Education 93*(2), 201–239.

Nickerson, R., Perkins, D., and Smith, E. (1985). *The teaching of thinking.* Hillsdale, NJ: Lawrence Erlbaum.

O'Neill, M. (1996, September 1). *New York Times Sunday Magazine.* p. 52.

Osborne, R., & Freyberg, P. (1985). *Learning in science: The implications of children's science.* Aukland, NZ: Heinemann.

Passmore, J. (1982). *The philosophy of teaching.* Cambridge, MA: Harvard University Press.

Peak, L., et al. (1996). *Pursuing excellence: A study of U.S. eighth grade mathematics and science teaching, learning, curriculum, and achievement in international context* (NCES 97-198). Washington, DC: U.S. Department of Education, National Center for Education Statistics.

Perkins, D. (1991, October). Educating for insight. *Educational Leadership, 49*(2), 4–8.

Perkins, D. (1992). *Smart schools: From training memories to educating minds.* New York: Free Press.

Perry, W. (1970). *Forms of intellectual development in the college years: A scheme.* New York: Holt, Rinehart and Winston.

Peters, R. S. (1967). *The concept of education.* London: Routledge & Kegan Paul.

Phenix, P. (1964). *Realms of meaning.* New York: McGraw-Hill.

Piaget, J. (1965). *The moral judgment of the child.* New York: Humanities Press.

Piaget, J. (1973). *To understand is to invent: The future of education.* New York: Grossman's Publishing Co.

Piaget, J. (1973/1977). Comments on mathematical education. In H. Gruber and J. Voneche (Eds.), *The essential Piaget.* New York: Basic Books. (Original work published 1973)

Poincaré, H. (1913/1982). *Science and method.* In *The foundations of science* (G. B. Halstead, Trans.). Washington, DC: University Press of America. (Original work published 1913)

Popper, K. (1968). *Conjectures and refutations*. New York: Basic Books.

Regional Laboratory for Educational Improvement of the Northeast & Islands. (undated). *The voyage of pilgrim '92: A conversation about constructivist learning* [newsletter], 1.

Ryle, G. (1949). *The concept of mind*. London: Hutchinson House.

Salinger, J. D. (1951). *The catcher in the rye*. Boston: Little Brown.

Saphier, J., & Gower, R. (1997). *The skillful teacher: Building your teaching skills* (5th ed.). Carlisle, MA: Research for Better Teaching.

Schank, R. (1990). *Tell me a story: Narrative and intelligence*. Evanston, IL: Northwestern University Press.

Schmoker, M. (1996). *Results: The key to continuous school improvement*. Alexandria, VA: Association for Supervision and Curriculum Development.

Schneps, M. (1994). *"A private universe" teacher's guide*. Washington, DC: The Corporation for Public Broadcasting.

Schoenfeld, A. (1988). Problem solving in context(s). In R. Charles & E. Silver (Eds.), *The teaching and assessing of mathematical problem solving*. Reston, VA: National Council on Teachers of Mathematics/Erlbaum.

Schon, D. A. (1989). *Educating the reflective practitioner: Toward a new design for teaching and learning*. San Francisco: Jossey-Bass.

School Curriculum and Assessment Authority. (1995). *Consistency in teacher assessment: Exemplifications of standards* (science). London: Author.

School Curriculum and Assessment Authority. (1997). *English tests mark scheme for paper two* (Key stage 3, Levels 4–7). London: Author.

Schwab, J. (1971). The practical: Arts of eclectic. *School Review, 79*, 493–542.

Schwab, J. (1978). The practical: Arts of eclectic. In *Science, curriculum, and liberal education: Selected essays*. Chicago: University of Chicago Press.

Serra, M. (1989). *Discovering geometry: An inductive approach*. Berkeley, CA: Key Curriculum Press.

Shattuck, R. (1996). *Forbidden knowledge: From prometheus to pornography*. New York: St. Martin's Press.

Shulman, J. (1992). *Case methods in teacher education*. New York: Teachers College Press.

Singh, S. (1997). *Fermat's enigma: The epic quest to solve the world's greatest mathematical problem*. New York: Walker and Co.

Sizer, T. (1984). *Horace's compromise: The dilemma of the American high school*. Boston: Houghton-Mifflin.

Skemp, R. R. (1987). *The psychology of learning mathematics: Expanded American edition*. Hillsdale, NJ: Lawrence Erlbaum.

Spiro, R., et al. (1988). *Cognitive flexibility theory: Advanced knowledge acquisition in ill-structured domains*. Hillsdale, NJ: Lawrence Erlbaum.

Steinberg, A. (1998). *Real learning, real work: School-to-work as high school reform*. New York: Routledge.

Stepien, W., & Gallagher, S. (1997). *Problem-based learning across the curriculum: An ASCD professional inquiry kit*. Alexandria, VA: Association for Supervision and Curriculum Development.

Stepien, W., Gallagher, S., & Workman, D. (1993). Problem-based learning for traditional and interdisciplinary classrooms. *Journal for the Education of the Gifted, 16*(4), 338–357.

Stepien, W., & Gallagher, S. (1993, April). Problem-based learning: As authentic as it gets. *Educational Leadership, 50*(7), 23–28.

Stepien, W., & Pyke, S. (1997). Designing problem-based learning units. *Journal for the Education of the Gifted, 20*(4), 380–400.

Sternberg, R., & Davidson, J. (Eds.). (1995). *The nature of insight*. Cambridge, MA: MIT Press.

Stiggins, R. J. (1997). *Student-centered classroom assessment*. Upper Saddle River, NJ: Prentice-Hall.

Stigler, J., & Hiebert, J. (1997, September). Understanding and improving classroom mathematics instruction. *Phi Delta Kappan, 79*(1), 14–21.

Strong, M. (1996). *The habit of thought: From Socratic seminars to Socratic practice*. Chapel Hill, NC: New View.

Sulloway, F. (1996). *Born to rebel: Birth order, family dynamics, and creative lives*. New York: Pantheon Press.

Tannen, D. (1990). *You just don't understand: Women and men in conversation*. New York: Ballantine Books.

Tharp, R. G., & Gallimore, R. (1988). *Rousing minds to life: Teaching, learning, and schooling in social context*. Cambridge, UK: Cambridge University Press.

Thomas, L. (1983). *Late night thoughts on listening to Mahler's Ninth Symphony*. New York: Viking Press.

Trenton Times. (1997a, April 27). Who tops world education heap? International math and science study tests 41 nations.

Trenton Times. (1997b, December 29). Volatile trio changed history. pp. B1–2.

Tyler, R. W. (1949). *Basic principles of curriculum and instruction*. Chicago: University of Chicago Press.

USA Today. (1997, November 13). Simon's capeman cometh. Sec. D, p. 1.

U.S. Department of Education, National Center for Education Statistics (NCES). (13 March 1998a). *Third international math and science study* [On-line]. Available: <http://nces.ed.gov/timss/video/finding22.htm>

U.S. Department of Education, National Center for Education Statistics (NCES). (13 March 1998b). *Third international math and science study* [On-line]. Available: <http://nces.ed.gov/timss/video/finding3.htm>

U.S. Department of Health, Education, and Welfare. (1976). *The American Revolution: Selections from secondary school history books of other nations* (HEW Publication No. OE 76-19124). Washington, DC: U.S. Government Printing Office.

van Manen, M. (1991). *The tact of teaching: The meaning of pedagogical thoughtfulness*. Albany: State University of New York Press.

von Hippel, E. (1988). *The sources of innovation*. New York: Oxford University Press.

Warmington, E., & Rouse, P. (Eds.). (1956). *Great dialogues of Plato* (W. H. D. Rouse, Trans.). New York: New American Library.

Washington Post. (1997, December 23). Japanese director commits suicide. p. A1.

White, R., & Gunstone, R. (1992). *Probing understanding*. London: The Falmer Press.

Whitehead, A. N. (1929). *The aims of education and other essays*. New York: Free Press.

Whitehead, A. N. (1947). Harvard: The future. In *Essays in Science and Philosophy*. New York: Greenwood Press.

Wiggins, G. (1987a, Winter). Creating a thought-provoking curriculum: Lessons from whodunits and others. *American Educator, 11*(4), 10–17.

Wiggins, G. (1987b). *Thoughtfulness as an educational aim*. Unpublished doctoral dissertation, Harvard University.

Wiggins, G. (1989, November). The futility of trying to teach everything of importance. *Educational Leadership, 47*(3), 44–59.

Wiggins, G. (1993). *Assessing student performance: Exploring the purpose and limits of testing*. San Francisco: Jossey-Bass.

Wiggins, G. (1996, December–1997, January). Practicing what we preach in designing authentic assessments. *Educational Leadership, 54*(4), 18–25.

Wiggins, G. (1997, September). Work standards: Why we need standards for instructional and assessment design. *NASSP Bulletin, 81*(590), 56–64.

Wiggins, G. (1998). *Educative assessment: Designing assessments to inform and improve performance*. San Francisco: Jossey-Bass.

Wilson, J. (1963). *Thinking with concepts*. London: Cambridge University Press.

Wiske, M. S. (1997). *Teaching for understanding: Linking research with practice*. San Francisco: Jossey-Bass.

Wittgenstein, L. (1953). *Philosophical investigations* (Aphorism 125). New York: Macmillan.

Woolf, V. (1929). *A room of one's own*. New York: Harcourt Brace and World.

ABOUT THE AUTHORS

Grant Wiggins is the President and Director of Research for the Center on Learning, Assessment, and School Structure (CLASS), a not-for-profit educational organization in Pennington, New Jersey. CLASS consults with schools, districts, and state education departments on a variety of reform issues; organizes national conferences and workshops; and develops video, software, and print materials on assessment and curricular change. Wiggins is the author of two books, *Educative Assessment* and *Assessing Student Performance*. His many articles have appeared in journals such as *Educational Leadership* and *Phi Delta Kappan*. He can be reached by e-mail at gwiggins@classnj.org or at CLASS, 65 S. Main St., Pennington, NJ 08534.

Jay McTighe serves as Director of the Maryland Assessment Consortium, a state collaboration of school districts working together to provide professional development and to create and share performance assessments. McTighe has also been involved with school improvement projects at the Maryland State Department of Education. He has worked as a classroom teacher, resource specialist, and director of a state residential enrichment program. He has published articles in a number of leading educational journals and books. McTighe can be reached by e-mail at jmctigh@aol.com.